Dictionary of Foreign
Words in English

D0958266

The Wordsworth
Dictionary of Foreign Words in English

–

John Ayto

Wordsworth Reference

First published 1991 as *Making Sense of Foreign Words
In English* by W&R Chambers Ltd, Edinburgh.

This edition published 1995 by Wordsworth Editions Ltd,
Cumberland House, Crib Street, Ware, Hertfordshire SG12 9ET.

ISBN 1-85326-344-3

Printed and bound in Denmark by Nørhaven.

The paper in this book is produced from pure wood
pulp, without the use of chlorine or any other substance
harmful to the environment. The energy used in its
production consists almost entirely of hydroelectricity
and heat generated from waste materials, thereby
conserving fossil fuels and contributing little to the
greenhouse effect.

Contents

Foreword

The English language, in the form of Anglo-Saxon, had hardly arrived in Britain when it began to show the influence of other languages, in the form of early Welsh, Latin and Old Norse, the speech of the Viking invaders. By the early Middle Ages it had taken in large numbers of new words from French. Thereafter, the process of lexical borrowing is continuous and eclectic, with thousands of words and phrases being introduced from Arabic, Greek, Spanish, Portuguese, German, and many other languages. Today, over two-thirds of English vocabulary is ultimately of foreign origin. In the 1990s the borrowing process continues unabated – and it is this process which receives an up-to-date and detailed account in John Ayto's book.

Foreign Words in English is wide-ranging in its coverage of the words and phrases found in modern English which native speakers still feel to be foreign. Each entry provides a description of an item's linguistic history, and its present-day meaning and range of use. John Ayto pays particular attention to the subtle nuances and connotations which accompany the use of foreignisms, and his careful accounts will be especially helpful to those who are uncertain of the force of a particular item or unsure about how it should be used. His book is informed and informative, clear and succinct in its commentary, and steering well clear of the impressionism and pedantry that so often colours books in the genre. It is, above all, an *explanation* of what is a major area of contemporary usage, and in this respect the book is a welcome addition to the Chambers Making Sense of . . . series.

David Crystal

Preface

English is the way it is because it is such an inveterate borrower from other languages. As long ago as the 7th century AD, Old English was adopting words such as *abbot, alms*, and *mass* from ecclesiastical Latin. To the basic Anglo-Saxon bedrock have been added over the last 1200 years successive layers of acquisitions from Scandinavian (from the 9th to the 12th centuries), from French (in the centuries following the Norman Conquest), from classical Latin and Greek (mainly in the 16th and 17th centuries), and eventually, in the period of commercial and imperial expansion, from virtually all the major languages of the world, and many minor ones.

Most loanwords that have been in the language for several centuries have become thoroughly naturalized. We use them without any conscious feeling that they are, or once were, foreignisms. To the English-speaker of the 20th century, *anger* (acquired from Old Norse in the 12th century) and *rage* (borrowed from Old French in the 13th century) are every bit as 'English' as the native *wrath* – and indeed are considerably commoner. This linguistic kleptomania has given the language an extraordinary richness of vocabulary, enabling English in many cases to make subtle distinctions lexically, where other languages must have recourse to circumlocutions: to quote an example from Simeon Potter's *Our Language*, English has its own *sleeplessness* and has taken *insomnia* from Latin, whereas French has only *insomnie* and German *schlaflosigkeit*.

But this borrowing has not stopped. It is an ongoing process. And many of the words and other expressions acquired during the past couple of hundred years have not yet become thoroughly anglicized. Perhaps some never will. They retain an aura of 'foreignness'. When they appear in printed texts, they are often italicized, as if they are not quite fully paid-up members of the language. When we say them, we often attempt to reproduce their pronunciation in their original language. If they have accents or other diacritic marks in the language they came from, these are generally retained. *Foreign Words in English* records around a thousand of the most widely used of such words in present-day English.

It represents, of course, only a fraction of the total of non-native words that appear in English from time to time. On the basis of what criteria was this selection made? The first was a matter of sheer frequency of occurrence. Speakers of English constantly have recourse, when referring to artefacts produced in a foreign culture, phenomena occurring in a foreign country, and so on, to the names applied to these things in the local language. But in the majority of cases the word is used once or twice, as needed, and then forgotten about. For instance, in the *New York Times*, 15 January 1989, the Portuguese word *açorda* appeared, denoting a sort of Portuguese bread soup; and an article in the *Observer Magazine*, 4 December 1988, used *bonzak*, a Czech slang term for someone who informs on dissidents to the authorities. These and thousands of words like them show no sign of taking up permanent residence in English. If the occasion arises they can be pressed into service again, but no continuity of usage has been established. Items of this sort are not included in the book.

Certain types of thing or areas of activity tend to provoke a disproportionate amount of lexical borrowing in English. It is extremely common, for example, for species of plants and animals to be named in English with the word used in their place of origin. Many of these have become naturalized (*budgerigar, okapi, wapiti*, etc), but hundreds of others are used so seldom by non-specialists that they retain a 'foreign' flavour (for instance, *sakabula*, a Zulu name for a species of bird, and *sasankwa*, a Japanese name for a species of shrub). To have recorded every one of these would have turned the dictionary into a zoological and botanical catalogue. Similarly, in the field of gastronomy, English has borrowed an enormous number of terms from French (*frisée, gratin dauphinois, hollandaise, julienne*, and so on). A complete listing of these would have unbalanced the dictionary, as would exhaustive coverage of Italian musical terminology adopted by English. On the whole, therefore, *Foreign Words in English* concentrates on loanwords that are part of general English vocabulary, rather than those that are restricted to the specialized language of a particular field.

Few of the world's languages have altogether escaped the attentions of English, but by far the leading contributors of unanglicized foreignisms are French and Latin. In the case of French, a main reason for this is presumably that the language has a certain cachet. Many of the areas of activity in which French terminology predominates are thought of as part of the world of sophistication and high fashion: clothing and hairdressing, for example (or should that be *couture* and *coiffure?*), fine art, ballet, and, as we have seen, food and wine. But even in the case of more general vocabulary, the dropping of a French phrase (*pièce de résistance, embarras de richesse*) may lend an air of cultivation and worldly polish – albeit sometimes spurious.

If larding one's English with French suggests sophistication, the use of classical tags and other Latinisms – now surely in terminal decline as the teaching of Latin winds down – may be taken as an indication of solider intellectual virtues, of a mind steeped in the literature of ancient Rome, or at least retaining some fragments of school Latin. Since Latin is not a living language, with a continuing spoken tradition to reinforce its 'foreignness', individual Latin words borrowed into English tend to become naturalized fairly quickly (*sanatorium, consensus, moratorium,* and *referendum* are all 19th-century acquisitions). So quite a large proportion of the Latin terms included here are not words but phrases, prepositional (*ex cathedra, ex libris, pro rata, pro tempore*) and others (*mutatis mutandis, non sequitur, nunc dimittis, prima facie*). English legal terminology is particularly rich in Latinisms.

Other leading contributors to English include Italian (*duce, grosso modo, numero uno*), Spanish (*aficionado, duende, mañana*), German (*autobahn, heurige, weltanschauung*), Russian (*apparatchik, glasnost, kolkhoz*), Yiddish (*nebbich, schlock, schmaltz*), and Japanese (*banzai, karaoke, seppuku*).

What is the future outlook for foreign borrowings in English? The answer must be – bright. Compared with a hundred years ago, the broad mass of English-speakers in Britain have vastly greater contacts with other languages, thanks to the teaching of such languages in school and the advent of package tours to foreign parts. A further factor that will surely come into play in the future is the closer links between Britain and its EC partners. All this means that not only is there no let-up in the flow of foreignisms into English, but that there is far less tendency to anglicize them once they have arrived. Greater awareness of other languages means that English-speakers feel more comfortable using their words.

They do not always get them completely right. This applies particularly in the area of pronunciation. Half-remembered phono-logical principles tend to get stretched beyond their limit. The first vowel in *ingénue* and *lingerie*, for instance, is often turned by English-speakers into a nasalized *o* (as in *hot*), this being the commonest nasal vowel in words borrowed from French. And it is far from uncommon to hear the final consonant of *Munich* pronounced like the *ch* of *loch*, as if it were a German word (the German name of the city is *München*). Nor does English stop at 'reinterpreting' the pronunciation of foreign words. Sometimes it even invents new 'foreign' words. The best-known is the pseudo-French *bon viveur*.

English-speakers' proverbial resistance to foreign languages, their inability to learn them, may occasionally mean that borrowed words end up rather mangled, but the influx shows no sign of slowing down.

John Ayto

Pronunciation Guide

Vowels

i:	need	/ni:d/
ɪ	pit	/pɪt/
i	very	/'vɛri/
ɛ	pet	/pɛt/
æ	pat	/pæt/
ʌ	other	/'ʌðəʳ/
ʊ	book	/bʊk/
u:	too	/tu:/
u	influence	/'ɪnfluəns/
ɒ	cough	/kɒf/
ɔ:	ought	/ɔ:t/
ɜ:	work	/wɜ:k/
ə	another	/ən'ʌðəʳ/
ɑ:	part	/pɑ:t/

Glides

eɪ	plate	/pleɪt/
aɪ	sigh	/saɪ/
ɔɪ	ploy	/plɔɪ/
oʊ	go	/goʊ/
aʊ	now	/naʊ/
ɪə	hear	/hɪəʳ/
ɛə	fair	/fɛəʳ/
ʊə	poor	/pʊəʳ/

Consonants

p	pit	/pɪt/
b	bit	/bɪt/
t	ten	/tɛn/
d	den	/dɛn/
k	cap	/kæp/
g	gap	/gæp/
ʃ	shin	/ʃɪn/
ʒ	pleasure	/'plɛʒəʳ/
ʧ	chin	/ʧɪn/
ʤ	budge	/bʌʤ/
h	hit	/hɪt/
f	fit	/fɪt/
v	very	/'vɛri/
θ	thin	/θɪn/
ð	then	/ðɛn/
s	sin	/sɪn/
z	zones	/zoʊnz/
m	meat	/mi:t/
n	knit	/nɪt/
ŋ	sing	/sɪŋ/
l	line	/laɪn/
r	rid	/rɪd/
j	yet	/jɛt/
w	quick	/kwɪk/

ʳ indicates an 'r' pronounced only before a following vowel
' precedes the syllable with primary stress

A

à bas

French *à bas* is the equivalent of the native English *down with*. It literally means 'to the bottom' (the elements of which it is made up are ultimately the same as those which lie behind English *abase*), and is used to express disapproval of someone or something, or to call for their removal or expulsion. Although never completely naturalized, it has been sporadically used in English as a more rhetorical alternative to *down with!*

abbé

The French word *abbé* has a long history in English, going right back to the early 16th century. Formally it is the same word as English *abbot* (both are descended from Latin *abbātem*), but in French its meaning has spread out far more widely, encompassing virtually any Roman Catholic secular cleric. English uses it specifically for a 'French' priest.

The whole family of *abb-* words, including also *abbey*, *abbess*, and *abbacy*, goes back ultimately, via Latin and Greek, to Aramaic *abb(a)*, which means literally 'father'. It was used in the Eastern Church for all monks, but in the West its descendants came to be narrowed down to the 'head of a monastery'. *Abba* itself, incidentally, has been used by English Biblical writers and translators down the centuries to denote 'God the Father' (on the model of *abba* in the Greek New Testament).

ab initio

Latin *ab initio* means literally 'from the beginning'. Latin *initium* 'beginning' is a derivative of a verb meaning literally 'go in', so its underlying sense is of 'entering on something'; it has also given English *initial*, *initiate*, and *initiative*. English has used *ab initio* since at least the early 17th century (the first occurrence of it on record in an English text is from Ben Jonson's *Every Man out of his Humour*, 1600), often with connotations of the unformedness or lack of experience that attend the beginnings of any undertaking. The 20th century has seen it increasingly pressed into service as an adjective. The RAF, for instance,

1

speaks of '*ab initio* trainers' – aircraft in which beginners are taught to fly.

à bon marché

French *bon marché*, literally 'good market', denotes 'cheapness', and *acheter* or *vendre quelquechose à bon marché* is to buy or sell something cheaply, at a bargain price. Without ever fully naturalizing it, English has occasionally commandeered the term, particularly when a French flavour is desired. The synonymous *à bon compte* has put in an appearance from time to time too. *Bon marché* has also been taken up in English as a noun, with the twin meanings 'bargain' and 'shop which sells goods at bargain prices'.

abonnement

French *s'abonner* means 'take out a subscription' (for example, if one *s'abonne à un journal*, one 'subscribes to a newspaper'). Derived from it is the noun *abonnement*, which denotes both 'subscription' in the abstract and also the reusable ticket to which such a subscription entitles one – a 'season-ticket'. It has a range of applications in French, including 'railway season-ticket', but it is in two particular contexts that it has come to be used in English: first, in the 1890s, for a subscription entitling one to seats at a particular theatre, concert hall, etc for a season; and second, from the 1960s, for season-tickets for the use of ski slopes, lifts, etc at continental ski resorts. English also uses the noun *abonné*, for a person who has taken out such a subscription.

ab ovo

Ab ovo is in effect a synonym of *ab initio*. It means literally 'from the egg', and hence by metaphorical extension, 'from the beginning'. Latin *ovum* 'egg', which is probably distantly related to English *egg*, has also given English *oval* and *ovary*. The use of *ab ovo* in English dates back to the late 16th century. It appears to be a simple allusion to the fact that the egg is symbolic of the beginning of life, but its occurrence in the expression *ab ovo usque ad mala* in Horace's *Satire* iii.6 suggests an alternative explanation. This means literally 'from the egg right through to the apple', and refers to the Roman custom of starting a meal with eggs and typically having apples for the dessert course (the English equivalent would be *from soup to nuts*). Horace adds a further strand to the history of *ab ovo* in his *Ars poetica*, where he writes *nec gemino bellum Trojanum orditur ab ovo* 'nor was the Trojan War begun from a twin egg' – an allusion to the fact that the Trojan War was brought about by Helen, who was born from one of the two eggs 'laid' by Leda after her liaison with the swan (Castor and Pollux came out of the other one), but that Homer did not begin his account of the war from this 'egg'.

absit omen

Absit omen is a superstitious formula intended to dispel any possibility that by referring to some unpleasant event in the past, one could in some sense be predicting or even bringing about its repetition in the future (eg 'The last time we came here, we all went down with flu. *Absit omen!*'). It means in Latin literally 'may the omen be absent' (*absit* is the third-person singular present subjunctive of *abesse* 'be away, be absent', which has also given English *absent*); but here 'being absent' is interpreted in the sense 'being ineffective, having no force'. Its use in English dates back to the late 16th century.

ab urbe condita

Latin *ab urbe condita* means literally 'from the foundation of the city' (that is, Rome), and it was frequently used in the ancient Roman world to designate a point in time from which dates were calculated. Legend has it that Romulus and Remus were the founders of the city, and the Roman author Marcus Terentius Varro (116–27 BC) reckoned that it came into being in 753 BC – the date usually referred to by *ab urbe condita*. The phrase was often abbreviated to *AUC*, which was also taken as standing for *anno urbis conditae* 'in the year of the foundation of the city'.

a cappella

A cappella (or *a capella*, as it is often erroneously written in English) is a musical term, denoting choral music performed without an instrumental accompaniment. In Italian it means literally 'in the style of the chapel', a reference to 16th-century church music, which was always performed unaccompanied. English originally acquired it in the middle of the 19th century as *alla cappella*, but the form *a cappella* is recorded from the 1870s and rapidly became dominant.

accouchement

The 19th century, ever anxious to put screens round the disturbing realities of life, sought to hide the process of childbirth behind impenetrable French. So English acquired the French term *accouchement*, which in its origins resembles the now obsolete English expression *be brought to bed of a child*: it is a derivative of *coucher* 'put to bed', which is also the source of English *couch*. Along with it came *accoucheur* 'male obstetrician' and *accoucheuse* 'midwife', and even a verb *accouche* 'assist a woman in childbirth'. The latter did not last very long, and *accouchement* itself now has a decidedly dated air. Its pronunciation nowadays is an approximation to French, but when it was commoner it was often anglicized to /əˈkʊʃmənt/ or even /əˈkaʊtʃmənt/.

à cheval

À cheval is a betting term, used particularly in roulette. It denotes a bet that is placed on two numbers (or, if the game is cards, on two cards). The phrase means literally in French 'on horseback', and its metaphorical use is based on the manner of placing the bet: the chips, coins, etc are positioned on the line separating two numbers, as if sitting astride a horse with the legs hanging down on either side, and if either comes up when the wheel is spun, the bet is won. Use of the term in English dates back at least to the 1880s, and it has also been pressed into figurative usage: in 1919 T. E. Lawrence wrote in a letter 'If we pay half the Hejaz expenses direct to Mecca, and another share direct to the Government of Syria, we seem reasonably *à cheval* upon all possible contingencies'.

achtung

Achtung is one of those German words that owe their presence in, or on the fringes of, English mainly to their use in the stereotypical portrayal of German soldiers, airmen, etc in pulp fiction, comics, and other popular materials dealing with the two World Wars. When danger threatens, the cry is *achtung!* – meaning roughly 'Look out!, Take care!' In its own language, *achtung* is not just an exclamation; it is an ordinary noun too, meaning 'attention', and also 'esteem, respect'. It is part of a family of words derived from *acht*, which denotes 'attention, heed, consideration'.

acte gratuit

An *acte gratuit* is an action performed impulsively, without any apparent motivation. As a concept it was formulated and celebrated by the French writer André Gide (1869–1951), who was much concerned in his writing with the conflict between self-fulfilment and what one is compelled to do by duty and convention. By the mid-1930s the term was being used in English.

acushla

Acushla is a term of Irish endearment, spoken when addressing a loved one. English has used it since the mid-19th century to give a convincing flavour to dialogue between Anglo-Irish speakers. The initial *a-* is simply an exclamation, equivalent to English *oh*; *cushla* represents Irish Gaelic *cuisle*, which means literally 'vein', hence 'pulse'. The key to this rather odd metaphor may be found in the Irish Gaelic expression *cuisle mo chroidhe*, literally 'my heart's pulse', which is also used as a term of endearment – as it were comparing one's darling to that which sustains one's own life. An alternative version of the word occasionally used in English is *macushla*, where *ma-* represents Irish Gaelic *mo* 'my'.

addendum, plural addenda

Addendum began life as a noun use of the gerundive of the Latin verb *addere* 'add' (source of English *add*), and so it means literally 'that which is to be added'. English adopted it towards the end of the 18th century, usually with the specific sense 'something added to a book at a late stage, after the main text has been printed, often supplying material that had been left out by mistake' (to begin with only the plural, *addenda*, seems to have been used; the singular does not come on the scene until the mid-19th century). Over and above this, *addendum* is used as a technical term in mechanics, applied to various dimensions of toothed wheels in gears.

à deux

A quiet little dinner *à deux* is one attended by only two people – the implication being of an intimate occasion, quite possibly candle-lit, conducive to private conversation, typically of a romantic nature. In French literally 'for two', the expression made its first appearance in English in the 1870s as a musical term, denoting a piece or passage composed for two performers or instruments, but by the end of the century it had broadened into its current general use.

ad hoc

Literally, Latin *ad hoc* means nothing more than 'towards this', but it is in the extended sense 'for this purpose' that it has become a familiar component of the English language (the first record of it in English dates back to the mid-17th century). Its central application is to things created in response to a specific need, but the implied contrast with things created in advance, anticipating such a need, has lent it derogatory connotations of hastily cobbled-together solutions to problems that ought to have been foreseen. In this mode it has spawned jocular derivatives such as *ad-hoc-ness* and *ad hoc-ery* (*The Economist* in October 1961 opined that 'Britain thrives on "anomalies" and "ad hoc-eries"').

ad hominem

An '*ad hominem* argument' is one that appeals not to logic or reason but to personal preferences or feelings (the Latin phrase means literally 'to the man' – *hominem* is the accusative form of Latin *homō* 'man'). There is evidence that the term was in use in English by at least the end of the 16th century. In modern English usage there is a tendency to extend its underlying meaning of 'personal' away from considerations of formal logic to the more mundane 'personally abusive' (as in 'The minister was subjected to a vicious *ad hominem* attack' – implying that his personal conduct or character were the target rather than his policies).

ad infinitum

When John Bunyan in his *Pilgrim's Progress* (1678) wrote 'I'll put you by yourselves, lest you at last should prove *ad infinitum*' – the first recorded use of the expression *ad infinitum* in English – he was referring to ideas for his book, which were threatening to become infinite in number, too many to handle. That is a fairly far cry from the accepted modern usage of the term, which is better represented by Jonathan Swift's famous lines 'So, naturalists observe, a flea / Hath smaller fleas that on him prey; / And these have smaller fleas to bite 'em, / And so proceed *ad infinitum*' (*On Poetry*, 1733). *Ad infinitum* denotes wearisomely endless repetition, expansion, or recursion (in its original Latin it means literally 'to infinity').

ad litem

If someone involved in a legal action is unable or unfit to take responsibility for his or her part in the proceedings (because of insanity, for example, or because of insufficient years), the court may appoint a guardian *ad litem* to act on his or her behalf. Latin *ad litem* means literally 'for the lawsuit' (Latin *lis* 'strife, lawsuit' lies behind English *allege* and *litigation*), and it has been part of English legal terminology since at least the middle of the 18th century.

ad nauseam

Latin *ad nauseam* means literally 'to the point of sickness'. Latin *nausea* 'sickness', which itself became an English word in the 16th century, came from a Greek word which originally denoted 'sea-sickness', and is related to English *navy* and *noise*. English has used it since at least the early 17th century to express the idea of something continuing for so long or being repeated so often that it becomes tedious or even sickening.

ad referendum

Ad referendum is, or was, part of the terminology of international diplomacy. Literally in Latin 'for reference', it denotes that a particular proposal put to diplomatic representatives in negotiations is provisionally accepted by them, but must be referred for confirmation to the government, ruler, etc that they represent. Its use in English dates back to the late 18th century.

ad rem

English occasionally uses *ad rem* as a Latinate alternative to the vernacular *to the point*. Literally 'to the matter', it denotes that something is relevant or pertinent to the matter in hand. It is first recorded in English as long ago as the early 17th century, in Thomas Middleton's comedy *The Family of Love* (1608): '*Ad rem, ad rem*, master Poppin: leave your allegories ... and to the point'.

ad valorem

Latin *ad valorem* means literally 'to value' – that is, 'according to what it is worth'. (*valorem* is the accusative case of late Latin *valor* 'value, worth', from which English gets *valour*). English uses it, and has done since the early 18th century, as a taxation term, denoting that duties, taxes, etc are to be levied on an item on the basis of the value that it is stated to have. It began life as an adverbial phrase, but it is now probably more commonly used as an adjective (as in '*ad valorem* duties'). It can be abbreviated to *ad val* or *av*.

advocatus diaboli

An *advocatus diaboli*, literally in Latin the 'devil's advocate', was originally an official appointed in the Roman Catholic Church to present reasons against a proposal to make a particular person a saint. The official title of such a person is *Promotor Fidei* 'Promotor of the Faith'. Metaphorically, though, the term came to be applied to a person who deliberately opposes an argument in order to expose any flaws in it. The anglicized version of the term, *devil's advocate*, dates back to the mid-18th century, but *advocatus diaboli* is not recorded in English before the 1840s.

affaire

English has taken over French *affaire* on two separate occasions. The first time it crossed the Channel was in the 13th century, in its original sense 'that which is to be done, matter, business' (etymologically it means 'to do, to be done', for it is a nominalization of the phrase *à faire* 'to do'). This has long since been naturalized as *affair*. But at the beginning of the 19th century it was borrowed again, this time in the phrase *affaire de coeur*, denoting a sexual relationship, and by the middle of the century *affaire* was being used on its own in this sense (the parallel use of the native *affair* dates back at least to the early 18th century). Another synonym occasionally encountered in English is *affaire d'amour* 'love affair'. English has also borrowed from French *affaire d'honneur* 'affair of honour', which denotes a 'duel'.

affiche

An *affiche* is a poster put up in a public place, typically advertising some forthcoming event. The word is French in origin, and its use in English (which dates from the early 19th century) often refers specifically to French contexts – for example, to the cylindrical billboards plastered with *affiches* that are such a feature of French city streets. It is a derivative of the verb *afficher* 'put up in a public place, display' (which is related ultimately to English *affix*, although they do not share a common source).

afflatus

The 'divine *afflatus*' is inspiration that descends from on high and galvanizes the wilting poet, painter, composer, etc. Latin *afflatus* originally meant literally a 'blowing or breathing on something' (it is derived ultimately from the verb *flāre* 'blow', which also gave English *flatulent*), but it was extended metaphorically to the 'creative impulse', thought of as being 'breathed into' someone by the gods, and it was in this sense that English took the word over in the mid-17th century. From the 17th to the 19th centuries it was often anglicized as *afflation*, but this has not survived. The notion of the creative impulse being 'breathed in' is replicated in the word *inspiration* itself, which comes from Latin *inspīrāre* 'breathe into'.

aficionado

An *aficionado* is a very keen and knowledgeable devotee of a particular area of interest – for example, a 'chess *aficionado*', or an '*aficionado* of big-band music'. English borrowed the word, in the 1840s, from Spanish, where it denotes an 'amateur' – both in the original sense of an 'enthusiast, one who does something out of love', and as contrasted with 'professional'. It is a noun use of the past participle of the verb *aficionar* 'become fond of', which in turn is derived from *afición* 'affection' (a relative of English *affection*). English-speakers aware of its Spanish origin often essay a /-fiθ-/ for the second syllable, rather than the usual anglicized /-fiʃ-/ or /-fis-/, but few go the whole hog and pronounce the *d* as /ð/ rather than /d/. Semantically, English often uses it specifically for a 'devotee of bullfighting'.

a fortiori

Fortiori is the ablative case of Latin *fortius* 'stronger', the comparative form of *fortis* 'strong'. So *a fortiori* means literally 'from the stronger'. It is short for *a fortiori argumento* 'from the stronger argument', and it is used to signify that if one proposition holds good, then on the same grounds a further proposition is even more valid (eg 'If a rich country like America can't afford a space programme, then *a fortiori* Britain can't'). Its use in English dates back to the early 17th century.

agent provocateur

An *agent provocateur* is someone who incites others to commit crimes. Typically he or she would be a person sent incognito by a government, the police, etc to associate with a group of people suspected of being up to no good, and particularly of planning seditious activities, in order to egg them on to commit criminal acts so that they can be arrested. The morality and legality of this sort of activity are clearly dubious, and *agent provocateur* is a decidedly derogatory term. English borrowed it from French (where it means literally 'provocative agent') in the late 19th century.

aggiornamento

Etymologically, Italian *aggiornamento* is virtually the same as English *adjournment* (both are formed from descendants of Latin *ad* 'to' and *diurnum* 'day'), but there the resemblance ends. *Aggiornamento* means 'modernization' – literally 'bringing up to today', from *a* 'to' and *giorno* 'day' – and it owes its fairly recent introduction into English to the liberalizing policies of Pope John XXIII. It was he who convened the Second Vatican Council in 1962 to consider proposals to reform the Roman Catholic Church's institutions, and by the following year *aggiornamento*, the Italian term for this modernizing impulse, had made it into English. Nor was it long before its use was being extended more widely, to cover political reform.

agiotage

Agiotage is a term of the stock and currency markets. Broadly speaking, it denotes dealing in foreign exchange or in stocks and shares. English borrowed it from French in the early 19th century, but it is a term with quite a complex linguistic history. It was derived from the verb *agioter* 'speculate in stocks and shares', which itself was formed from the noun *agio* 'stock-brokering'. This was borrowed from Italian *agio* or *aggio* (which English acquired in the 17th century as *agio*). The Italian word may have been an alteration of the dialectal *lajjë*, which came from Medieval Greek *allagion* 'exchange'. And *allagion* was descended from Greek *allagē* 'change', a derivative of *allos* 'other' (to which English *alien* and *else* are distantly related).

à gogo

Far apart as they now seem, English *agog* and *à gogo* may have the same ultimate source. *A gogo*, borrowed from French in the 1960s, means 'in abundance, galore'. It has never really caught on to any extent, and probably remains most familiar in *Whisky à gogo*, once popular as a nightclub name. French *gogo* may have originated as a reduplicated form of the first syllable of obsolete French *gogue* 'merriment', which itself was perhaps imitative of the sound of noisy chatter or roistering. And Old French had the expression *en gogues* 'merrily', which it is thought is probably the source of English *agog* (first recorded in the mid-16th century).

agora

Greek *agorā́* originally meant 'assembly' (it was derived from the verb *ageirein* 'assemble'), but it spread out metaphorically to encompass first 'place of assembly' and then 'market-place' and 'open space' (whence English *agoraphobia*, which signifies 'fear of open spaces'). Like the *forum* in the Roman world, the *agora* formed a key central public space in ancient Greek cities, and contained most of the important public buildings. The best known is the one in Athens, to the north of the Acropolis, whose most notable building is perhaps the 5th-century-BC Theseum, a temple. Use of the term *agora* in English dates back to the late 16th century. It should not, incidentally, be confused with *agora*, the name of a former Israeli unit of currency, which is a derivative of the Hebrew verb *āgōr* 'collect'.

agrément

English originally acquired French *agrément* in the 14th century, since when it has become anglicized to *agreement*. But towards the end of the 17th century it crossed the Channel again, in the plural, in the specialized sense 'agreeable features, pleasant qualities'. At first it was often translated as *agreements*, but by the mid-18th century it was commoner to use the French form, which in writing was frequently rendered as *agrémens*: 'We talked about the *agrémens* of the place. It was very agreeable for the English', William Thackeray, *Vanity Fair* (1848). A specialized application of the term was to musical grace notes, such as trills and appoggiaturas.

That plural usage has now died out, but in the 20th century *agrément* returned to English via international diplomatic terminology, in the sense 'approval given by a government to the appointment of another country's ambassador'.

aguardiente

The offer of a glass of *aguardiente* should be treated with caution. The contents are liable to be fiery. The word is Spanish in origin, and is a compound of *agua* 'water' and *ardiente* 'burning' – the nearest native English equivalent would be *fire-water*. A variety of generally coarse spirits share the name. Originally in Spain and Portugal it was used for a rough-and-ready local brandy. In Spanish America it came to be applied to rum. It was mainly this connection that brought it into English, in the 19th century, and once there it was also pressed into service for an anise-based liqueur and, in the south-western USA, for the local variety of whiskey.

aide-de-camp

An *aide-de-camp* was originally and literally in French a 'camp-assistant' – that is to say, a junior officer who performed various duties to help a senior officer in camp. English adopted the term in the late 17th century, since when it has become formalized as a designation for an officer who acts as a confidential personal assistant for an officer of high rank, such as a general or admiral. It is often abbreviated to *ADC*.

aide-mémoire

French *aide-mémoire* means literally 'help-memory'. It has a range of applications: it is used for a small book containing a digest of useful information, such as a list of formulae; for a memorandum; and, in international diplomacy, for a summary of the items in an agreement. French being historically the language of diplomacy, it was in the last of these senses that *aide-mémoire* became more widely known, and English adopted it in the mid-19th century.

à la

French *à la* has taken on a life of its own in English, in the sense 'in the style of' – for example, 'wiggling her hips *à la* Marilyn Monroe'. The earliest known examples of this sort of usage come in the letters of Jane Austen, written in the early 19th century – this one, for instance, from 1808: 'Yesterday passed quite *à la* Godmersham'. Its inspiration, of course, is the large number of

French expressions beginning *à la* that have been introduced into English over the centuries. Particular exposure to the construction has been in the field of gastronomy: *à la meunière*, for instance, denotes a dish in which a fish is lightly coated in flour and then fried in butter, and *à la provençale* signifies a dish in which olive oil, tomatoes and garlic predominate. Purists sometimes object, misguidedly, to expressions like 'batting à la Tom Graveney', on the grounds that French *la* is feminine, and should not be used with reference to males; but in fact *à la* is short for *à la mode de* 'in the manner of'.

à la carte

If you order a restaurant meal *à la carte*, you order it item by item from a typically extensive menu (*carte* is the standard French term for 'menu'). Each item is individually priced. This contrasts with a *table d'hôte* menu, where the range of choices is far smaller, and an overall inclusive price is charged for the meal, regardless of the dishes selected. Use of the term *à la carte* in English dates back at least to the early 19th century. Of roughly equal antiquity is the English use of *carte* for 'menu', although it has never caught on to the same extent as *à la carte*. Metaphorical uses of the term occasionally crop up, suggesting choice from an array of options: 'The law is the law . . . there can be no dining *à la carte* with the law of the land', Michael Heseltine (December 1990).

à la mode

French *à la mode* means 'in fashion, fashionable'. English adopted it in the 17th century (it crops up in the title of Dryden's tragi-comedy *Marriage-à-la-mode*, 1672), and before long was well on the way to anglicizing it: between the 17th and 19th centuries it was commonly spelled *alamode*, and it was not unusual to find *all-a-mode*, as if it contained English *all*. There was even a noun coined from it – *alamodality* 'the quality of being fashionable' (described by the poet Robert Southey as 'a good and pregnant word', 1834). The present-day form *à la mode* represents a reassertion of the original French.

As well as its general sense of 'fashionable', *à la mode* has two particular meanings in the field of gastronomy: it denotes a method of preparing meat, and especially beef, by braising it with vegetables and then serving it in a rich brown sauce; and

13

in American English it signifies 'served with ice-cream' (as in 'apple pie *à la mode*').

à la page

In French, *être à la page* is to be up to date or in the know, *ne pas être à la page* to be behind the times (*à la page* literally means 'at the page'). It was in the 1930s that *à la page* first put in an appearance in English, and it has cropped up sporadically ever since.

al dente

Al dente is an Italian culinary term applied particularly to the cooking of pasta. Literally 'to the tooth', it denotes a cooking period sufficient for the pasta to be done, but not over-soft – still retaining some firmness when bitten. It made its first appearance in English texts in the 1930s, and in a culture where excessive boiling of food is a popular vice, it has in recent decades supplied a gap in the lexicon when describing vegetables, and sometimes even fruit, as 'boiled but still firm'.

al fresco

Italian *fresco* means 'fresh' (indeed it is closely related to English *fresh*). *Al fresco*, literally 'in the fresh', has come into English in two distinct guises. First, as part of the terminology of artistic technique: it denotes painting that is done on freshly applied plaster, while it is still wet (the resulting paintings are, of course, called *frescoes*). Second, and much more commonly, it means 'in the fresh air, in the open' (as in 'lunching *al fresco*'). Both usages date back in English to the middle of the 18th century, but it is the latter that has become firmly naturalized, to the extent of being used as an adjective ('an *al fresco* lunch').

alma mater

Latin *alma mater* means literally 'bountiful mother'. The adjective *almus* is related to the verb *alere* 'nourish', from which English gets *alimentary*, *alimony*, and indeed *alumnus*. The Romans used *alma mater* as an epithet of various goddesses thought of as bestowing nature's bounty on humanity, notably Ceres and Cybele (mention of it in English in this sense dates back to the 14th century). In the modern era it has been adopted as a term for one's former school, college, or university, thought of as being the place where one received one's intellectual nourishment. In American English it is additionally used for an 'official college or university song'.

aloha

Perhaps it is the accidental resemblance to *hallo*, but few Polynesian words have entrenched themselves so firmly in English as *aloha*. It is instantly recognizable as the all-purpose salutation in Hawaii and elsewhere in the South Pacific, doing service for both 'hallo' and 'goodbye' (its original literal meaning in Hawaiian is 'love'). It has been used in English since the mid-19th century in Hawaiian contexts, and the linkage is now so firm that it is almost symbolic of Hawaii: the islands are often termed 'the Aloha State', and there is a type of luridly coloured and extravagantly patterned short-sleeved shirt, originally worn by holiday-makers in the Pacific, that is widely known in American English as an *aloha shirt*.

alumnus, plural alumni

An *alumnus* of a college is someone who used to be a student there. In Latin the word denoted simply a 'pupil' or 'foster son' (it is derived from the verb *alere* 'nourish, bring up', which also lies behind the *alma* of English *alma mater*), and that is how English first used it, in the 17th century. The term's modern usage emerged in the USA, in the 19th century, and even today is largely restricted to American English. The equivalent word for a female former student is *alumna*.

ambiance

Etymologically, *ambiance* denotes 'surroundings': it goes back ultimately to Latin *ambīre* 'go round', a compound verb formed from *ambi-* 'round' and *īre* 'go'. English acquired it from French towards the end of the 19th century, since when it has led rather a double life: it was quite common originally to find it anglicized to *ambience*, with a pronunciation to match its spelling, but its original French form survived, and in recent years seems to have made a comeback, complete with quasi-French nasalized vowels. In meaning, too, it has evolved from the concrete 'surroundings' to the more intangible 'atmosphere or character of a place'. In this sense Italian and Spanish *ambiente* are also sometimes used in English.

âme damnée

In French, *être l'âme damnée de quelqu'un* is to be someone's tool, their willing accomplice (*âme damnée* means literally 'damned soul'). English adopted the usage as 'be someone's *âme damnée*', and it is first recorded in the works of that enthusiastic expander of the English language, Sir Walter Scott ('He is the *ame damnée* of every one about my court', *Peveril of the Peak*, 1823).

amende honorable

An *amende honorable* is a public apology, particularly one which rehabilitates the reputation of the person who has been wronged. In French the term means literally 'honourable compensation, honourable reparation' (*amende* is the singular form of the word from which English got *amends* 'reparation'). At first it was used literally to denote a situation in which someone had to stand up in public and make a humiliating admission of the wrong he had done, but now such a personal appearance is not implied. The term probably began to be used in English in the 17th century, and at first it was usual to anglicize it, either partially (to *amend honourable*) or wholly (to *honourable amends*), but since the 19th century English has gone back to the original French.

a mensa et thoro

In former times, when it was desired to put an end to a marriage (on grounds of adultery, for instance), an ecclesiastical court could declare the two parties divorced *a mensa et thoro*. Literally 'from table and bed' (Latin *thorus*, or *torus*, originally meant 'swelling, bulge', and is the source of English *toroid*; 'bed' is a later extended sense), this signified that the couple would no longer live together, although legally they would remain married. Marriages at that time could be annulled only on grounds such as bigamy, consanguinity, etc. It was in 1857 that the law was changed, introducing the modern concept of divorce, and what was until then known as 'divorce *a mensa et thoro*' came to be termed 'legal separation' or 'judicial separation'.

amicus curiae , plural amici curiae

An *amicus curiae* is someone, typically a lawyer, who is invited by a court to give his opinion on a point of law in a case to which he is not a party. The term means literally in Latin 'friend of the court', and is first recorded in English in one of Francis

Bacon's essays, at the beginning of the 17th century. In American law, an '*amicus* brief' is a legal submission by someone who is not a party to a case, but has an interest in its outcome.

amour

French *amour* 'love' has a long history in the English language. It goes back as far as the 13th century, and by the 15th century it seems to have become thoroughly naturalized (pronounced like *hammer* without the *h*). At this stage it was simply a synonym for the native *love* (*in amours with* was used for 'in love with'). But by the 17th century this generalized sense was well on the way out, leaving the more suggestive usage of love affair, especially a clandestine or illicit one', which survives today. It was presumably the connotations of French naughtiness that contributed to this development, as also to the reversion to a Frenchified pronunciation, which happened at about the same time.

French *amour* is descended from Latin *amor* 'love' – and in the 16th and 17th centuries *amor* often replaced *amour* in English.

amour propre

French *amour propre* means literally 'own love, self-love'; it denotes both a 'legitimate self-esteem', and also 'vanity, conceit'. English acquired it in the latter part of the 18th century, and uses it mainly to suggest the sort of prickly good opinion of oneself that is easily flattered but also easily offended.

amuse-gueule

An *amuse-gueule* is a small snack – such as a bite-sized pizza, a tiny tartlet filled with a quiche mixture, or a simple cracker topped with caviare – that is served with drinks at a cocktail party or before a meal, or, increasingly these days, as a complimentary pre-first course to consume while pondering the menu at up-market restaurants ('In the drawing room beforehand [before lunch] there were signs of the excellence to come by way of the warm filo pastry amuse-gueules', *Decanter*, November 1990). The term means in French literally 'amuse-gob' – that is, something tasty to keep your mouth happy – and has started to become more familiar to English-speakers in recent years with the upsurge of interest in French gastronomy.

ancien régime

The original *ancien régime* was the pre-Revolutionary system of government in France. A feudal society persisted long after the passing of the Middle Ages, and the Bourbon kings still ruled with absolute power. All this 'old régime' was swept away in 1789, and it was not long before references to the *ancien régime* began to appear in English texts (the earliest on record dates from 1794). Translated versions have also been common – *ancient régime* (which predates *ancien régime* in English by two years) and *old régime* – but the original French version has retained its place in the English language. Indeed, it is now used more widely, to denote any political system or ruling elite that has been superseded and now seems outdated. *The Guardian* of 7 March 1961, for instance, wrote of '*ancien* (pre-Nasser) *régime* Egyptian politicians', and *The Observer* of 9 December 1990 suggested that 'if ... Sarah Hogg [a relative of Tory grandees] ever conspires to organise a coup d'état by the Tory Party *ancien régime* from her Downing Street office, she will be able to keep it in the family.'

anglice

Anglice originated as a medieval Latin adverb based on the adjective *anglicus* 'English', meaning 'in English'. English took it over in the 17th century, and uses it both when introducing an English translation of a foreign expression ('That baptism shall, nevertheless, be administered to it by injection – *par le moyen d'une petite canulle* – Anglicè *a squirt*', Laurence Sterne, *Tristram Shandy*, 1760) and, perhaps more commonly, when introducing a plain English explication of a piece of circumlocution.

angst

It was not until the middle of the 20th century that English felt the need to import the word *angst* 'anxiety' from German. There are sporadic examples of its occurrence before then, as a conscious Germanism or as an untranslated technical term in English versions of philosophers and psychiatrists such as Heidegger and Freud, but it was the 1940s that was the true foster-decade of *angst*. There is more to it than simple *anxiety* (a word to which it is distantly related): it is a gnawingly persistent but unsettlingly ill-defined fear, often mixed with elements of guilt and remorse, which assails modern man, cast adrift in the existential void of an irreligious age. An early and enthusiastic user of the term was Cyril Connolly. One of its commonest manifestations these days is in the compound adjective *angst-ridden*.

anno Domini

Latin *anno Domini* means literally 'in the year of the Lord' (it is in the ablative case), and it is used in giving dates of the Christian era, counting forward from the year in which Christ is traditionally accepted as having been born. It is said to have been introduced by the monk Dionysius Exiguus in the 6th century. Its use in English dates back at least to the 16th century, although in this literal role it is usually represented by the abbreviation *AD* (purists insist that this should precede the date, but it is standard practice nowadays to put it after, following the pattern of *BC*). However, in its metaphorical mode, as a jocular reference to the effects of advancing years on brain and body ('Can't get up the stairs like I used to; it's *anno Domini* catching up with me!'), it is still very much around. This is of quite long standing, dating back to the late 19th century.

Alternatives to *anno Domini* sometimes encountered are *anno Christi* 'in the year of Christ' and *anno humanae salutis* 'in the year of man's redemption'. Other Latin *anno*-formulations used in English include *anno Hegirae* 'in the year of the Hegira', dating the Muslim era from Muhammad's flight from Mecca in 622 AD; *anno lucis* 'in the year of light', used by Freemasons in counting the years that have passed since 4000 BC; and *anno mundi* 'in the year of the world', counting back from the year when God created the world, which theologians calculated as 4004 BC.

annus mirabilis

Latin *annus mirabilis* means literally 'wondrous year'. Its original application appears to have been to 1588, during which a series of disasters was forecast to happen, but its decisive boost came when John Dryden used it as the title of a poem, published in 1667, which had as its subject the stirring events of the year 1665–6. This period included the catastrophic Great Fire of London and also the defeat of the Dutch fleet off Lowestoft, so clearly the term was still being used with reference to any amazing or momentous happenings, bad as well as good. In modern usage, however, it is used only for a remarkably successful or auspicious year.

anschauung

German *anschauung* 'way of looking at things, point of view' was introduced into English in the 1860s from the terminology of Kantian philosophy. In this context it denotes 'sense perception' (Kant held that knowledge of the world comes via the perception of the senses, interpreted by the conceptual apparatus of human understanding). The concept is alternatively rendered in English by the term *intuition*. English began to use *anschauung* in its more general sense 'attitude, point of view' at the beginning of the 20th century. (See also **weltanschauung**.)

anschluss

German *anschluss* denotes generally 'joining together, union' (it is a derivative of the verb *anschliessen* 'join'). But it took a much more specific application of the term to bring it into English. The occasion for this, mooted after World War 1, was the union of Austria with Germany. In German, the concept was termed *anschluss*, and English seems to have been using the word as early as 1924. The actual annexation of Austria by Hitler did not take place until 1938. There are sporadic examples of the use of *anschluss* in English as a verb in the mid-1940s, meaning 'subject to *anschluss*, annex'.

ante-bellum

Latin *ante bellum* means literally 'before the war' (Latin *bellum* 'war' has given English *bellicose* and *belligerent*, and is related to English *duel*). But in English it is generally used to refer to a specific war. Its earliest, and still by far its commonest application, was to the period before the American Civil War (as in 'a fine ante-bellum mansion'). In British English it was used with reference to the Boer War, and it enjoyed a brief currency after each of the world wars, but it is the original American usage that has kept it in the language.

ante meridiem

Latin *meridies* meant 'midday' (it was descended from an earlier unrecorded adverbial phrase **mediei die* 'at the middle of the day'). *Ante meridiem* 'before midday' is the standard formula used in English (usually in its abbreviated version *am*) to designate any hour of the day between midnight and midday. The first record of it in an English text is in the diary of the Elizabethan mathematician and astrologer Dr John Dee, in an entry dated 28 September 1563.

anti-roman

French *anti-roman* means literally 'anti-novel'. Many French novelists of the mid-20th century, among them Alain Robbe-Grillet, Nathalie Sarraute and Marguerite Duras, became increasingly disaffected from the traditional forms and techniques of the novel. They rebelled against the way in which its narrative structure and the voice of an apparently all-knowing narrator conspire to suggest a cohesion and significance that does not really exist. And so the *anti-roman* was born, which eschews moral judgment and concentrates instead on a meticulous cataloguing of external circumstances. Examples of the genre include Robbe-Grillet's *Le Voyeur* and Sarraute's *Les Fruits d'or*. Given their French provenance, such works are often called *anti-romans* in English, although the vernacular *anti-novel* is also used; an alternative term is *nouveau roman*.

à outrance

French *outrance* means 'excess' (it is a derivative of the verb *outrer* 'carry to excess', which goes back ultimately to Latin *ultra* 'beyond'). English adopted it in the 15th century, often using it in the anglicized form *utterance*, but it has long since died out. However, in the 19th century it made a reappearance, in the very specific context *à outrance*, which means 'to the bitter end, unsparingly' (familiar particularly in the French expression *guerre à outrance* 'war to the bitter end'). Then, perhaps prompted by some half-remembered school-French injunction to insert the definite article between *à* and a noun beginning with a vowel, a quite new form emerged, *à l'outrance*, which is completely unknown in French.

aparejo

Aparejo is a term of the south-western USA, introduced there in the mid-19th century from American Spanish. It denotes a pack-saddle, particularly one made of well-stuffed leather or canvas that protects the animal carrying the burden. The word is a derivative of the Spanish verb *aparejar* 'make ready' (a relative of English *apparel*), and originally in Spanish meant literally 'preparation'. It then came to be used for 'harness, tackle', as being the equipment with which horses are prepared for work, and finally passed from there to 'pack-saddle'.

aperçu

French *aperçu* is a noun use of the past participle of the verb *apercevoir* 'perceive'. Its original literal meaning was 'brief view, glimpse', but when English first took it over, in the early 19th century, it was in the extended sense 'summary, brief exposition' (the semantic link being 'brevity'). This meaning is still recorded in most large dictionaries of English, but in practice is very seldom encountered nowadays. Its place has been taken by 'insight' (as in 'The book provides some fascinating *aperçus* of court life in the 17th century'). An isolated example of this survives from the mid-19th century, but it is essentially a mid-20th-century introduction.

à point

French *à point* is a general term meaning 'into the right condition', but it is as a very specific culinary term that it has recently begun to make inroads into English. It denotes that food has been cooked to the point of perfection. 'Done to a turn' might be the nearest vernacular equivalent, although (as with the parallel Italian *al dente*) the traditional English way with roast meat and boiled vegetables has been to cook them well beyond the point that would be considered 'done' in France: a steak cooked *à point* in France might well strike a British eater as on the rare side.

À point also formed the basis of the Old French verb *apointer* 'put in good condition', from which English gets *appoint*.

a posteriori

An argument formulated *a posteriori* is one that is put together on the basis of known or observed facts, and proceeds from them to generalized conclusions – in other words, an 'empirical' or 'inductive' argument. The term in Latin means literally 'from the later, from the subsequent' (that is, one argues from the effect, the 'later' thing, to the cause, rather than the other way round), and its use in English dates back to the early 17th century. It is specifically contrasted with *a priori*, which denotes deductive reasoning, from cause to effect, based on general priciples rather than particular facts.

A posteriori is also used more loosely, to denote 'open to revision (since based on contingent facts rather than on general principles)'. In the 18th and 19th centuries there was a vogue, based on the similarity to *posterior* 'buttocks', for using it humorously to mean 'on the buttocks': 'One of them clapped a furze-bush under the tail of Gilbert, who, feeling himself thus stimulated *a posteriori*, kicked and plunged and capered' (Tobias Smollett, *Sir Launcelot Greaves*, 1762).

apparatchik, plural apparatchiki or apparatchiks

In the Communist party of the Soviet Union, the organizational and administrative machinery has historically been known as the *apparat* (the word comes via German *apparat* 'apparatus, instrument' from Latin *apparatus*). From this word was formed the Russian derivative *apparatchik*, signifying 'someone who belongs to an *apparat* (the suffix *-chik* can denote a 'member or supporter' of something). English acquired the word in the 1940s, and since then has broadened out its application to cover a 'Communist spy or secret agent'. It also serves as a grimly humorous term to denote any bureaucratic hack, analogous to those who laboured for party and government in Eastern Europe.

apparatus criticus

Apparatus criticus is a modern Latin term meaning literally 'critical apparatus'. It is used both for a collection of materials used in scholarly research, such as manuscripts, particularly as presented as an addendum to an edition of a text; and for the aggregate of commentary, glossary, footnotes, appendices, etc that accompany a scholarly edition of a text. Use of the term *apparatus* on its own, in this sense dates back at least to the early 18th century, but *apparatus criticus* itself is not recorded before the mid-19th century.

appellation contrôlée

French *appellation contrôlée* (literally 'certified name') is an official designation, issued by the Institut National des Appellations d'Origine, guaranteeing that a particular wine was made in the stated area, to the standard and from the grape varieties stipulated for that area: thus a wine certified as *appellation Margaux contrôlée* is a claret produced in the Margaux commune of Bordeaux. Short for *appellation d'origine contrôlée*, the term has become a familiar part of English since the 1950s, both on wine labels and in newspaper wine columns (the certification system itself dates back to 1932). In addition to wine, some French foodstuffs have their own *appellation contrôlée*, including *présalé* lamb and Bresse chicken. The term is often abbreviated to *AC*.

Equivalent designations in other wine-growing countries include Italian *denominazione di origine controllata (DOC)* and Spanish *denominación de origen (DO)*.

après-ski

For the socially-minded, the *après-ski* activities at a ski resort are more important than what actually happens on the slopes. These include dining, drinking, socializing, and various sorts of partying, to which the day's skiing is merely a prelude. The term *après-ski*, literally 'after-ski', was introduced into English from French in the early 1950s. It can be used both as an adjective ('an *après-ski* party', '*après-ski* clothes', etc) and as a noun, denoting the 'evening social scene at a ski resort'. There have been some signs in recent years of the French preposition *après* 'after' becoming more generalized in English as a combining form denoting the 'period after an activity' (eg *après-swim*).

a priori

A priori means literally in Latin 'from the previous', and it is used as a term in logic to denote argument 'from that which came before' (ie the cause) to that which comes afterwards (ie the effect); in other words, deductive reasoning that starts from general principles and works towards a necessary conclusion based on them. It is opposed to *a posteriori*, which signifies reasoning in the other direction, from effect to cause. As an English term it dates back to the early 18th century, and it is now frequently used (in the general language rather than as part of the terminology of logic) in the extended sense 'claimed as true (based on accepted principles) but not proved by experiment or analysis'. Philosophers also employ it to denote the concept of knowledge existing independent of experience, in which sense the derivative *apriorism* has been coined from it.

à propos

French *à propos* means literally 'to the purpose', and is used in a variety of contexts signifying suitability, timeliness or relevance (it has also been turned into a noun, meaning 'suitability' or 'opportuneness'). English took it over in the mid-17th century, as both an adverb and an adjective, and since then it has become partly naturalized to *apropos* (although now, with wider knowledge of French, the original version seems to be making a comeback). In addition, English uses it, either on its own or in the phrase *à propos of*, as a preposition, meaning 'on the subject of, speaking of', where French would use *à propos de*.

French *à propos des bottes*, literally 'on the subject of the boots', is used to denote a subject introduced inconsequentially or without any apparent reason. It has made sporadic appearances in English over the past two-and-a-half centuries.

Arcades ambo

Virgil in his *Eclogues* wrote *Arcades ambo, et cantare pares et respondere parati* 'Both Arcadians, both ready to sing in even contest, both ready to reply' (*Arcadian* here connotes a composer or performer of pastoral lyrics). It was Byron in his *Don Juan* who introduced the term into English: ' "Arcades ambo", *id est* – blackguards both'. Taking its cue from this, English took to employing it in the 19th century as a derogatory reference to a pair of similar people.

arrière-ban

In feudal France, when the king was about to go to war, he summoned all the vassals who owed him military service. This summons, and the vassals summoned, were known as the *arrière-ban*. The word is an example of folk etymology, the process by which an unfamiliar loan-word is changed in its host language so as to resemble a native form. The loan-word in this case was Old High German *heriban*, a compound formed from *heri* 'army' and *ban* 'summons'. Old French borrowed this as *herban*, but over time it evolved to *arrière-ban*, helped partly by the mis-apprehension that the men summoned were *arrière-vassals* or 'lesser vassals' (French *arrière* meaning literally 'behind'). English took the word over in the early 16th century, and at first essayed some outlandish anglicizations, including *arrear-band* and *arrear-van*. The authentic French form did not decisively establish itself until the 19th century.

25

arrière pensée

An *arrière pensée* is a thought or motive which one does not reveal – an ulterior motive, or a mental reservation. The term means literally in French 'behind thought', and seems first to have been used in English in the early part of the 19th century.

arriviste

If a *parvenu* has just arrived, an *arriviste* is trying hard to get there. Both of these English borrowings from French exploit the metaphor of journeying or travelling to a new and higher status, particularly on the social scale. An *arriviste* is someone whose efforts are concentrated, with complete tunnel-vision, on elbowing his or her way to the top, and thereby earns the scorn of those who are already there and of those who get trodden on in the process. The French word is a derivative of *arriver* 'arrive', and was acquired by English at the beginning of the 20th century. English has also taken over the noun *arrivisme*, which denotes the characteristics or methods of *arrivistes*. Both are occasionally anglicized, to *arrivist* and *arrivism*.

assimilado

In the days when Portugal still had an empire in Africa, it was possible for favoured blacks to gain official admittance into white society in colonies such as Angola and Mozambique by being granted Portuguese citizenship. Such people were termed *assimilados* (*assimilado* is a noun use of the past participle of Portuguese *assimilar* 'assimilate'). The expression came into English in the 1950s.

atelier

An artist's *atelier* is the place where he or she works, a studio. English borrowed the word from French as long ago as the 17th century, but probably its infrequency of use and its association with the bohemian world of continental painters and sculptors have inhibited its naturalization. It originated as a derivative of Old French *astelle* 'splinter, chip of wood, thin board'. At first it denoted a 'woodpile', but it eventually came to be used for a 'carpenter's workshop', and from there it moved on to 'artist's studio'.

à tort et à travers

French *à tort et à travers*', literally 'wrongly and across', is used to mean 'at random, without any logical plan'. Lord Chesterfield in the mid-18th century is the first on record as using it in an English text, and although it has never made great headway in the language, sporadic examples continue to crop up into the 20th century.

au contraire

French uses *au contraire*, literally 'to the contrary', in circumstances where English would normally employ *on the contrary*. English-speakers occasionally have recourse to *au contraire* as a piece of elegant variation: 'It is common knowledge ... that Reagan's dealings with the Bureau [FBI] were anything but passive. *Au contraire*, they were regular enough for him to be given an informer's code number' (*The Observer*, 9 December 1990).

au courant

French *au courant* means literally 'in the current' (English *current* is a 13th-century borrowing of the Old French ancestor of *courant*), and it has a range of metaphorical applications: *être au courant* can, for instance, mean 'be in the swing of things'. But it is in the very specific sense of 'being up to date with what is going on, being aware of the latest developments' that English has adopted it. The first record of its use in an English text is in the diaries of the historian Edward Gibbon, in the year 1762. In French it is used with the preposition *de* (*être au courant de quelque chose*), and in English this is now usually rendered as *with* (presumably on the model of *up-to-date with*), although in the past the more literal *of* has been used.

au fait

If you are *au fait* with something, you are either highly skilled at or knowledgeable about it, or you are familiar with it even though it is a relatively recent development. The term is borrowed from French, where it means literally 'to the point'. English acquired it in the mid-18th century, and has had some trouble settling on a translation of *de*, the preposition used with it in French. At first a simple and literal *of* was used, but this has now largely been abandoned. Other stabs at it have included *at*, *in*, and even *to*, but now *with* is the preferred usage. 'Put someone *au fait* of something', a direct translation of French *mettre quelqu'un au fait de quelque chose*, enjoyed some currency in the 19th century; it meant 'inform someone fully'.

Aufklärung

German *aufklärung* means literally 'clarification, elucidation, enlightenment', and is used as the name of the 18th-century philosophical movement generally known in English as the Enlightenment or the Age of Reason. The guiding principle of the movement was the primacy of rational thought and enquiry, and it questioned traditional political and social conventions. A leading German figure of the period was the dramatist and philosopher Gotthold Ephraim Lessing (1729–81). The first English writer on record as using the term *Aufklärung* (in 1801) was Henry Crabb Robinson, who travelled extensively in Germany and did much to popularize German culture in Britain.

au fond

French *au fond* means literally 'at the bottom' (*fond* 'bottom' comes from the same Latin source as produced English *foundation* and *fundamental*). It is used to mean 'fundamentally, when all superficial or extraneous considerations have been removed', and that is how English borrowed it in the 18th century. Its first recorded use in English displays a withering scorn for the people from whose language it had been abstracted: in a letter dated 1 January 1782 Lady Derby wrote, referring to Prince Ernest of Prussia, 'Prince Hen: says he is charming, but *au fond* he is french'. The equivalent English *at bottom* appeared around the same time, and it could well be that this was inspired by *au fond*.

au naturel

French *au naturel* means literally 'in the natural state', and it is with two specific applications that it has been taken over into English. The first is as a euphemistic circumlocution for 'naked' (Mrs Humphry Ward referred in her *Marriage of William Ashe* (1905) to 'ankles *au naturel*'). But it is also used as a culinary term, denoting either 'cooked very simply' or 'uncooked, raw', or, in relation to salads, 'without dressing'. Its use in English dates from the early 19th century.

au pair

French *pair* means 'equal' (its Old French ancestor was the source of English *peer*), and so *au pair* means literally 'on an equal basis'. It is applied to certain categories of household helper (eg an *institutrice au pair*, an '*au pair* governess'), and it signifies that the householder and the helper are on an equal basis: the helper performs certain services in exchange for board and lodging, but no wages are paid. As long ago as 1897 the *Girl's Own Paper* was explaining to its readers how English girls could go and spend time *au pair* in French, German, and Swiss schools, joining in the classes there in return for doing some English teaching, and there are sporadic examples of the term in English in later decades; but it was not really until the 1950s that the *au pair* phenomenon really took off in Britain. Countless thousands of British middle-class households had their French, German or Scandinavian teenage girl, working often as little better than an unpaid nursemaid in return for an opportunity to learn English, and it is around 1960 that the use of *au pair* as a noun in English, denoting such a person, first emerges.

au pied de la lettre

Au pied de la lettre, in French literally 'to the foot of the letter', means 'with strict literal accuracy'. English has used it sporadically since the late 18th century, usually with the connotations of an excessive or obsessive literalism.

au sérieux

French *prendre quelque chose au sérieux* means 'take something seriously', and English took the prepositional phrase over in such contexts as 'take something *au sérieux*', 'intend something *au sérieux*', etc. For additional emphasis the term is *au grand sérieux* 'in all seriousness'. Both expressions were borrowed into English in the early 19th century and, while never making great headway, have retained niches in the language ever since.

autobahn

The idea of wide straight roads specially built for fast motor transport is virtually as old as the 20th century (in 1903 the magazine *Car* was saying 'the Motor-way is *bound* to come!'), but Britain did not get into the act until the 1950s. Between the two world wars it was on the continent of Europe that the building of such roads began. It was the Italian term for them, *autostrada* (literally 'motor road'), that first found its way into English, around 1927, and German *autobahn* (also literally 'motor road') followed a decade later. After World War 2 came French *autoroute* and Spanish *autopista*. When such roads were still just an idea in Britain, they were often called *speedways*, a term that originated in America, but when they actually came to be built, *motorway* won the day.

auto-da-fé

An *auto-da-fé* was originally a public pronouncement of a sentence imposed on someone by the Inquisition, the Roman Catholic tribunal which from 1231 inquired into charges of heresy and sought to stamp out all infractions of the Christian faith. The term is of Portuguese origin, and means literally 'act of the faith' (the 'act' consists of the action taken by the tribunal in making the announcement). English adopted it in the early 18th century, and since then it has come to be used mainly in its secondary sense – the carrying out of the Inquisition's sentence by the civil authorities, which in the case of heresy often involved burning the convicted person at the stake.

avant-garde

The *avant-garde* is literally the 'front guard', and when English originally borrowed the term from French in the 15th century that is just what it meant – the 'front part of an army', which went into battle first. But in English this gradually became eroded to *vanguard*, and it was not until the early 20th century that the word was re-acquired in its original French form. But now its associations were far from military: it was used for those who were in the forefront of an artistic movement, pushing at the boundaries of creativity in such a way as to seem eccentric or incomprehensible to the lay public. By the 1920s it was in common use as an adjective, perhaps its commonest role today, and in the 1940s the derivatives *avant-gardism* and *avant-gardist* were added to the language.

ave atque vale

Latin *ave atque vale* means 'hail and farewell' (*ave* also appears in English in *Ave Maria* 'Hail Mary', and *vale* has given English *valediction*). The phrase appears to have been coined by the Roman poet Catullus, and certainly its survival into English depends on its use in his *Lyric* 101, in which he mourns his dead brother: *Nunc tamen interea haec prisco quae more parentum / Tradita sunt tristi munere ad inferias, / Accipe fraterno multum manantia fletu, / Atque in perpetuum, frater, ave atque vale* 'Yet take these gifts, brought as our fathers bade / For sorrow's tribute to the passing shade; / A brother's tears have wet them o'er and o'er; / And so, my brother, hail, and farewell evermore.' English has adopted it as a valedictory formula.

B

babushka

Russian *babushka* means 'grandmother'. It is a diminutive form of *babu* 'old woman'. Variations on *baba* are common throughout the Slavic languages as terms for 'old woman' or 'grandmother' – Serbo-Croat, for instance, has *baba*, Czech *babička*, and Polish *babka*. It is one of a wide range of Indo-European words, many of them terms for 'mother' or 'father', that are formed from syllables typical of infants' first attempts at speech; English *baby* is probably of parallel origin. One of the characteristic garments of old Russian peasant women is a scarf folded into a triangle and worn over the head, tied beneath the chin, and English has adopted the word *babushka* as the name for such a scarf. The first record of its use in English texts comes from just before World War 2.

backfisch

German *backfisch*, literally 'fish for baking', is used metaphorically for a 'teenage girl', one who is just on the point of emerging into adulthood. It enjoyed a brief vogue in English towards the end of the 19th century, and continued in sporadic use thereafter, generally in German contexts.

bagnio

Italian *bagnio* means 'bath' (it is descended from Latin *balneum* 'bath', which also produced French *bain*). English adopted it in the early 17th century, using it not for the sort of bath you sit in, but for a 'public bath-house', containing not just facilities for washing but also steam rooms, rest rooms, the services of masseurs, etc – what in later times came to be known as a *Turkish bath*. Applied particularly to such establishments as found in Italian and Turkish cities, it has long since gone out of use, but it lingers on as an archaic euphemism for a brothel. Clearly the patrons of *bagnios* expected more services than just a wash and brush-up, and their reputation as houses of ill fame led to a change in the meaning of the word (the same thing happened in the case of the now obsolete *stews*, which originally denoted 'public steam-baths', but later came to be used for a brothel). Another, unexplained application of *bagnio*, also now defunct, was to an oriental prison for slaves.

bain-marie

A *bain-marie* is a double saucepan. The bottom half, containing water, is placed on the source of heat, and the upper saucepan rests in the heated water. It is used for preparing foods, particularly sauces, that need slow and gentle cooking, and also for keeping things warm. Its name goes back to a medieval Greek alchemical term, *kaminos Marias*. This meant 'Mary's furnace', and referred to Mary, or Miriam, the sister of Moses, who according to medieval legend was a skilled alchemist and wrote a book on the subject. It was mistranslated into medieval Latin as *balneum Mariae* 'Mary's bath', which became in French *bainmarie*. English acquired the term in the early 19th century.

baksheesh

Baksheesh is used in English as a term for money given as a tip or as a charitable gift, particularly in Turkey, Egypt and other countries in that area. The term was acquired in the mid-18th century from Persian *bakhshīsh*, a derivative of the verb *bakhshīdan* 'give'. It has had a wide variety of spellings over the centuries, and several alternatives still remain, notably *backsheesh, bakshish*, and *backshish*. In the late 19th and early 20th centuries it was used as a verb, meaning 'give *baksheesh* to'. It has retained an aura of foreignness, so much so that a demotic English version emerged among British soldiers serving in the Near East in World War 1: *buckshee*. This remained a slang term for 'free' for many decades, but is now obsolescent.

bal costumé

A *bal costumé* is a dance to which all the guests come in various fanciful costumes, representing historical figures, characters from literature and legend, etc – in other words, a fancy-dress ball. The term is first recorded in English in the 1820s, and remained popular in fashionable society throughout the 19th century. It is sometimes translated as *costume ball*, but the usual vernacular equivalent is *fancy-dress ball*. There are no actual records of this before the 1880s, the earliest known term being the now defunct *fancy ball*, dating from the 1820s. English *ball* 'dance' itself was acquired from French in the 17th century (it goes back ultimately to the Greek verb *ballizein* 'dance'). Another *bal* compound borrowed from French is *bal masqué* 'masked ball', which crossed the Channel in the mid-18th century.

ballon d'essai

French *ballon d'essai* means literally 'trial balloon' – that is, a balloon launched experimentally to see if it will stay up. It is used metaphorically for an idea or suggestion that is mooted tentatively to gauge people's reactions to it, and can be strategically withdrawn if its reception is unfavourable. English appears to have acquired the term in the late 19th century, and by the 1930s there is evidence of the translation *trial balloon* being used in its stead. The association of ideas behind the parallel metaphorical use of the expression *fly a kite* is very much the same.

ballon-sonde

A *ballon-sonde* is a device used by meteorologists and others to make measurements in the upper atmosphere. It is a hydrogen-filled balloon that carries recording instruments up to heights at which it would be impractical to operate aircraft. The term means in French literally 'sounding-ballon', and that indeed is a vernacular name for the device in English (the other is *registering balloon*); it was borrowed around the turn of the 20th century.

bal musette

French *bal*, like English *ball*, denotes a 'dance', but a *bal public* is a 'dance-hall', and a *bal musette* is a dance-hall at which the music is provided by a band featuring the *musette* – that most prototypically French of instruments, the accordion. The term, with its connotations of cheap and cheerful entertainment, began to be used in English in the 1920s.

bambino

Bambino is Italian for 'infant, little boy'. It is a diminutive form of *bambo* 'child', a nursery word related to *bimbo* 'child', which gained some currency in British English in the late 1980s as a term for a beautiful but brainless young woman. English has taken *bambino* over in two distinct modes. First, as a term for a 'child' – often, naturally, an Italian one, but the word is also used as a heartily facetious synonym for *infant* in general ('How are the bambinos?'). In this role it was introduced into English in the mid-18th century. But it is also a term in art criticism, and denotes a representation in painting or sculpture of the infant Jesus, typically wrapped in swaddling clothes.

banzai

When pulp World War 2 comics feature Japanese soldiers fearsomely charging, they are always pictured yelling *banzai!*; but in fact this was not originally so much a battle-cry as a loyal greeting to the emperor. It means literally 'ten thousand years' (the force of it being 'may you live ten thousand years'), and it was actually borrowed from Chinese: Chinese *wàn* means 'ten thousand' and *sùi* means 'year'. The first records of the term in English, in the late 19th century, are in this pacific sense, and it was not until the 1940s that the now more familiar 'war-cry' meaning took hold. In the early part of the 20th century, naval slang had the term *banzai party* for a group of sailors going ashore to paint the town red, but after Pearl Harbor this compound gave place to *banzai attack* or *banzai charge*, denoting a suicidally desperate attack by Japanese forces.

barre

As with most of the terminology of ballet, *barre* is a French introduction to English. It denotes the rail attached at waist height to the wall of a ballet rehearsal room, often backed by a mirror, which the dancers hold on to while they practise their leg movements. Etymologically *barre* is the same word as *bar*, which was originally borrowed from French in the 12th century. As a ballet term it was adopted by English in the late 19th century, and it is frequently anglicized to *bar*.

barrio

Spanish *barrio* means 'district, suburb'. Like many Spanish words, it is of Arabic origin; it comes from the Arabic adjective *barrī*, a derivative of *barr* 'open country'. English took it up in the mid-19th century to designate a district or quarter of a city in a Spanish-speaking country, but it is in 20th-century American English that its use has really blossomed. There it denotes an area of a city that is populated by Spanish-speaking immigrants or their descendents, particularly a poor or run-down district.

bas bleu

The original bluestockings were English. At intellectual gatherings in England in the mid-18th century it was customary for men to wear not formal dress, which included black silk stockings, but more casual clothes. Here, the worsted stockings were of a greyish colour conventionally termed 'blue'. The women who attended such meetings were regarded with scorn in some quarters, and came to be termed sarcastically 'Blue Stocking Ladies'. The insult stuck, and female intellectuals have been derogatorily known ever since as bluestockings. French soon took the name over in translated form as *bas bleu* (French *bas* means 'lower part', and by extension 'stocking'), and as early as the 1780s English had borrowed *bas bleu* back as an alternative to *bluestocking*.

basho

Probably the biggest influx of Japanese terms into English in the 1980s was inspired by the sport of sumo wrestling which, thanks to prolonged exposure on Channel 4 television, achieved considerable popularity in Britain. Amongst them perhaps the most widely familiar is *basho*, which denotes a 'sumo wrestling tournament'. There are six bashos a year in Japan, at two-monthly intervals, each lasting 15 days. The first, in January, is known as the *Hatsu Basho*, the last, in November, as the *Kyushu Basho*.

batik

Batik is a method of dyeing cloth which involves drawing patterns on the fabric with wax. The cloth is then steeped in the dye, which only takes in the areas where there is no wax. When the wax is removed, the pattern remains. The technique is of Southeast Asian origin, and the word itself comes from Javanese *batik* 'painted'. English acquired it via Malay in the late 19th century.

bâton de commandement

Bâton de commandement is a paleoanthropological term that denotes an artefact fashioned out of a deer's antler, examples of which have been found in many early Stone Age sites. It has a rod-like shape with a hole at one end and is often elaborately decorated, and the earliest French anthropologists to examine such objects thought that they looked like a staff of office that might be carried by a military leader – hence the name. However, it is now believed that they were used for making the shafts of arrows and spears.

Bauhaus

The Bauhaus was a school of architecture and design founded in Weimar, Germany in 1919 by the architect Walter Gropius (1883–1969). Its aim was to create a unified, simple, clean modern style across the whole spectrum of art, design, architecture and crafts. Amongst the famous names associated with it were Klee, Kandinsky, and Mies van der Rohe. In 1925 it moved to Dessau, and in 1933 was closed down by the Nazis, who found it ideologically abhorrent, but its principles live on today. The first record of the term *Bauhaus* (in German literally 'architecture house') in English dates from 1923.

beau geste

French *beau geste*, literally 'beautiful gesture', denotes a 'magnanimous action'. English borrowed it in the 1920s and used it quite frequently for a time, but now, although it is still occasionally encountered ('We live in an unromantic age in which the *beau geste* is little understood or admired', *The Observer*, 2 December 1990), it is probably most familiar as the title of a novel by P. C. Wren. Published in 1924, this was a romantic adventure story set in the world of the French Foreign Legion. Its commercial success inspired a series of sequels with titles like *Beau Ideal* and *Beau Sabreur*.

beau idéal

French *beau idéal* has become transformed out of all recognition following its transference into English, largely due to the different placement of adjectives in the two languages. In French, the adjective generally follows the noun, so *beau idéal* means 'ideal beauty, beauty in its most perfectly imaginable form' (*beau* here is being used as a noun, signifying 'the beautiful, beauty'). English, however, puts the adjective before the noun, and this, together with the perception that French *beau* is prototypically an adjective, was enough to ensure that the phrase got reinterpreted as 'beautiful ideal' – that is, the 'perfect model' of a particular quality, kind of person, etc ('The Highlanders came

to regard him as the very beau-idéal of a minister', Hugh Miller,
My Schools and Schoolmasters, 1854).

beau monde

The *beau monde* is 'fashionable society', the sort of people who
are hounded by paparazzi and whose most trivial doings are
lovingly recorded by newspaper gossip columnists. The phrase
means literally 'beautiful world', and was borrowed from French
in the 18th century. The first English writer on record as using
it is Alexander Pope. At the end of his *The Rape of the Lock* (1714)
he pictures the purloined lock of hair ascending to the firmament
as a new star, and describes how 'This the Beau-monde shall
from the Mall survey, / And hail with music its propitious ray'.
English *beautiful people* 'the young, fashionable, rich section of
society', first recorded in the mid-1960s, may well have been
inspired by *beau monde*. Similar terms adopted from French are
haut monde and *grand monde*, which connote aristocracy rather
than fashionability.

beau sabreur

The original *beau sabreur* was Joachim Murat (1767– 1815), a
French cavalry officer (and brother-in-law of Napoleon). He led
his forces with great distinction during Napoleon's campaigns in
Italy and Egypt and fought at the battles of Marengo and
Austerlitz, and his exploits earned him the nickname *beau
sabreur*, literally 'beautiful wielder of a sabre, fine swordsman'
(French *sabreur* carries connotations of one who is an excellent
and dashing fighter but is not too strong when it comes to
strategy). Murat was made king of Naples in 1808, but in the
upheavals following Napoleon's defeat he was captured and
finally executed. English has used the term *beau sabreur* sporadically since the early 19th century for any dashing soldier, or
any dashing handsome adventurer in general.

beauté du diable

French *beauté du diable*, literally 'devil's beauty', denotes the
bloom of youth, which confers attractiveness on women who
might not otherwise be considered beautiful. However, when
English took the expression over, in the middle of the 19th
century, it was in the sense 'captivatingly beautiful exterior that
disguises the mischief underneath', which is how it has been used
ever since.

beaux arts

French *beaux arts* means 'fine arts', and English has occasionally used it in that sense since the early 19th century, but perhaps its commonest application in English is as a shorthand term for the style and philosophy of the École des Beaux-Arts. This school of art and architecture in Paris was the inheritor and guardian of the classical decorative style, and sought to pass this on to its pupils. In the 20th century, however, *beaux arts* has come to used as a term of contempt, signifying the artificial imposition of moribund stylistic features from the past.

bêche-de-mer

French *bêche-de-mer* means 'sea-slug' (it is an alteration of an earlier *biche de mer*, which was borrowed from Portuguese *bicho do mar* 'sea worm'). English acquired the word in the early 19th century. The sea-slug is regarded as a great delicacy in the southwest Pacific, and in the 19th century it was an important trading item. It thus came about that its name began to be used to denote an English-based creole used as a trading language in that area. This was commonly in the form *Beach-la-mar*, which may be a corruption of either *bêche-de-mer* or *bicho do mar*, but nowadays linguists more usually use the term *bêche-de-mer*. It is still spoken in Vanuatu and Fiji.

bel esprit, plural beaux esprits

French *bel esprit*, literally 'fine mind', is used for 'wit, wittiness', and hence also for a 'witty person'. English took the word over in this latter sense as long ago as the early 17th century, and has used it consistently ever since; but of the former meaning there is no evidence in English beyond a couple of isolated instances in the 19th century.

belle époque

The decade or two immediately preceding World War 1 has been dubbed the *belle époque*, literally the 'beautiful epoch'. It was a time when, at least for those with enough money, life was comfortably easy. An extended period of peace and prosperity seemed to beckon, and even for the less well-off there was the prospect of stability. World War 1 savagely shattered this idyll, but its golden glow, nostalgically enhanced by retrospection, earned it the sobriquet *belle époque*.

belles lettres

Belles lettres sounds as though it ought to be a complimentary term. It means literally in French 'fine letters', and indeed it was originally coined to complement *beaux arts* – 'fine literature' as opposed to 'fine art'. That is how it came into English, in the early 18th century. But over the years its stock seems imperceptibly to have sunk, so that by the end of the 19th century it was being used for 'prose writing considered for its aesthetic qualities, rather than for its instructive or moral content' – often, by implication, writing that is elegant, affecting, or witty but essentially slight or trivial. The derivatives formed from it – *belletrist* 'writer of such works', the adjective *belletristic* – inherit these connotations. To modern sensibilities perhaps the epitome of the belletrist is the Edwardian essayist, typified by E. V. Lucas.

beneficiaire

A *beneficiaire* is a sports player who receives or is about to receive a benefit – that is to say, a sum of money collected from or subscribed by admirers in recognition of several years' outstanding service for a particular club. English borrowed the term from French *bénéficiaire* in the first half of the 19th century and was still using it in the 1920s ('Sandham's Benefit Match ... [Andrew Sandham was a Surrey cricketer] ... The beneficiaire was not destined to do well', *Daily Telegraph*, 23 August 1927), but nowadays it has been replaced by the vernacular *beneficiary*.

ben trovato

The Italians have a saying, *Se non è vero, è (molto) ben trovato* 'If it is not true, it is (very) well found' – that is to say, even if a particular story is not true, it is a very appropriate invention, which captures the spirit of the truth. It has been dated back to at least the 16th century, and there are references to it in English from the late 18th century, but it does not seem to have been until the end of the 19th century that English began to use the abbreviated form *ben trovato* to encapsulate its sense of apt fabrication: '*Trovato* though the story no doubt is, it is very *ben*, and thus, by means of fiction, conveys fact' (E. F. Benson, *As We Were*, 1930).

bersagliere, plural bersaglieri

A *bersagliere* is a member of a crack regiment of sharp-shooting riflemen in the Italian Army. The term, acquired by English from Italian in the mid-19th century, is a derivative of Italian *bersaglio* 'target'. This in turn was borrowed from Old French *bersail*, a derivative of the verb *berser* 'shoot at'. A *bersaglieri hat* is a hat decorated with a plume of cock's feathers, such as *bersaglieri* wear.

bête noire

French *bête noire*, literally 'black beast', denotes someone's pet aversion – a person or thing whose very mention is guaranteed to annoy, upset or exasperate someone, or which regularly frustrates someone's intentions. Its use in English dates back to the mid-19th century.

bibelot

A *bibelot* is a small decorative object, a curio, knick-knack, or trinket – for instance, a porcelain figurine, or an enamelled snuff-box. The word is French in origin, and goes back to Old French *beubelet*, which was a reduplicated formation based on *bel* 'beautiful', the ancestor of modern French *beau*. English acquired the word in the second half of the 19th century, and has generally used it as a somewhat dismissive term, suggestive of fussy daintiness and low-brow taste. Ouida, for instance, wrote of someone whose 'soul never rises above brocades and *bibelots*' (1882), and the effeminate Georgie Pillson in E. F. Benson's 'Mapp and Lucia' stories has a collection of *bibelots* which he dusts in moments of stress. French has the derived verb *bibeloter*, never passed on to English, which means 'collect trinkets' and, by metaphorical extension, 'do odd jobs'.

bidet

The original, literal meaning of French *bidet* is 'small horse, pony' (English, too, once used it in this sense: 'I will return to myself, mount my bidet, in a dance, and curvet upon a curtal', Ben Jonson, *Chloridia*, 1631). It is thought that it may derive from the Old French verb *bider* 'trot'. A *bidet de toilette* (or *bidet* for short) originated as a basin supported on four legs, one at each corner, on which one sat astride, as if on a horse, for the purpose of washing the genital and anal areas. English acquired the term, as *bidet*, in the 18th century. Francis Grose included it in his *Dictionary of the vulgar tongue* (1785): '*Bidet*, commonly pronounced biddy, a kind of tub, contrived for ladies to wash themselves, for which purpose they bestride it like a little French pony, or post horse, called in France bidets'.

Biedermeier

Biedermeier originated as a fictitious name invented by the German poet Ludwig Eichroth (1827–92). This Gottlieb Biedermeier, a Swabian schoolmaster, was the supposed author of various dreary, pedestrian, conventional poems (actually composed by Eichroth himself and others to satirize bourgeois middle-brow tastes of the time). The term came to be applied to a style of furniture favoured by the middle classes in Germany, Austria and Scandinavia in the early 19th century, which, thanks to new mass-production techniques, brought French Empire-style ornateness within the reach of the general public. It is also used for a style of German and Austrian painting which flourished at the same time, marked by a painstaking realism. English adopted the term at the beginning of the 20th century, and additionally employs it as a general derogatory adjective denoting bourgeois philistinism.

bien pensant

People who are *bien pensant* are 'right-thinking' – that is to say, have the same set of attitudes and assumptions as oneself. In practice, the term is generally used in English to connote orthodoxy and conservatism ('in her world, Catholic, royalist, *bien pensant*', Nancy Mitford, *The Water Beetle*, 1962). Literally in French 'well-thinking', English borrowed it in the early 20th century, and also uses it as a noun, meaning 'right-thinking person'.

bildungsroman

A *bildungsroman* is a novel which charts its hero's early life, showing how his formative years and the experiences of his youth made him into the person whom he eventually became (the term means literally in German 'education novel'). The genre is particularly popular in German – Goethe's *Wilhelm Meisters Lehrjahre/Wilhelm Meister's Apprenticeship* (1796) and Thomas Mann's *Der Zauberberg/The Magic Mountain* (1924) are notable examples – but some English writers have also used it (eg Thomas Carlyle's *Sartor Resartus*, 1834). English acquired the term in the early 20th century, and also occasionally uses the synonymous German *erziehungsroman* 'education novel'.

billet doux

English acquired French *billet doux* long enough ago (in the 17th century, in fact) for it to have become colloquially anglicized over the years to *billy-do*, but in modern usage the original French form has reasserted itself. It means in French literally 'sweet letter, sweet note', and denotes a 'love letter'. Nowadays it is rarely used in English except facetiously or ironically.

blasé

French *blasé* originated as the past participle of the verb *blaser* 'cloy, surfeit (with pleasure)', the source of which is variously cited as Provençal *blazir* 'cloy' and Middle Dutch *blasen* 'blow up, cause to swell'. If one is surfeited with pleasure then by implication, if the opportunity for further pleasure comes along, one feels one can take it or leave it; hence the use of *blasé* to suggest the indifference or lack of enthusiasm of one who has seen or experienced it all before. English acquired the word in the early 19th century. Byron is the first English writer on record as using it, in his *Don Juan* (1819): 'A little "blasé" – 'tis not to be wonder'd at, that his heart had got a tougher rind').

Blaue Reiter

Der Blaue Reiter was the name of a loosely organized group of expressionist painters founded in Munich in 1911. When Vasili Kandinsky had one of his pictures rejected by the committee of the *Neue Künstlervereinigung*, he and his fellow painter Franz Marc set up a rival exhibition, which led to their forming a group of like-minded painters. They named it after one of Kandinsky's paintings, *Le Cavalier bleu* 'The Blue Horseman'. Its membership, which also included Paul Klee and August Macke, covered a wide range of styles and approaches, but a common strand running through them all was their concern to express the spiritual side of human nature, which they thought had been neglected by the Impressionists. Amongst other artists to exhibit with them were Delaunay, Braque, Derain, Vlaminck and Picasso. The group disbanded during World War 1.

blitzkrieg

The original sense of the German *blitzkrieg* (literally 'lightning war') was of a sudden massive surprise attack by ground and air forces, pressed home at such speed and in such numbers as to be irresistible. This was the tactic that overwhelmed Poland in 1939, and many other European countries thereafter. When the assault on Britain began in 1940, it was by aerial bombardment only, in the attempt to soften the country up for an invasion by sea, so when English took the term over it was often implicitly restricted to 'series of air-raids'. In particular its shortened version *Blitz* was used for the intensive bombing of London between July and December 1940, when over 23 000 civilians were killed. In more recent times, *blitz* has also come to be used humorously for a 'brief period of intensely concentrated effort' (as in 'have a blitz on the housework').

bloc

Bloc has crossed the English Channel twice. English originally acquired it, from Old French, in the 14th century as *block* (it is ultimately of Germanic origin, and Old French got it from Middle Dutch *blok* 'tree-trunk'). Then, at the beginning of the 20th century, it was borrowed again, this time in the specialized sense of a grouping of political parties which, under the political systems of various Continental European countries, keeps the government in power. From this it has broadened out to its present-day meaning 'grouping of countries, organizations, etc united by a common interest' (as in the 'Soviet bloc' and the 'Communist bloc').

Boche

Boche was the contemptuous term used by French soldiers in World War 1 for the Germans, and their British comrades-in-arms soon took it over. It is short for *alboche* 'German', which may have originated as a blend of French *allemand* 'German' and *caboche* 'head, pate' (whose Old French ancestor gave English *cabbage*). It was pre-eminently a World War 1 word – in World War 2 the preferred term was *Jerry* – but it has remained available in the language for anyone who wants to be rude to Germans.

bodega

In Spain, a *bodega* is a shop that sells wine, and usually groceries as well; it is also a building where wine is stored. English took the term over in the mid-19th century, and has mainly used it in the context of Spain and other Spanish-speaking countries (although there does seem to have been a vogue, in late 19th-century Britain, for applying it to indigenous varieties of wine bars and saloons). The Spanish word is descended from Latin *apotheca* 'storehouse', which also produced English *apothecary*. *Apotheca* in turn goes back to Greek *apothēkē* 'storehouse' (a derivative of the verb *apotithenai* 'put away'), which is also the ancestor of French *boutique*, borrowed by English in the mid-18th century.

bois brûlé

In former times in Canadian English, *bois brûlé* was a term applied to a person of mixed native American and white (typically French-Canadian) ancestry. It means in French literally 'burnt wood'. In popular parlance it often became contorted to *bob ruly*.

boîte

French *boîte*, literally 'box', is also used figuratively for a 'night-club' (in full, *boîte de nuit*) or 'small restaurant'. English writers began to pick it up after World War 1, at first usually in the context of French niteries (typically of the low-life Montmartre variety), but gradually also with reference to such establishments elsewhere.

bona fides

Latin *bona fides* means literally 'good faith' (English *faith* is descended ultimately from Latin *fides*). English has used it since the mid-19th century, originally as a legal term, to mean 'lack of intent to deceive'. It is a singular noun, but its -*s* ending frequently lures people into treating it as a plural. This is further encouraged by the existence in English of the adjective *bona fide* 'sincere, genuine' (as in 'a bona fide offer'), which comes from the Latin adverbial phrase *bona fide* 'in good faith', the ablative case of *bona fides*, and which may subconsciously be thought of as a singular underlying the 'plural' *bona fides*.

Irish English uses *bona fide* colloquially as a noun, signifying a pub that is allowed to stay open after hours to cater for bona fide travellers.

bona vacantia

Latin *bona vacantia* means literally 'ownerless goods'. *Vacantia* is derived from the verb *vacare* 'be empty or unoccupied', in the extended sense 'be ownerless', which also provided English with *vacant* and *vacate*. English has used it since the mid-18th century as a legal term denoting 'property that has no apparent owner'. For example, treasure trove is *bona vacantia*. Under English law, the ownership of anything declared *bona vacantia* reverts to the Crown.

bonhomie

French *bonhomie* means 'good nature, affability'. It is an alteration of an earlier *bonhommie*, which was derived from *bon-homme* 'good-natured man'. English adopted the term at the beginning of the 19th century, and by the early 20th century it was well enough established to have the adjective *bonhomous* 'full of bonhomie' formed from it.

bon mot

A *bon mot* (in French literally 'good word') is a 'witty remark', a 'witticism'. English started using it in the early 18th century, giving it a considerable head-start over the synonymous *mot* that it has never relinquished. The term connotes a witticism that is at once pithy and particularly apt.

bonne

French uses *bonne*, the feminine form of *bon* 'good', as a noun meaning 'female servant, maid'. The English radical politician John Wilkes is the first on record as using it in an English text, in a letter written in 1771, and since then it has come and gone in the language as a transient visitor, chiefly deployed in French settings.

bonne bouche

The term *bonne bouche* certainly exists in French, but French-speakers would be hard put to recognize it as it has come to be used in English. Literally 'good mouth', in French it denotes a 'pleasant taste' (*avoir bonne bouche* means 'taste nice', and *avoir mauvaise bouche* correspondingly signifies 'taste disagreeable').

However, English-speakers of the 18th century evidently encountered it mainly in the context *morceau qui fait bonne bouche* 'titbit which has a pleasant taste', hence 'tasty morsel', and taking the part for the whole, adopted *bonne bouche* with the meaning 'tasty morsel'. Over the years it has become specialized in meaning to an 'additional delicious titbit eaten at the end of a meal', and by metaphorical extension to an 'especially nice extra item at the end': 'As a bonne bouche [after other wines], the team tasted a Zind Humbrecht Gewürztraminer Vendange Tardive, AC Alsace 1986 ... which met with great approval', *Decanter*, November 1990.

bonnet rouge
The sans-culottes during the French Revolution wore distinctive red hats known as *bonnets rouges*. They were soft brimless affairs with a floppy crown. Before long the term was coming to be used metaphorically to denote an 'ardent revolutionary or extreme radical', and this usage began to make some inroads into English in the early 19th century.

bonsai
Bonsai is the Japanese art of growing miniaturized versions of trees and shrubs. This is done by planting the seeds in a small pot, which restricts root growth, and by regular pruning of the branches. It is the pot-growing that gives *bonsai* its name: Japanese *bon* means 'pot, bowl' and the verb *sai* means 'plant'. The term was introduced into English around 1950, and is now also applied to the dwarf plants grown by the *bonsai* method.

bon ton
French *bon ton* (literally 'good tone') denotes 'stylishness, sophisticated manners'. English took it over in the mid-18th century, and by the end of the century was also using it extensively for the 'fashionable world, fashionable society' – the more widespread application of the term today. A near-synonym occasionally used in English is *haut ton*, literally 'high tone'.

bon vivant
A *bon vivant* is someone who enjoys and appreciates to the full the fine things of life, particularly good food and wine. English acquired the expression from French, but there it is a rather more general term: literally 'good living (person)', it denotes

'someone who enjoys life', without any specifically gastronomic overtones. It crossed the Channel in the late 17th century, and was evidently an 'in'-word: 'The truth is, the habit of such *Bons vivants*, which is the fashionable word, maketh a suspicion so likely', Lord Halifax (1695). It was perhaps towards the end of the next century that it began to narrow down in meaning: Byron, using the rare feminine form, wrote 'But though a "bonne vivante" ... her stomach's not her peccant part' (*Don Juan*, 1824). *Bon vivant* is at least a genuine French expression, but was the inspiration for a most curious Frenglish term, the synonymous *bon viveur*, which is a pure English invention (dating from the middle of the 19th century). *Viveur* is indeed a French word, but it does not simply mean 'liver'; it has connotations of rather dissolute living.

bon voyage

English has used French *bon voyage* as an expression of farewell and good wishes for a safe and pleasant journey since at least the 15th century. At first it was anglicized to *boon voyage* (French *bon* 'good' was in quite common usage in English between the 14th and 17th centuries as *boon*, but it now survives only in *boon companion*). *Boon voyage* remained in the language for a couple of hundred years but then died out, and it does not seem to have been until the early 19th century that *bon voyage* was reintroduced from French. It is perhaps most frequently encountered in the expression 'wish someone *bon voyage*'.

bouclé

French *bouclé* means literally 'buckled, curly' (*cheveux bouclés* is 'curly hair'). English adopted the term at the end of the 19th century with specific reference to a type of yarn with one thread looser than the others, giving a looped effect, or to fabric woven from such yarn, which has an uneven tufted surface.

bouffant

French *bouffant* made its debut in English in the 1880s, as a fashion term. It is used of skirts, sleeves, and suchlike, and means 'puffed out, with a rounded outline'. But it is for its second adoption into English, at the hands of hairdressers, that it is perhaps better known today. Although this began in the mid 1950s, the 1960s were pre-emininently the decade of the *bouffant* hair-style, in which a shock of puffed-out hair was achieved by back-combing and liberal applications of lacquer. The French word is the present participle of *bouffer* 'swell, puff out the cheeks'.

boules

Boules, thought of as quintessentially the French game, began to make some inroads in Britain towards the end of the 20th century. It is very similar to the game of bowls, but the balls are thrown at the target through the air rather than rolled along the ground. This means that it can be played on any convenient piece of rough terrain (known as the *piste*). The *boules* themselves are metal balls, somewhat bigger than tennis balls; the target ball is called a *cochonnet*. With ever closer British links with the Continent and the advent of the Channel Tunnel, boules is beginning to make an appearance as a pub game in Kent and elsewhere, taking the place of the traditional skittles. In 1987 there were 3500 licensed players in Britain. Particularly in the southern part of France the game is also known as *pétanque*.

boulevardier

A *boulevardier* is literally someone who frequents the boulevards – that is to say, a man about town, a sophisticated man who habitually visits fashionable night-spots, restaurants, casinos, etc and in former more expansive times would have been seen strolling nonchalantly from one to the other along the boulevards. English borrowed the word from French in the late 19th century, and at first occasionally anglicized it to *boulevardeer*.

bourgeois

Someone who is *bourgeois* literally lives in a 'town'. The French word is a derivative of *bourg* 'town', which is related ultimately to English *borough*. English originally acquired it in the 13th century, and has since anglicized it to *burgess*, but then borrowed it for a second time, as *bourgeois*, in the late 16th century. Originally it was used in specifically French contexts, to denote the free city-dwelling class in French society, as contrasted with the peasantry and the gentry. But gradually it came to be more generalized, and now it has a range of applications centred on the concept 'middle class'. In Marxist thought, it signifies the capitalist system, which exploits the working class; while as a more general term of opprobrium, it connotes the supposed narrow, philistine, strait-laced provincialism of the middle classes. The derivative *bourgeoisie* dates in English from the early 18th century. (See also **petit bourgeois**.)

boutonnière

French *boutonnière* means literally 'button-hole' (it is a derivative of *bouton* 'button'), but it was in two metaphorical senses that English adopted it in the late 19th century. Like English *button-hole*, it is used for a flower or small spray of flowers worn in the button-hole of a coat lapel (it is the preferred term for this in American English, while British English adheres to the vernacular). It is also applied to a very small straight surgical incision: English used it in this sense for a while, particularly with reference to incisions in the urethra, but it was gradually ousted by the native *button-hole*.

Brumaire

When the new Republic was declared in France in 1792, it was to sweep away all ecclesiastical influence in the revolutionary state. One of the ways it set about doing this was to replace the old Gregorian calendar with a new Republican calendar. The old months were to disappear, and in their place came twelve entirely new ones, each exactly 30 days long. They received new names, based on the characteristics of their times of year. Amongst these names was *Brumaire*, which covered the period 23 October to 21 November in the old calendar (etymologically this denotes the 'misty' month; it is derived from French *brume* 'mist'). In 1806 France returned to the Gregorian calendar, and *Brumaire* and its eleven companions became redundant.

brutum fulmen, plural bruta fulmina

It was the Roman author Pliny in his *Natural History* who wrote of the *bruta fulmina et vana, ut quae nulla veniant ratione naturae* 'thunderbolts that strike blindly and harmlessly, being traceable to no natural cause'. *Brutum fulmen* came to be used metaphorically for a 'blustering threat or display of force that is ultimately futile or empty'. Its use in English texts dates back at least to the early 17th century.

bwana

Bwana is a characteristic term of East African English, and has spread into the general language in that context: typically in colonial tales of explorers and white hunters in old Kenya, Tanganyika, and so on. It is roughly equivalent to English *sir*, and is used as a term of address or respect to an employer or other superior (in practice, generally a white man). It is a Swahili word, and goes back ultimately to Arabic *abūna* 'our father'. Its use in English dates from the mid-19th century.

C

cabotin

French *cabotin* denotes an actor, particularly a second-rate one who hams it up histrionically and is better at self-advertisement than at the dramatic portrayal of character. Its original meaning was 'strolling player', and it is thought that it may have been derived from the verb *caboter* 'sail along a coast carrying cargo' – the underlying connection being between the itinerant way of life of such actors and the trading voyages of coasters. The term begins to appear in English texts around the turn of the 20th century, and it has been joined by the feminine form *cabotine* and the derivative *cabotinage*, which denotes the behaviour or way of life of *cabotins*.

cache-sexe

French *sexe* means not just 'sex' but also by extension 'genitals'; combine it with the verb *cacher* 'hide' and you have a *cache-sexe*, a device for concealing the genitals. Specifically, the term denotes an exiguous garment, in the manner of a G-string, worn by someone otherwise naked (eg a photographic model) in order to cover the genitals. Its use in English dates back to the 1920s.

cacoethes scribendi

The Latin phrase *cacoethes scribendi* was coined by the Roman author Juvenal. He used it in the seventh of his *Satires*: *Tenet insanabile multos scribendi cacoethes et aegro in corde senescit* 'An inveterate itch of writing, now incurable, clings to many, and grows old in their distempered body'. Literally 'mania for writing, incurable passion for writing' (Latin *cacoethes* was a borrowing of Greek *kakoēthēs* 'bad habit, mania', a noun use of an adjective formed from *kakos* 'bad' and *ēthos* 'character'), it probably began to be used in English in the 16th century, and it survives to this day: 'The Mann family was possessed of the *cacoethes scribendi* to a quite obsessive degree. Indeed when Thomas Mann's wife Katja was prevailed upon to chronicle her recollections, she emphasised her distinction as the only member of the clan who had not so far written a book' (*The Observer*, 6

January 1991). Parallel Latin phrases sometimes encountered in English are *cacoethes carpendi* 'mania for fault-finding' and *cacoethes loquendi* 'mania for talking'; and *cacoethes* is also used with English collocations (eg 'a *cacoethes* for painting').

cafetière

French *cafetier*, a derivative of *café*, means 'café-owner'. Its feminine form, *cafetière*, is used for a 'coffee-pot'. This was taken over by English in the mid-19th century, and is now mainly used specifically with reference to the sort of pot in which hot water is poured over ground coffee and a plunger is pushed down when the infusion is sufficiently advanced, isolating the grounds at the bottom of the pot and leaving clear, strained coffee.

cahier

French *cahier* has a number of applications, including 'note-book', 'exercise book', 'pamphlet', and 'report of the proceedings of a meeting (as originally recorded in a notebook)' (it is descended from Old French *quaier*, which gave English *quire*). The *Oxford English Dictionary*, noting it in 1888, described it as 'hardly in English use', but several 19th-century English dictionaries recorded it, including Benjamin Smart's (1849), Joseph Worcester's (1860), and Webster's, and by the 20th century it had clearly become an established, if seldom used, part of the language. It has the full range of French meanings, and is perhaps particularly familiar in the names of learned journals (eg *Cahiers du cinéma, Cahiers de lexicologie*). It is also used specifically as the name of the instructions prepared for their delegates by each of the three estates of the realm participating in the French States-General in 1789.

camera obscura

Latin *camera obscura* means literally 'dark room' (*camera* is the ultimate source of English *chamber*). The term appears to have been coined in the 16th century, and it denotes a light-free container (originally a room, later a box) with an opening in one side. When light is admitted through the opening by way of a convex lens, an image of outside objects is produced at the focus of the lens. Such a device was first described by Leonardo da Vinci, in 1515, and was much used by painters as an aid to composition. But it was not until 1826 that the French doctor

Nicéphore Niepce hit on the idea of putting a pewter plate at the focus of the lens. After an eight-hour exposure, the world's first photograph was produced. *Camera* had been used as a shorthand term for *camera obscura* since the early 18th century, but the first record we have of its being used for a device we would today recognize as a camera dates from 1840.

A *camera lucida*, literally 'light room', is a device fitted to optical instruments such as microscopes which allows the simultaneous viewing of the object observed and a flat surface, so that the object can be drawn or traced.

canaille

The *canaille* is the rabble, the mob, the vulgar crowd. It is a French word, but it has been used in English since at least the late 17th century. It was originally adapted into French from Italian *canaglia* (itself used in English in the 17th and 18th centuries), which to begin with meant literally 'pack of dogs' – it is a derivative of Italian *cane* 'dog'.

canard

French *canard* means literally 'duck', but it is also used figuratively for an 'untrue story put about to hoax or confuse people'. The origin of the metaphor is not entirely clear, although naturally there is no shortage of colourful suggestions. The likeliest explanation is that it comes from the old expression *vendre des canards à moitié*, literally 'half-sell ducks', that is, 'swindle someone' (the underlying notion being that if you only half-sell a duck, you haven't really sold it at all, even though the 'buyer' has parted with some money). Another, but rather improbable, story – probably a *canard* in itself – is that it originated in an attempt to prove how greedy ducks are. According to this version, a man called Cornelissen put it about that he had twenty ducks, one of which he killed and fed to the rest. They devoured it enthusiastically. He then killed another and fed it to the eighteen ducks left, and so on until in the end the twentieth duck had eaten the nineteen others. English appears to have taken the term over in the first half of the 19th century.

English also uses French *canard* for an arrangement in which the small horizontal wings that normally go at the rear of an aircraft, forming the tailplane, are placed in front of the main wings. And in the early part of the 20th century there was a vogue for applying *canard* to a bright deep iridescent blue colour, like that on a mallard's wing.

carabiniere, plural carabinieri

A *carabiniere* is a member of the Italian police force, which is under military command but acts as a civil police. English began to use the term as long ago as the mid-19th century, but it is probably only since World War 2 and the exponential increase in Continental holidays that it has become at all well known. It means literally 'someone armed with a carbine or light rifle'. English has its own (now archaic) word *carabineer*, which signifies precisely that, and indeed it has also sporadically used the corresponding Spanish *carabinero*, which stands for a 'customs officer' or 'frontier guard'.

The history of the word *carbine*, incidentally, is rather bizarre. It goes back ultimately to Old French *carabin* 'soldier armed with a light musket', and it is thought that this may originally have been a contemptuous term derived from *escarrabin* 'person who lays out the corpse of someone who has died of the plague'. This in turn was based on *scarabée* 'dung beetle', a relative of English *scarab*.

carpe diem

Carpe diem is a warning to enjoy the pleasures of the present moment while they are available, without worrying too much about the future. It means in Latin literally 'pluck the day' (*carpe* is the imperative form of *carpere* 'pluck'). The aphorism was coined by the Roman poet Horace. He used it in one of his odes (Book I, Number 11), in which he warned against believing in soothsayers and fortune-tellers and encouraged people to take each day as it came: *Dum loquimur fugerit invida aetas: carpe diem quam minimum credula postero* 'While we speak the hateful age will flee: pluck the day, as little as possible believe in the future'. The metaphor rests on the notion of 'plucking' the day like a ripe fruit, ready for consumption. The first record of its use in English (where it is usually rendered as 'seize the day') dates from the early 19th century, in the works of Byron.

carte blanche

French *carte blanche* means literally 'blank sheet of paper', and its passage into metaphor began with the notion of giving someone a blank sheet of paper (often signed by oneself) on which they were free to write down any conditions or stipulations they chose (for instance in making the terms of an agreement or treaty). English appears to have taken the term over in this sense at the beginning of the 18th century ('I threw her a *Charte Blanche*, as our News Papers call it, desiring her to write upon it her own terms,' Joseph Addison, *Spectator* 299, 1712), and it was not long before it was being used entirely figuratively, as it is today, for 'complete freedom to act at one's own discretion'. It usually occurs in the phrases *have* or *give someone carte blanche to do something*.

casus belli

A *casus belli* is an act which is taken as a justification for starting a war – for example, an armed annexation of another country's territory. The Latin phrase means literally 'occasion of war' (*casus* 'fall, chance, occasion' is the ancestor of English *case*, and the resemblance to *cause*, which might seem to be semantically appropriate, is merely fortuitous). Use of the term in English dates from the mid-19th century, and it is now often employed figuratively, for an 'act or event which sparks off a quarrel'.

casus foederis

Casus foederis is part of the terminology of international diplomacy. Literally in Latin 'occasion of a treaty', it denotes a 'circumstance that calls into force the provisions of a treaty, requiring the parties to the treaty to take action' (Latin *foedus* 'treaty, covenant' has given English *confederate* and *federal*). Its use in English dates from the late 18th century.

catalogue raisonné

A *catalogue raisonné* is in French literally a 'reasoned catalogue' – that is to say, a catalogue which has been thought out methodically. The term denotes a catalogue (for example, of the items in an exhibition) which has been classified into various categories, and usually contains notes on or descriptions of some or all of its contents: 'In lieu of the retrospective it looks as though London will never have, Kallir's magnificent biographical account and *catalogue raisonnée* confirms [Schiele's] place as one of the century's finest draughtsmen' (*The Observer*, 23 December 1990). Its use in English dates from the late 18th century.

caudillo

Spanish *caudillo* means 'chieftain, leader' (it comes from late Latin *capitellum*, a diminutive form of Latin *caput* 'head'). There are sporadic instances of the use of the word in English from the middle of the 19th century, with reference to heads of state in Latin American countries, but it was its adoption in 1938 by Franco (1892–1975) as his title (*El Caudillo*) as Spanish head of state that established its place in the language. It generally has the connotation of a military leader in a Spanish-speaking country who acts as a dictator.

cause célèbre

Cause célèbre was originally, if not a legal term, at least an expression associated with the law and with law-courts. It meant, and indeed still means, a 'trial which arouses enormous public interest'. English borrowed it, in the mid-18th century, from French, where *cause* still means 'law-suit, trial' (it used to do so in English too, but nowadays it is largely restricted to the term *cause list* 'list of cases waiting to be tried'). Over the years a more general meaning has taken over from the legal sense of *cause célèbre* in English, so that now it is usually used for a 'controversial matter which gives rise to heated debate'.

causerie

French *causerie* means 'talk, chat, of a light, inconsequential type'. It is a derivative of the verb *causer* 'talk', which is descended from Latin *causari* 'discuss, dispute'. English adopted it in the early 19th century, particularly in the context of discussions on literary topics held in the fashionable salons of the day. It is also used for a short article – a review, say, or a piece on a literary topic – which treats its subject in a light, conversational tone.

caveat emptor

The injunction *caveat emptor* means 'let the buyer beware' (Latin *emptor* is a derivative of the verb *emere* 'buy', which has also given English *pre-empt* – etymologically 'buy something before anyone else has a chance to' – while *caveat*, the third person singular present subjunctive of *cavere* 'beware', has been taken over by English as a noun, meaning 'warning, caution'). It signifies that it is the responsibility of buyers to examine carefully the article they are about to purchase, so that if afterwards they are dissatisfied with it, they cannot justly claim that they were misled by the seller. The first record of its use in English dates back to the early 16th century: '[The horse] is no chapmans ware yf he be wylde: but and he be tame and haue ben rydden vpon then caueat emptor be ware thou byer' (John Fitzherbert, *Treatise for all husbandmen*, 1523).

certiorari

Certiorari is the passive form of the Latin verb *certiorare* 'inform, certify', and so it means 'be informed'. It occurs in the opening words of a Latin writ issued by a superior court commanding that the records of a case heard by a lower court should be sent to it, so that the case can be reviewed. In English, the writ begins: 'We, being desirous for certain reasons that the said record should be certified to us'. Such a legal instrument is therefore known as a 'writ of *certiorari*' (or in legal parlance simply a *certiorari*). Use of the term in English dates back at least to the early 16th century.

c'est la vie

C'est la vie is a French expression of resignation that in the 20th century has made considerable headway in English. Literally 'that's life', it fatalistically recognizes the tendency of life to visit one with trials great and small. Vernacular versions of the saying, including *such is life, that's life*, and *life's like that*, go back at least to the late 18th century. A not dissimilar function is served by *c'est la guerre* 'that's war', originally used to put the blame on war when things go wrong, but now in English often employed as a near synonym to *c'est la vie*.

ceteris paribus

Latin *ceteris paribus* means 'with other things [being] equal'. *Ceteris* is the ablative plural of *ceterus* 'remaining over', and used here as a noun denotes 'other things, the rest'; its neuter nominative plural form, *cetera*, appears in English *et cetera*. It is a relatively modern expression, not dating back to classical Latin, and it appears to have come into English towards the end of the 16th century. It is sometimes abbreviated to *cet. par.* As far as is known, its vernacular equivalent *other things being equal* began to be widely used in the 19th century.

chacun à son goût

French *chacun à son goût* (or simply *chacun son goût*) signifies 'each to his own taste'. *Goût* is descended from Latin *gustus* 'taste', which also produced English *gustatory* and *gusto*. Usually said with a real or figurative shrug of the shoulders, it expresses surprise at what seems to be another person's odd choice, with the implication 'I certainly wouldn't have chosen that myself!' Its use in English dates from the late 18th century, and over the years it has become more common there than in its native tongue. It is sometimes erroneously analysed as *chacun a son goût*, as if it meant 'everyone has his own taste.' See also **de gustibus non est disputandum**.

chalutz, plural chalutzim

A *chalutz* (or *halutz*) was one of the early pioneers of the state of Israel. It was in the 1920s that the word began to appear in English texts, recording the exploits of Jews from various parts of the world (eg Russia) who were going to Palestine to set up co-operative societies for building homes, starting agricultural settlements, etc, with the long-term aim of building up a Jewish state. In Hebrew the term means literally 'pioneer, fighter'.

chambré

Chambré is the past participle of French *chambrer*, which means literally 'put into a room' (it is a derivative of *chambre* 'room'). However, it has a very particular and specific signification in relation to wine, which is the role in which it has been acquired by English (it is first recorded in 1956). It denotes 'brought to room temperature', and is used mainly of red wines that are taken in advance from a cool cellar to the room in which they are to be consumed, so as to rise gradually to a temperature suitable for drinking. (It should be noted, though, that the term originated at a time when the average dining room was noticeably cooler in winter than its modern centrally heated counterpart, and a consequence of following the *chambré* rule is that lighter red wines are often drunk nowadays at a higher temperature than is ideal.) English now uses *chambré* as a verb, meaning 'bring to room temperature', more often than as an adjective (although, as with *flambé* and *sauté*, this creates problems when trying to form the past tense and past participle).

chametz

In the Jewish religion it is forbidden to eat during Passover any bread that has been caused to rise by leavening. The term for such bread, or for the leavening itself, is *chametz* (or *hametz*). It came into English from Hebrew in the late 19th century, together with the form *chometz*, filtered through Yiddish.

champlevé

Champlevé denotes a type of enamelwork in which areas are hollowed out by incising into a metal base (typically of silver) and then filled with various coloured enamels which are fused by firing. Notable *champlevé* work was produced in Celtic England, and in more modern times in India. The term *champlevé* was acquired from French in the mid-19th century. It is a compound of *champ* 'field' and *levé* 'raised'. (The other main type of enamelwork, which involves constructing compartments with wire, is called **cloisonné**.)

chanteuse

French *chanteuse* denotes a 'female singer', particularly one who sings popular songs in a nightclub or cabaret. It first appears in English texts at the end of the 19th century. Its use is largely restricted to French contexts, although in American English (where the exaggeratedly anglicized pronunciation /ʃanˈtuːz/ is sometimes encountered) it is a more general term.

chapelle ardente

French *chapelle ardente*, literally 'burning chapel', denotes a chapel or other room in which the body of a king, queen, president, etc lies in state before its burial. 'Burning' refers to the flaming torches that in former times lined the walls of such a chamber, illuminating it, or to the candles often placed at each corner of the catafalque. The first record of the term in English dates from the 1820s, and it has made sporadic reappearances since then.

chargé d'affaires

A *chargé d'affaires* is in French literally someone who has been 'charged with affairs' – that is, given the job of looking after matters. The term is used specifically for an 'ambassador's deputy', and, French being the traditional international language of diplomacy, it has made its way into English (it is first recorded in the 1760s). It is applied to two distinct types of diplomatic official: to someone temporarily in charge of a diplomatic mission while the ambassador or minister is away or incapacitated; and to someone in charge of a diplomatic mission of relatively small size, which does not warrant someone of the rank of ambassador at its head. The term is sometimes abbreviated to *chargé*, and in the 18th and 19th centuries *chargé des affaires* was occasionally used instead.

châtelaine

A *châtelaine* was originally the mistress of a castle. It is the feminine form of French *châtelain*, the equivalent of English *castellan* 'keeper or governor of a castle', both of which go back ultimately to Latin *castellum* 'castle'. English adopted the term in the mid-19th century, virtually as an archaism, but before long was using it in the updated sense 'mistress of a household, particularly a grand one': 'The chatelaine of 17, Hertford Street, was hereditarily qualified to preside over a home whose natural atmosphere was one of culture' (*New Century Review*, 1900). The French word is also used for a chain worn suspended from the waist by women in former times, used for holding keys, a purse, a handkerchief, etc. A *châtelaine watch* is one attached to a *châtelaine*, or attached to a lapel or bib. The word is frequently spelled *chatelaine* in English, especially when it refers to the waist-chain.

chazan

A *chazan* is someone who leads the singing in a synagogue – that is, a cantor. The word is used particularly for someone who does the job professionally. It came into English from Hebrew as long ago as the mid-17th century, and it has had a variety of different spellings over the years: *hazan, hazzan, chazzan, chazzen, hazzan'n*, amongst others. It sometimes keeps the Hebrew plural form *chazanim*. It may go back ultimately to Assyrian *hazannu* 'overseer, governor'.

cheder

A *cheder* (or *chedar*, or *heder*) in Jewish communities is an elementary school where children are taught the Jewish religion, Hebrew history, etc. The word came into English from Hebrew (where it means literally 'room') in the late 19th century, and in English-speaking Western countries is applied chiefly to religious-education classes for young Jewish children, typically held outside ordinary school hours. It is also used colloquially for a 'prison'.

chef d'oeuvre

A *chef d'oeuvre* is a masterpiece, the best piece of work a particular artist, writer, etc has ever done. In French the term means literally 'chief [piece] of work' (*oeuvre* is descended from Latin *opus* 'work', which English has also taken over). English has been using it for quite some time: the first record of it goes back to the early 17th century.

Other French terms incorporating *chef* to have been acquired by English include *chef de cabinet* 'principal private secretary to a political leader', *chef d'orchestre* 'leader or conductor of an orchestra', and of course *chef de cuisine*, usually abbreviated to *chef* (which dates from the first half of the 19th century).

cherchez la femme

The injunction *cherchez la femme!* (in French literally 'look for the woman!') encapsulates the notion that there is always a woman at the bottom of any problem or mystery, and that if she is found, a solution will soon follow. Its originator appears to have been the French novelist Alexandre Dumas (1802–70), although the form in which he used it in his *Les Mohicans de Paris* (1864) is slightly different from the canonical expression that has come down to us: *cherchons la femme* 'let's look for the woman'. The earliest records of its use in English date from the 1890s.

cher maître

In French, if one wants to butter up an author, to build up his self-esteem as a leading literary light, one addresses him as *cher maître*, literally 'dear master'. The term began to find its way into English in the 1920s, both as a form of address and as a noun, a complimentary word for 'writer': 'It's a rare French author who can ... dash off a note to his bank without being conscious of his literary duty as a "cher Maître"' (*The Guardian*, 29 July 1968). (See also **petit maître**).

chez

French *chez* means 'at the home of (someone), at (so-and-so's) place' (it goes back via Old French *chiese* to Latin *casa* 'house'). English adopted it in the mid-18th century. Originally it was used mainly in French contexts, but gradually it has expanded its role, and in present-day English it functions as a useful shorthand way of saying 'at the home of'. When it is used with pronouns, the French form is retained (*chez moi*, not *chez me), but it can precede English names ('chez Dave', Iris Murdoch, *Under the net*, 1954). It is quite common in the names of restaurants (*Chez Nico*), and *Chez Nous* has enjoyed a certain vogue as a house-name.

chic

The ultimate origins of French *chic* 'smart(ness), stylish(ness)' are uncertain. It first appeared in 19th-century artists' slang, and it may have come from German *schick* 'skill'. Another possibility is that it was a shortening of *chicane* 'chicanery'. But whatever its source, it turned up in English in the middle of the 19th century. It was at first a noun, and it did not shift into its now more familiar role as an adjective until the 1870s (it seems that French may have borrowed it back from English as an adjective).

chicano

The term *chicano* denotes either a 'Mexican worker who is living in the USA' or an 'American of Spanish descent'. It is Spanish in origin, and is a reduced and altered form of *mejicano* 'Mexican'. The feminine version of the word is *chicana*.

chumash

The Jewish Torah consists of the five books of Moses: Genesis, Exodus, Leviticus, Numbers and Deuteronomy. A printed book containing any one of these books is called a *chumash*. The word in Hebrew means literally 'fifth' – hence, a 'fifth part of the Torah'.

chutzpah

Chutzpah, or *chutzpa*, is the sort of shameless audacity and self-confidence one needs to do or say outrageous things without turning a hair. The word is a Yiddish contribution to the language, and entered American English in the late 19th century (it has yet to make much headway in British English). It goes back ultimately to late Hebrew *huspāh*. It is pronounced /'hu:tspa:/.

chypre

At the turn of the 20th century, the in perfume was *chypre*, a heady concoction based on sandalwood: 'No woman who uses *chypre* has any sense of proportion' (*Westminster Gazette*, 2 December 1901). It owes its name to its supposed origins in Cyprus (*Chypre* is French for 'Cyprus'), and the word is first recorded in English in 1898.

cicisbeo, plural cicisbei

Cicisbeo is an elegant but now dated euphemism for a married woman's lover. The word comes from Italian (where it also means 'walking-stick'), but its origins are uncertain: one suggestion, no longer given much credence, is that it was based on French *chiche beau* 'beautiful chickpea' (the modern French equivalent is *sigisbée*). It was much used in English in the 18th century, but since then has become virtually a historical term, referring back to 18th-century Italy.

ci-devant

French *ci-devant* is an adverb, meaning 'formerly' (its constituent parts are *ci* 'here' and *devant* 'before'). But English took it over at the end of the 18th century as an adjective, in the sense 'former' or (referring to people no longer alive) 'late' (as in 'her *ci-devant* lover'). It has also been used as a noun, referring to former aristocrats at the time of the French Revolution, whose erstwhile titles had been abolished.

cinéma-vérité

The term *cinéma-vérité* denotes a style of film-making which sets out to capture as closely as possible the appearance of real life (it means literally in French 'cinema-truth'). Amongst the techniques employed are the use of hand-held cameras, which are minimally intrusive and give a less artificial, 'finished' feel than conventional cine-cameras; and as little use as possible of editing and other post-production processes which compromise the actuality of the film. *Cinéma-vérité* is usually used in documentary films, but its methods can be applied to feature films too. Use of the term *cinéma-vérité* in English dates from the 1960s. An alternative often encountered is *ciné-vérité*.

cinquecento

In the Italian system of designating centuries the *cinquecento* is the 1500s, or the 16th century. The term is used in English mainly with reference to Italian art and literature of that period. In the visual arts, the first half of the century saw the flowering of the high Renaissance, dominated by Michelangelo, Raphael, Titian and Giorgione. This gradually evolved into the mannerism of the second part of the century, exemplified by such painters as Parmigianino and Bronzino. Tintoretto and Veronese also belong to this period, as do the architects Palladio and Giulio Romano. The most notable writers of the century were Ariosto, Machiavelli and Tasso.

circa

Just like English *around*, Latin *circa* originally meant literally 'surrounding', but it gradually came to be used metaphorically for 'in the neighbourhood of', and hence 'almost, approximately'. The Roman historian Livy is the first writer on record as employing *circa* in this way (the usual prepositions for expressing this concept had hitherto been *ad* and *circiter*). English apparently started using it in the mid-19th century, and it is now comparatively common, especially in the abbreviated form *c* as prefixed to dates. In this role it serves to indicate that the year of a particular occurrence is not known with absolute certainty.

cire perdue

French *cire perdue* means literally 'lost wax' (*cire* 'wax' is related to English *cerement* 'waxed cloth for wrapping a corpse'). It is used to denote a method of casting bronze in which a model is made consisting of a heat-proof core with an outer layer of wax; the model is then surrounded with a heat-proof mould; the wax is melted out; and finally molten bronze is poured into the space left by the wax. The technique dates back to ancient Egyptian times. English began to use the term in the latter part of the 19th century, and nowadays often replaces it with the vernacular *lost wax*.

cliché

The original and literal meaning of French *cliché* is 'stereotype printing block'. It is a noun use of the past participle of the verb *clicher* 'stereotype'. The stereotype printing process involves making a cast-metal printing plate from a mould, and *clicher* appears to have originated as a printers' slang term imitative of the sound which the matrix makes when it is dropped into the molten metal. This *ur*-sense of the word has been sporadically used in English since the early 19th century. But it is in its metaphorical guise that it has had its greatest impact on the language. Like English *stereotype*, the French word has come to have connotations of the hackneyed, the unoriginal, and it was in this sense that English reborrowed *cliché* at the end of the 19th century. It has subsequently produced its own derived adjective, *clichéd*.

cloisonné

Cloisonné is a term used in the making of enamel-ware. Wires or thin strips of metal are attached to a surface. The arrangement of lines forms a pattern of compartments. In these compartments powdered enamel is placed, producing a coloured design when the whole is fired in a furnace. English acquired the word from French in the mid-19th century. It is the past participle of French *cloisonner* 'partition', which goes back ultimately to Latin *claudere* 'close'. (The other method of making enamel patterns, in which the design is cut into the metal base, is known as **champlevé**, in French literally 'raised field.')

cloqué

French *cloque* denotes a 'swelling, lump', particularly a 'blister', and the past participial adjective *cloqué* means 'blistered'. A particular application of this is in the context of textile fabrics: it refers to a sort of cloth that has an embossed surface. It was in this sense that English took it over – at first, in the 1920s, in the curiously anglicized form *cloky*, but from around 1950 in the original French version.

cogito ergo sum

Cogito ergo sum 'I think therefore I am' was the Latin formula used by the French philosopher René Descartes in his *Meditations* (1641) to establish his existence. Starting from the question 'How and what do I know?', he was able by a series of logical steps to reach the conclusion that because he possessed awareness and was capable of rational thought, he must exist; and he went on from this to prove the existence of God and the rest of the universe. The aphorism has become a familiar one in English, and its abbreviated form *cogito* is used by philosophers as a noun to designate Descarte's principle or any similar one, or more broadly still, conscious awareness in general.

cognoscente, plural cognoscenti

The *cognoscenti* are those who have a combination of expert knowledge and well-informed taste – particularly when viewed as an exclusive group who possess inside knowledge not shared by outsiders ('The cognoscenti know that going to a Wagner opera involves a certain routine,' *Radio Times*, 17 November 1990). English acquired the word in the late 18th century from Italian (where it has since died out). It goes back to Latin *cognoscens* 'knowing person, one who knows', a noun use of the present participle of the verb *cognoscere* 'come to know' (which also lies behind *connoisseur*, borrowed by English from French in the early 18th century).

coitus interruptus

English has used Latin *coitus* to clothe sexual intercourse in medical obscurity since the early 18th century, but *coitus interruptus* is a relatively new term, first recorded in English in *Studies in the psychology of sex* (1900) by the sexologist Havelock Ellis. It means literally 'interrupted intercourse', and denotes intercourse in which the penis is deliberately withdrawn from the vagina before ejaculation, typically as a form of contraception. It is also widely employed metaphorically to suggest anticlimax when something is prematurely terminated.

Another sexological Latinism used in English is *coitus reservatus*, literally 'intercourse held back', which signifies intercourse in which the man deliberately delays or avoids reaching orgasm.

cojones

Spanish *cojones* means literally 'testicles': it is related to Italian *coglione* and French *couillon*, which gave English the now archaic *cullion* 'testicle, scurvy knave', and it goes back ultimately to Latin *coleus* 'scrotum'. But it was in the metaphorical sense 'manly courage' (shared by the vernacular *balls*) that it first came into American English in the early 20th century: 'It takes more cojones to be a sportsman where death is a closer party to the game' (Ernest Hemingway, *Death in the Afternoon*, 1932). It has subsequently also come to be employed in the anatomical sense. It is pronounced /kə'hoʊnes/.

comédie humaine

The name *Comédie humaine* (literally 'human comedy') was originally given by the French author Honoré de Balzac to a series of novels and stories he wrote between 1827 and 1847. There were 91 of them, including *Eugénie Grandet* and *Le Père Goriot*. Balzac's ambitious aim was to give a complete and authentic fictionalized picture of French society in the late 18th and early 19th century, and so it gradually came about that the general title he had chosen came to be used in the language at large for any literary portrait of the diversity of human affairs, and indeed for those affairs themselves. It began to be used in English in the second half of the 19th century.

comme il faut

French *comme il faut* means literally 'as it is necessary' (*faut* is the third-person present singular of *falloir* 'be necessary'), and it is used in the sense 'proper, properly'. English borrowed it in the middle of the 18th century, and employs it particularly to convey the notion of infractions of social nicety or etiquette: 'I make large allowance for the difference of manners; but it never can have been *comme il faut* in any age or nation for a man of note ... to be constantly asking for money' (Lord Macaulay, 1857).

commis

French *commis* is a noun use of the past participle of the verb *commettre* 'commit, appoint', and so its etymological meaning is 'someone appointed to do a task' – particularly in the role of a deputy or subordinate. Amongst its specific applications is 'clerk', and it was used sporadically in this sense in English from the 16th to the 18th centuries. Its current status in English is a culinary one, designating an assistant, deputy or apprentice to a chef or waiter (it is often used attributively, as in a '*commis* chef'); in this sense its introduction dates from between the two world wars. English has occasionally also employed the French compound *commis-voyageur* 'travelling salesman'.

compos mentis

Latin *compos* meant 'having control of' (it was a compound adjective formed from the prefix *com-* 'with' and *potis* 'having power'), and it was used in the phrase *compos mentis* 'having control of one's mind', hence 'sane'. English took this over in the 17th century, and uses it mainly in non-assertive contexts – that is to say, in negatives (its usual environment: 'I don't think she's entirely *compos mentis*') and in questions. It belongs to colloquial rather than technical usage, and is frequently shortened to simply *compos*.

compte rendu

French *compte rendu*, literally 'account rendered', denotes a 'report' on or 'account' of something – as it might be, a statement of events or a review of a book (*faire le compte rendu d'un ouvrage* is 'to review a book'). English began to use the term, with this range of senses, in the early 19th century, and also occasionally employs it in the financial sense 'statement of account'.

con amore

Italian *con amore* means literally 'with love', and English has occasionally used it like that ('She sat and cried *con amore*', Jane Austen, *Mansfield Park*, 1814), but more usually English seems to employ it with the connotation of 'done out of enthusiasm or emotional commitment rather than for commercial motives' (as in 'a book written *con amore*'). The first records of it date back to the early 18th century, and although Charles Lamb in 1826 dismissed it as 'a coxcombical [foolish, pretentious] phrase', it survives to this day. It is also used specifically as a musical direction, meaning 'tenderly'.

concierge

Grainily realistic stories set in modern low-life France would not be complete without the character of the *concierge*, the caretaker or janitor of a block of flats or other large building who lurks like Cerberus in a cubbyhole by the entrance and watches all comings and goings with a suspicious and jaundiced eye. The word *concierge* goes back to **conservius*, a Vulgar Latin variant of Latin *conservus* 'fellow slave', and originally denoted a relatively exalted figure – the custodian of a large house, the warden of a castle, etc. In France and certain other countries it was used as the title of the man in charge of a royal palace, fortress, etc. English has occasionally employed the term in this historical sense, but the modern 'janitor' did not become firmly established until the 19th century.

concours d'élégance

The French were pioneers of motoring as a hobby, and it is fitting that English is indebted to them for this term redolent of the days of wire-spoked wheels and leather string-backed driving gloves. Literally 'contest of elegance', it denotes an event in which proud car-owners put their vehicles on display alongside others, and the most immaculate or best turned-out is adjudged the winner. There are also *concours d'élégance* for other sorts of vehicle, such as motorcycles. The term came into English after World War 2, and latterly the abbreviation *concours* has come to be used as an adjective for cars that are well enough preserved to be worthy of exhibition, in the phrase 'in *concours* condition'.

consolatio

The term *consolatio* (literally in Latin 'consolation') denotes a genre of literature, predominantly medieval and earlier, whose purpose is to provide comfort and solace against the tribulations of human existence. It could manifest itself in many forms – verse or prose, or a mixture of the two, as brief as a letter or in complete book form. It can be traced back to ancient origins in Greece, but its most celebrated manifestation is probably *De consolatione philosophiae* 'Concerning the consolation of philosophy', written by the philosopher Boethius (c 480–524 AD) while incarcerated in the prison of the Gothic emperor Theodoric.

conte

French *conte* means broadly 'story', or more specifically 'short story' (it is related to English *account* and *recount*). It has been used in English since the late 19th century as a literary critical term for 'short story', particularly as written by French authors such as Guy de Maupassant. But for medieval scholars it has a more specific application still: it denotes a narrative tale, particularly of the sort identified by the 12th-century French poet Marie de France as the source for her lays ('De cest cunte ke oi avez / Fu Guigemar le lai trovez, / Que hum fait en harpe e en rote: / Bone est a oir la note'). English occasionally also uses the derivative *conteur* for the composer or narrator of such tales.

contra mundum

Latin *contra mundum*, literally 'against the world', is used in English to denote defiant perseverance in the teeth of universal criticism and discouragement, a proud isolation proclaiming the justice of its position: 'Housman, at first almost *contra mundum*, fought and ultimately discredited that fashion' (*The Listener*, 21 December 1961).

contretemps

The etymological notion underlying the word *contretemps* is that of being 'against time' – that is, 'unseasonable' or 'inopportune'. It was formed in French from the preposition *contre* 'against' and *temps* 'time', and was originally borrowed into English towards the end of the 17th century as a fencing term, denoting a 'thrust or attack made at the wrong moment' (in this context it was also used as a verb in English, meaning 'make a *contretemps*'). The modern sense 'untoward or embarrassing occurrence, mishap' did not arrive until the beginning of the 19th century, and the now quite common 'mildly hostile confrontation' appears to have been a 20th-century development. *Contretemps* is also used in ballet for a 'step performed ahead of the musical beat'.

convenance

French *convenance* means 'conformity, agreement, propriety' (it is related to English *convenient, convention*, and *covenant*). It made brief appearances in English in the 15th century (in the sense of 'covenant') and in the 17th century (in the sense of 'agreement'), but its current presence in the language dates from the mid-19th century, when it was reborrowed in the sense of 'suitable behaviour, propriety'. It is also used in the plural to denote the prescribed conventionalities of social intercourse: 'her utter ignorance of London *convenances* and proprieties' (*Spectator*, 9 April 1881).

conversazione

When Crabtree in Richard Sheridan's *The School for Scandal* 1777 asked Sir Benjamin Backbite to 'repeat the charade you made last night extempore at Mrs Drowzie's conversazione', he was not implying that the lady was simply having a chat. In late 18th- and early 19th-century England a *conversazione* was a private party held at one's home. The term has come a long way since English originally borrowed it from Italian in the early 18th century. There, it denoted a fashionable assembly held in the evening, at which one had pleasant conversation with one's fellow guests and amused oneself in various other ways. At first, that is how English employed it, using it strictly in Italian contexts. But by the end of the century it was being used for home-grown parties. Then it began to narrow down in application to parties at which topics of an intellectual or cultural nature were discussed, and by the middle of the 19th century it had evolved into its present-day meaning: 'seminar or similar meeting held by a learned body to discuss a particular topic'.

coram populo

The Latin preposition *coram* meant 'in the presence of'. A number of phrases incorporating it have been used in English legal vocabulary in former centuries denoting various sorts of appearance in court, including *coram judice* 'before a judge', *coram nos* 'before us' (that is, in the court of King's Bench), and *coram paribus* 'before one's peers'. But the only one to spread out into the general language is *coram populo*, which means 'in the presence of the people, publicly' – often with the implication of being judged in the tribunal of public opinion. Such expressions were common enough in the 16th century for *coram* virtually to be reinterpreted in English as 'judgment' – *call to coram*, for instance, was used for 'bring to book'.

cordon bleu

A *cordon bleu* (in French literally a 'blue ribbon') was originally the sky-blue sash worn by knights-grand-cross of the Order of the Holy Ghost, the highest order of chivalry in Bourbon France, which was instituted by Henry III in 1578. The term hence came to be applied to the highest order of excellence in any of several fields. Among them was cookery, and it is this usage that has stuck, both in its native French and, by borrowing, in English. The first record of the term in English in the sense 'chef of the first rank' dates from the early 19th century, and it has since also come to be used adjectivally, to denote food cooked to the highest standard ('That *boeuf bourguignon* was a real *cordon bleu* effort'). In addition, *cordon bleu* is a culinary term denoting a dish made with ham and cheese and a white sauce (as in 'veal *cordon bleu*').

English has its own version of the term, *blue ribbon* or *blue riband*, originally applied in the 17th century to the sash of the Order of the Garter. In the USA, blue ribbons are worn by advocates of teetotal temperance. In modern usage the term is most often encountered in the context of the record time for crossing the Atlantic Ocean held by a passenger ship (in British English, *blue riband* is the preferred form in this sense).

cordon sanitaire

In French, *cordon sanitaire* means literally 'sanitary line', and its original application was to a system of guarded installations set up round an area in which there was an outbreak of an infectious disease in order to enforce a quarantine, preventing any spread of the disease. The first trace of the expression in English is in the abbreviated form *cordon* (James Mill in the *Westminster Review* of 1826 enquired 'if a cordon against the ordinary plague is an expedient measure'). But by the middle of the 19th century there is evidence that *cordon sanitaire* itself had come into general use in English (the translated version *sanitary cordon* has often been used too). However, it is the metaphorical application of the term that has really established its place firmly in the language. In this role it is used for a buffer zone between two countries that are not on good terms – for example, a series of states set up to separate two ideologically opposed nations, preventing armed incursion or clandestine infiltration from one to the other.

corniche

English got *cornice* in the 16th century from the obsolete French *cornice*, whose modern form *corniche* was reborrowed in the 19th century. Literally a 'projecting part', either a projecting moulding at the top of a wall or a ledge of rock on a cliff or mountainside, it came to be used in the South of France for a 'road along the edge of a cliff' (as also did its Italian equivalent, *cornice*). English began to use it in this sense in the early 19th century, at first usually in the compound *corniche road*. As early as this it was being applied specifically to the often precipitous coastal road between Nice and Genoa, which winds along cliffs overlooking the blue Mediterranean, and it has since come to be used for any similar scenic cliff route.

corpus delicti

The term *corpus delicti* has come a long way since its introduction into English in the early 19th century. In Latin it means literally 'the body of the crime' (*delicti* comes from the past participle of Latin *delinquere* 'be at fault, offend', from which English gets *delinquent*). It was originally used as a legal term for the whole aggregate or 'body' of material circumstances that constitutes evidence that a crime has been committed. In the case of murder, the evidence would generally be a corpse, and this opened the door to a folk-etymologizing transformation of the meaning of *corpus delicti*: '*corpus* means "body" (never mind about *delicti*), it's a legal term that often crops up in murder cases, so therefore the *corpus delicti* must be the murder victim's corpse'. That is the way the term is most commonly used today.

corpus vile, plural corpora vilia

A *corpus vile* is something that is fit only to be used for experimental purposes, and has no other profitable application. The term had its origins in the Latin maxim *Fiat experimentum in corpore vili* 'Let the experiment be done on a cheap body', observed by economical anatomists in the 18th and early 19th centuries. At first the reference was unequivocally to physical bodies, dead or living, but it gradually broadened out to any object of experimentation: 'Ireland may be tried as a *corpus vile* for experimentation on Government management of railways and telegraphs' (letter from John Stuart Mill, 1867).

corrida

Corrida is the Spanish word for 'bullfight', and since the end of the 19th century English has used the word when attempting to conjure up a genuine Hispanic atmosphere (it was also formerly used in Britain as a brand name for a type of Spanish wine). It is short for *corrida de toros*, which literally means 'running of bulls' (*corrida* is related to English *corridor*, which is etymologically a 'place for running').

couchette

French *couchette* (a diminutive form of *couche* 'bed, couch') can refer to a child's cot or to a berth on a ship, but it is its application to sleeping accommodation on trains that has brought it into English. It denotes a bed in a railway carriage, particularly one (as found in Continental trains) formed from a folded-down seat. English also uses it for a carriage containing such beds (in French, *wagon à couchettes*). It is an early 20th-century borrowing.

coup de foudre

French *coup de foudre* means literally 'flash of lightning' (*foudre* comes from Latin *fulgur* 'lightning', and its verbal derivative *foudroyer* 'strike with lightning' has given English the rare adjective *foudroyant* 'dazzling, stunning'). Figuratively it is used, rather like English *bolt from the blue*, for a 'sudden astounding event or action which takes one's breath away'. It can also denote 'love at first sight'. English began to use it in these metaphorical senses in the late 18th century.

coup de grâce

The original application of *coup de grâce* was to a sword-thrust, a gun-shot, etc that puts an end to the suffering of a wounded or tortured person or animal by killing them (in French it means literally 'blow of mercy'). But already by the time English took it over, in the late 17th century, its now more familiar metaphorical meaning had come to the fore: 'decisive action which finally puts an end to some ailing or troubled undertaking or enterprise'. The pronunciation of the term has undergone some vicissitudes in English in recent years. Perhaps as a result of hearing it rather than reading it, some English-speakers seem to have fallen under the misapprehension that it ends in an *s*, and that since '*s* is silent at the end of French words', *grâce* should be pronounced to rhyme with *blah*.

coup de main

A *coup de main* is a forceful action performed suddenly, particularly to take the enemy by surprise – a raid, a surprise attack. The Duke of Wellington is recorded as remarking 'This place can be taken by a *coup de main*, and probably in no other manner' (1801). In French the term means literally 'blow of hand, blow with the hand', and it started to appear in English in the mid-18th century.

coup d'état

French *coup d'état* means literally 'blow of state', and at first it was used broadly for any brilliant and unexpected stroke of statecraft. That is the sense in which English originally borrowed it in the 17th century: 'These were the two first *Coups d'estat*, stroaks of State that he [Richelieu] made' (James Howell, *Life of Lewis the XIII*, 1646). Its connotations were of an action taken in support of the régime in power, and it does not appear to be until the 19th century, at least in English, that it underwent a *volte-face* and began to be used for a sudden and often violent overthrow of a government, its present-day sense (the first notable *coup d'état* was the one in which Louis Napoleon seized power in France in 1851). Usé of *coup* on its own in the same sense dates from the mid-19th century.

Several other French expressions in English contain *coup* 'blow, stroke' (which is descended from medieval Latin *colpus* 'blow', source also of English *coppice* and *copse*). These include *coup d'éclat* 'sudden bold move', *coup de dés* 'throw of the dice', *coup de force* 'sudden violent action', *coup de maître* 'master-stroke', *coup de plume* 'satirical attack in writing', *coup de soleil* 'sunstroke', *coup d'essai* 'first attempt', *coup de tête* 'rash or impetuous action', and *coup de vent* 'gale, whirlwind'.

coup de théâtre

Coup de théâtre (in French literally 'blow of theatre') has a range of applications, both within the theatre and outside. As a theatrical term it signifies a 'sudden unexpected turn of affairs which completely transforms the action of a play', and it is also used for a 'play or other theatrical production which is a smash hit'. It is the first of these which has provided the basis of its metaphoricization to the more general 'sudden dramatic action which turns a situation on its head or seizes everyone's attention'. English acquired the expression in the mid-18th century.

coup d'oeil

French *coup d'oeil* means both 'view' and 'quick look, glance' (it is literally a 'blow of the eye'). English has used it in both these senses since taking it over in the mid-18th century, and additionally in the 19th century adopted it into military terminology, signifying 'capacity for making a swift tactical assessment of a situation': 'He was but a mediocre general, lacking the *coup d'oeil* of a genius.' (Harrison Ainsworth, *John Law*, 1864).

coupé

The original *coupé* was a four-wheeled horse-drawn carriage
with two covered passenger seats and an outside seat for the
driver. Its name was short for *carrosse coupé*, in French literally
'cut carriage' – the notion being that it resembled a berlin (a
similar sort of carriage with an extra seat at the back) with the
extra seat cut off. The word came into English in this sense in
the 1830s. Then at the beginning of the 20th century it began
to be applied analogously to cars. *Coupés* are up-market elegant
vehicles with streamlined bodywork and two doors. Fixed-head
coupés have four seats and a fixed roof that slopes down at the
back; drophead *coupés* have a roof that can be folded back and
typically seat only two. Then there was the *coupé de ville*, a sedate
vehicle popular in the 1920s and 30s in which the passengers sat
in a covered compartment but the chauffeur was exposed to
the elements. In American English the acute accent is often
dispensed with, and the word pronounced /ku:p/.

coûte que coûte

French *coûte que coûte*, literally 'cost what cost', is equivalent
to English *at all costs*. It is used for emphasizing that something
is essential, and must be done no matter how great the sacrifice.
Writers of English began using it as long ago as the beginning
of the 18th century, but in the early years tended to be rather
cavalier with it, producing inauthentic forms like *coûte qui coûte*
and *coûte qu'il coûte*.

crème de la crème

When Jean Brodie, teacher at the Marcia Blaine School for Girls
in Muriel Spark's *The Prime of Miss Jean Brodie* (1961), described
the select group of her favoured 16-year-old pupils as her 'crème
de la crème', she was identifying them as the pick of the best,
representing the very pinnacle of excellence. English acquired
the term from French (where it means literally 'cream of the
cream') in the middle of the 19th century, and often uses it to
suggest 'out of the top drawer of society'. (Metaphorical use of
the vernacular *cream* for 'best part' dates back to the 16th
century. The nearest English equivalent to *crème de la crème* is
cream of the crop.)

cri de coeur

A *cri de coeur* (literally in French a 'cry from the heart') is a heartfelt expression of distress combined with an appeal for assistance. English acquired it around the beginning of the 20th century, and it has often attracted journalists with its suggestion of the sensational and pathetic (indeed the earliest known example of its use in English is by G K Chesterton, writing in *The Daily News*, 1 July 1905).

crime passionnel

A *crime passionnel* is a crime which is held or claimed to have been committed out of extreme or uncontrollable feeling (rather than as a coolly calculated act prompted by a desire for gain or a wish to cause harm). In practice the term is usually applied to murder motivated by sexual jealousy, and in many cultures such a motive is often taken as a partial exculpation of the murderer ('In cases of what is termed "crime passionnel", French juries ... almost invariably find extenuation', *Encyclopaedia Britannica*, 1910). English adopted the term from French (where it means literally 'crime relating to the passions') at the beginning of the 20th century, and frequently substitutes for it the vernacular *crime of passion*.

cru

The French noun *cru* (or *crû*) is derived from *crû*, the past participle of the verb *croître* 'grow'. It denotes both a locality where wine is produced – a vineyard or a region – and by extension the wine itself, and the grade of quality to which the wine belongs. It is in the last of these applications that English has most commonly used the term since acquiring it from French in the 1830s. It typically occurs with some sort of descriptive epithet (*grand cru, cru exceptionnel, cru bourgeois*) or as part of a numerical categorization. English usually translates it as 'growth.' (See also **premier cru**.)

cui bono

Cui bono? is a question asked particularly by lawyers. It means in Latin 'To whose benefit?', and it is the sort of enquiry that suggests itself when a crime has been committed and the perpetrator is being sought. Who will profit, financially or otherwise, from the murder, the fraud, or whatever? The strong possibility must be that this person was responsible for the crime.

According to the Roman orator and writer Cicero, the Latin expression (which in full is *Cui bono est, fuit*, etc 'To whose benefit is it, was it', etc) was coined by one Lucius Cassius Pedanius, a judge. English often uses it additionally for 'What use is it? What good is it?', which is rather off beam as far as its original Latin meaning is concerned.

cuisine minceur

Cuisine minceur was a concept introduced by the French chef Michel Guérard. Taking the basic principles of the **nouvelle cuisine** (use of fresh ingredients, respect for natural flavours, avoidance of fats, etc), he sought to adapt them still further to the needs of people who wish to stay slim and healthy (the French expression means literally 'slenderness cooking'). Developed at his hotel at Eugénie-les-bains, in the Landes, *cuisine minceur* eschews most dairy products apart from fromage blanc, uses no sugar or flour, and concentrates on fat-free or low-fat ingredients such as game, shellfish and vegetables. Following the success of his *cuisine minceur*, Guérard went on to publish a book called *Cuisine gourmande*, which might be translated as 'Greedy cooking', and which successfully replaces the calories removed by *cuisine minceur*.

cul-de-sac

The literal meaning of French *cul-de-sac* is 'bottom of the bag', and when English first took it over, in the early 18th century, it was as an anatomical term, signifying a cavity or tube in the body that is open at one end only (eg the caecum, a part of the gut that ends in the appendix). Its more familiar present-day application, to a road that is closed off at one end, dates from the end of the 18th century; and it was not long before this was followed by the metaphorical 'dead end, course of action that offers no prospect of advancing matters'.

Other French terms incorporating *cul* that have been used in English include *cul-de-four*, literally 'bottom of the oven', an architectural term denoting a low spherical vault, and *cul-de-lampe*, 'bottom of the lamp', a cone- or pyramid-shaped decorative device.

cum laude
See **summa cum laude**

cum grano salis
Faced with an unpalatable dish, one way of transforming it into something eatable is to season it with salt. And so the mid-17th century, when it sought a metaphor to suggest the allowances necessary to give credence to a somewhat unlikely story, hit on Latin *cum grano salis* 'with a grain of salt'. It is first recorded in English in the mid-17th century, and it has since become a familiar Latin tag. Of the same vintage is the vernacular version *with a grain of salt*, but the now commoner *with a pinch of salt* appears to be much more recent (it is not recorded before 1948).

curiosa
The innocent-sounding term *curiosa* may seem to (and indeed sometimes does) suggest nothing more sensational than 'curiosities, oddities'. It is a noun use of the neuter plural of Latin *curiosus*, source of English *curious*. But when it turns up in booksellers' and librarians' catalogues, it is generally as a mincing concealment of 'pornographic material'. There are records of English *curious* itself being used in this euphemistic sense from the 1870s, and presumably *curiosa* is of roughly the same vintage. (Compare **facetiae**.)

curragh
The Celtic languages have given English two distinct words from *curragh*. First, in the 15th century, came Irish Gaelic *curach*, which denotes a type of small boat made from hides stretched over a frame (the related Welsh *corwgl* lies behind English *coracle*). Then in the 17th century it was followed by Irish *corrach* 'marsh' and Manx *curragh* 'moor, fen', which have become particularly familiar in the form 'the Curragh', the name of a racecourse in County Kildare, Ireland, which was built on a large area of flat open ground.

currente calamo
To write *currente calamo* is to write freely and fluently, without hesitation or the need to cogitate over what one is going to put. The Latin phrase means literally 'with the pen running on, with hurrying pen'. Latin *calamus*, from Greek *kalamos*, originally meant 'reed, cane', and so came to be used for a pen made from

a reed. Its use in English dates from the late 18th century. It has not been traced to any classical Latin source.

curriculum vitae

Latin *curriculum vitae* means literally 'course of life', and English has used the expression since the beginning of the 20th century for a 'list or summation of the chief events of a person's life'. In particular it denotes a summary of someone's educational qualifications and work experience, for presentation to a prospective employer. It is more familiar in its abbreviated form *CV*, and American English prefers *résumé* (borrowed from French). (Use of Latin *curriculum* in English for a 'course of study', incidentally, originated in the Scottish universities in the 17th century.)

cwm

Cwm is a Welsh contribution to English. It denotes a deep bowl-shaped depression on a mountainside, often containing a small lake, and was adopted by geologists in the mid-19th century. In Welsh it means simply 'valley', and ultimately is probably related to English *coomb* 'valley' (which may have been borrowed from a Celtic source). Other terms acquired by English for the same geological feature are *cirque* (a 19th-century borrowing from French) and *corrie* (adapted from Scots Gaelic *coire* in the late 18th century).

D

dacha

In Russia, a *dacha* is a country villa for the use of town-dwellers in the summer. The Russian word means literally 'act of payment, gift', and arrived at its modern application via 'land granted by a prince'. English began to use it towards the end of the 19th century. It is pronounced to rhyme with *thatcher*.

dame de compagnie

French *dame de compagnie* (literally 'lady of company') denotes that now virtually vanished breed, the paid female companion – a woman employed to live with, travel with, assist, etc her employer, typically an elderly woman, as a sort of mercenary friend. Her image, as distilled from 19th- and early 20th-century novels, is of a dim and downtrodden figure at the beck and call of a domineering old battle-axe. Use of the term *dame de compagnie* in English dates from the late 18th century, and in the 19th century it was sometimes partially anglicized to *damdecompany*.

danse macabre

In the art and literature of late medieval Europe, human mortality was often represented allegorically as a feverish dance in which a skeletal personification of death leads people to their graves, commonly in order of social precedence. English has two names for this dance, both dating back to the 15th century: the vernacular *dance of death* and, borrowed from French, *danse macabre*. The etymology of the latter is not entirely clear, but it is thought that *macabre* may be an alteration of an original *macabé*, disguising some sort of reference to the Maccabees, a family of Jewish patriots of the second and first centuries BC – possibly an allusion to II Maccabees 12:43–46, which contains prayers for the dead, or to a representation of the killing of the Maccabees in a miracle play. *Macabre* has since become generalized as an adjective denoting gruesomeness.

82

déclassé

Someone who is described as *déclassé* has come down in the world – demoted or relegated by circumstances to a lower rank of society. The word is a borrowing of the past participle of French *déclasser* 'lower in class', which English actually adopted and adapted at around the same time (the late 19th century) as the verb *declass*. For a time the anglicized form *declassed* vied with *déclassé* ('the declassed Judith Marsett' *New Review*, June 1891), but it is *déclassé* that has won out. In present-day English it is also used of things, with the sense 'no longer in favour with fashionable society'. The French feminine form *déclassée* is occasionally resorted to in appropriate circumstances.

décolleté

French *collet* means 'collar' (it is a diminutive form of *col* 'neck'), and addition of the prefix *dé-*, denoting removal, produced the verb *décolleter* 'cut out the neck of a dress'. Its past participle, *décolleté*, is used of a woman's dress, blouse, etc, signifying that it has a low-cut neckline, revealing the cleavage and often the shoulders as well. English acquired this in the early 19th century, and in its wake followed the noun derivative *décolletage* '(exposure of the upper body resulting from) a low-cut neckline', and also, in the early 20th century, the noun *décolletée* 'low-cut neckline'. French also applies the adjective *décolletée* to women wearing low-cut garments, and that used to be the case in English too ('a stout countess of sixty, décolletée', William Thackeray, *Vanity Fair*, 1848), but the usage seems to have gone out of fashion.

dedans

The French adverb *dedans* means 'inside' (the element *dans* 'in' goes back to an Old French compound formed from *de* and *enz*, a descendant of Latin *intus* 'inside'), but it is in a very specialized application that it has come into English. It is also used as a noun, meaning 'interior', and this came to be used as a term in the game of real tennis to designate the open gallery at the server's end of the court. The gallery is used by specatators, and *dedans* itself is sometimes employed to designate the 'spectators at a real-tennis match'. The term is first recorded in English in the early 18th century.

de dicto

Literally in Latin 'about the saying', *de dicto* is a term used in logic and philosophy to denote knowledge or belief acquired via a linguistic or other expression rather than via that to which it refers. The classic example of this is the so-called 'Electra paradox': Electra knew that Orestes was her brother (ie knew that she had a brother called Orestes), but did not know that the man before her (Orestes) was her brother, so her knowledge of him was *de dicto*. The term is specifically contrasted with *de re* 'about the thing'.

de facto

The adverb and adjective *de facto* denotes what is in fact or in practice the case, irrespective of what is legally or should in theory be the case. It means in Latin literally 'from the fact', and it probably began to be used in English in the 16th century. It is frequently employed to designate someone who actually wields power, even though someone else may nominally be in charge (as in 'the *de facto* head of state'). In this and other contexts it is often explicitly contrasted with *de jure*.

In the late 17th century, people who recognized William III as *de facto* king of England were popularly known as *defacto-men*. And in present-day Australian and New Zealand English, a *de facto* is a 'live-in lover', a 'common-law spouse'.

de fide

Latin *de fide*, literally 'of faith', is used in the Roman Catholic Church to denote that a particular doctrine must be embraced by all members of the Church as an article of faith, and may not be questioned. It is applied particularly in cases where a papal ruling has been promulgated. Its use in English dates back to the 17th century: 'Some [hold] that the Popes indirect Power over Princes in Temporalities is *de Fide*; Others the contrary' (William Chillingworth, *The Religion of Protestants*, 1638).

dégagé

Dégagé, an adjective based on the past participle of French *dégager* 'disengage, free', was borrowed into English as long ago as the late 17th century, in the sense 'relaxed, casual, unrestrained'. It led a fairly low-profile existence for 200 years and more, retaining its original meaning, but then in the middle of the 20th century it took on a new lease of life. As part of the language of artists, writers and the intelligentsia in general, it is now frequently used to mean 'lacking intense personal involvement, not committed to any artistic ideals, political ideology, etc'. It is contrasted expressly with **engagé**.

de gustibus non est disputandum

This Latin tag (often in English shortened for convenience to *de gustibus*) means 'there is no disputing about tastes' – that is to say, there is no sense in challenging people's preferences, no matter how strange they may appear, because they are not amenable to rational argument. *Disputandum* is the gerundive form of the verb *disputare* 'dispute', and therefore signifies 'to be disputed'. **Chacun à son goût** expresses much the same sentiments.

de haut en bas

De haut en bas, in French literally 'from high to low', denotes 'in a condescending or patronizing manner, as if speaking from a lofty or exalted position to someone whom one considers inferior': 'How odd of D. J. Taylor to describe the tone of J. K. Galbraith's novel as "snooty and *de haut en bas*", and then to end the review by complaining that the American spellings have not been "corrected"' (*The Sunday Times*, 6 January 1991). English borrowed the expression from French (where it also signifies more concretely 'downwards' and 'from top to bottom') as long ago as the late 17th century. It is sometimes used attributively ('Her *de-haut-en-bas* judgment of Macaulay is perhaps widest of the mark', W. R. Greg, *Miscellaneous Essays*, 1882).

déjà vu

When you go to a place you have never visited before and it seems strangely familiar, you experience a 'sense of *déjà vu*'. The term was taken up by psychologists from French (where it means literally 'already seen') at the beginning of the 20th century, and by the middle of the century had seeped out into the general language. The experience is a recognized psychological condition, and is characterized as a form of paramnesia, in which the memory is distorted. In more recent times, the term has been extended in general usage to connote 'something seen so often before that it has become tedious'.

de jure

Latin *de jure* means literally 'according to law'. *Jure* is the ablative form of Latin *jus* 'law', which has also given English *jury* and *just*. It found its way into English in the early 17th century, and its commonest role is as a term contrasting with *de facto*. *De facto* denotes 'in practice, actually', whereas *de jure* expounds the legal or theoretical position, which may not correspond with reality. It is frequently used in the context of control or power (as in 'Smith is the *de jure* leader, but his deputy wields all the power').

délassement

French *délassement* 'relaxation, rest' enjoyed a sporadic career in English in the 19th century, but seems to have gone gradually out of use in the 20th century. It is a derivative of the verb *délasser* 'rest, refresh', which etymologically denotes 'un-weary' (it is based on the adjective *las* 'weary', which also underlies English *alas*). The first record of it in an English text dates from 1804.

delirium tremens

Etymologically, Latin *delirium* describes a ploughman accidentally swerving aside from the straight line of his furrow. It was derived from the verb *delirare* 'go mad', which itself was formed from the prefix *de-* 'away from' and the noun *lira* 'ridge, furrow'. English adopted it as a word for 'madness' in the 16th century. The term *delirium tremens*, literally 'trembling delirium', was introduced around 1813 by a certain Dr T. Sutton. He used it for a sort of frenzied fit that could be alleviated by opium, but was made worse by bleeding the patient (a frequent procedure for madness at that time). It was not until later in the century that it began to be used in its present-day sense of 'psychotic condition caused by alcoholism, involving anxiety, shaking, hallucinations, etc'.

de luxe

French *de luxe*, literally 'of luxury', is used post-nominally in expressions such as *articles de luxe*, where it has the force of English *luxurious*. From this it developed into a quasi-adjectival role, as in *édition de luxe* 'edition with luxurious binding, high-quality paper, etc'; and indeed, the earliest record of the term in English, in 1819, was in the phrase *edition de luxe*. Its syntactic niche in English appears to have remained after the noun for a century or more (eg 'train *de luxe*'), and its more familiar modern attributive role (eg '*de luxe* train') does not seem to have evolved until between the two world wars. French *luxe* itself was acquired by English in the mid-16th century. It seems to have withered away after about 200 years, but it began to reappear at the beginning of the 20th century, often in an attributive mode, synonymous with *de luxe* ('hiring out luxe carriages' *Westminster Gazette*, 28 July 1908).

démarche

French *démarche* means literally 'way of walking, gait'. It is related to English *march*, but it is also used metaphorically to denote a 'step taken to achieve some end', and it was in this sense that English took it over in the late 17th century. It has come to be used particularly with reference to diplomatic manoeuvres, initiatives, or approaches ('to induce the Bonn Government to make a joint démarche to the four Foreign Ministers', *Annual Register*, 1956), and to the presentation of views, complaints, etc to a public authority.

déménagement

Déménagement is an up-market way of saying 'moving house'. It is the standard French term for the activity (derived from *ménage* 'household'), and it began to appear in English in the late 19th century. The first record of it in an English text is in Lady Charlotte Schreiber's journal (1875).

demimonde

The French term *demimonde* (literally 'half-world') was coined by the novelist and playwright Alexandre Dumas the younger (1824–95), best known for his play *La Dame aux camélias*. By it he meant to suggest a world half in and half out of respectable society, inhabited by women whose status was compromised by suspicions of sexual promiscuity; but over the years it has come more and more to have connotations of high-class prostitution. English acquired it in the mid-19th century, and it was followed towards the end of the century by *demimondaine*, signifying a 'woman belonging to the *demimonde*'. *Demimonde* itself is now often used in English in a broader, more general sense, denoting any group that inhabits the edge of respectability, success, fame, etc.

demi-pension

Demi-pension is a form of hotel or guest-house accommodation in which bed, breakfast and one main meal per day are provided. English borrowed the term (equivalent to the vernacular *half board*) from French in the mid-20th century. (See also **pension**.)

démodé

Démodé is the past participle of the French verb *démoder* 'put out of fashion' (a derivative of *mode* 'fashion'), and it is used as an adjective meaning 'out of date'. English began to take an interest in it in the late 19th century, and to begin with used it in the anglicized form *demoded* as well as the original French ('anything so demoded as bustifying', *Saturday Review*, 17 October 1891), but it is the latter which has won out. It has useful overtones of scorn, which make it much more satisfyingly dismissive than close synonyms such as *outdated, outmoded, unfashionable*, etc.

de nos jours

French *de nos jours* means 'of our days', and it is used quasi-adjectivally to suggest similarity between a living person or contemporary thing and a comparable one of a previous period. For instance, a distinguished lexicographer might be praised as a 'Larousse de nos jours'. English started to use the expression around the turn of the 20th century: 'I admire the Demosthenes *de nos jours*' (Max Beerbohm, *Yet Again*, 1909).

de novo

De novo denotes 'from the beginning, from scratch, afresh'. In Latin literally 'from new', it began to be used in English as long ago as the early 17th century. It usually functions as an adverb, but it is also occasionally used as an adjective.

deo volente

Latin *deo volente* is an ablative absolute expression denoting literally 'God willing'. *Volente* is the ablative form of the present participle of the verb *velle* 'will, wish'; it is sometimes incorrectly replaced with the nominative form *volens*. It is used in English, and has been since at least the mid-18th century, as a sort of good-luck talisman, rather like touching wood, for superstitiously warding off the effects of tempting fate when saying what one intends to do in the future. It is frequently encountered in the abbreviated form *d.v.*, as in 'I shall come back the following week, d.v.'

de profundis

Latin *de profundis* are the first words of Psalm 130 in the Vulgate: *De profundis clamavi ad te, domine* ('Out of the depths I have cried unto thee, O Lord', in the Authorized Version). They have been used in English from as far back as the 15th century as the name of this psalm, and of any penitential psalm in general, and also by extension for a 'cry of despair from the depths of misery, grief, or degradation'. Its best-known application is perhaps as the title given by Oscar Wilde to a vindication of the conduct that led to his imprisonment for homosexuality, originally written in prison as part of a letter to Lord Alfred Douglas but published in 1905.

déraciné

Someone who is *déraciné* has been plucked from his or her habitual environment and put down amongst unfamiliar people, ways of life, etc. The term implies etymologically a pulling up by the 'roots'; it is the past participle of French *déraciner* 'uproot', which goes back ultimately to late Latin *radicina*, a derivative of Latin *radix* 'root'. It is commonly applied to someone who has been transplanted into an alien culture, in a different country, but it is also used for people cast adrift in strange social environments, out of the class of their birth. English acquired the term in the early 20th century. The language had adopted and anglicized French *déraciner* as *deracinate* much earlier, in the late 16th century.

de re

The Latin phrase *de re*, literally 'about the thing', is used in the terminology of logic and philosophy to denote that knowledge, belief, etc is based on a thing itself rather than any linguistic or other representation of it. For example, if someone knew that a piece of domestic equipment was a machine for washing clothes, without knowing that it was called a *washing machine*, their knowledge of it would be *de re*. The term is contrasted with *de dicto*.

de rigueur

French *de rigueur* means literally 'of strictness', and originally denoted that 'according to strict etiquette, something is compulsory'. Today the underlying connotations of 'etiquette' remain: the expression is used for 'essential, compulsory', but almost always in the context of 'what is in accordance with social convention' ('The only place to be was in the cathedral-like expanse of the two-tiered restaurant. (Dinner jackets *de rigueur*.), an advertisement in *The Observer Magazine*, 18 November 1990). Use of the term in English dates from the mid-19th century.

dernier cri

If something is 'the *dernier cri*' (or '*le dernier cri*'), it is the very latest thing, the most up-to-date fashion, the last word. English borrowed the expression from French (where it means literally 'final shout') towards the end of the 19th century. It began as a noun, but French also uses it as an adjective (*des chaussures dernier cri* are 'ultra-fashionable shoes'), and English has followed suit: 'Any old necklace can be made modern and "dernier cri"' (*The Daily Express*, 9 November 1928).

derrière

French *derrière* means broadly 'behind' (it is related to English *rear* and *retro-*), but it is in one very specific colloquial sense that English has taken it over – as a noun meaning 'bottom, buttocks'. The borrowing dates from the late 18th century; and like the parallel vernacular *behind*, which seems to be of similar antiquity, its role is as a facetious euphemism (occasionally also exploiting the suggestion of French naughtiness).

déshabillé

English has borrowed French *déshabillé* twice. The first time was in the late 17th century, since when it has become anglicized to *dishabille*. But in the 20th century, in what is virtually a re-acquisition, *déshabillé* has crossed the Channel again. In either guise (and occasionally the in-between *déshabille*) the word means 'state of being only partially dressed, or of being casually dressed'. It is a noun use of the past participle of the French verb *déshabiller* 'undress' (which is distantly related to English *able*). To be *en déshabillé* is to be partially dressed, or casually dressed.

dessous

Underwear habitually attracts euphemism, and *dessous* is an (albeit modest) example. Originally an adverb, meaning 'beneath', French *dessous* came to be used as a noun denoting the 'lower part, underpart'; and this in turn formed the basis of a plural noun *dessous* 'underclothes, particularly women's underclothes'. This made an appearance in English at the beginning of the 20th century, but it does not seem to have survived very long.

de trop

If you find yourself seated at table with a newly married couple, you may well feel *de trop*. The expression (in French literally 'of too much') means 'excessive', and hence often 'more than is wanted, superfluous', and was acquired by English in the mid-18th century. Its use in English usually connotes the embarrassment caused by superfluity.

deus ex machina

Latin *deus ex machina* means literally 'a god from a machine' (it is a modern Latin rendering of Greek *theos ek mēkhanēs*). The *machina* was a piece of stage machinery used in ancient Greek and Roman drama for suspending actors in the role of 'gods' above the stage. It was often the function of these gods to intervene in the action of a play to resolve a difficulty, and so the term *deus ex machina* came to be used figuratively for any unexpected or artificial event, person, etc that suddenly comes on the scene to untangle a knotty situation or bring reconciliation all round.

diamanté

Fabric that is *diamanté* is encrusted with small paste diamonds or other artificial jewels, sequins, etc to give a glittering effect. The word is the past participle of the French verb *diamanter* 'stud with diamonds', a derivative of *diamant* 'diamond'. English acquired the word at the beginning of the 20th century, and also uses it as a noun denoting '*diamanté* decoration'.

dies non

A *dies non* is a day on which courts of law do not sit and no legal proceedings may be conducted. For example, Sunday is a *dies non*. The term is short for Latin *dies non juridicus*, literally 'day which is not set aside for the administration of justice'. Its beginnings in English legal vocabulary go back to the 17th century. Latterly it has occasionally been used figuratively, for any day when nothing happens or when things are closed down: 'This has been almost a "dies non" in the City, owing to the Stock Exchange being closed' (*The Daily News*, 19 April 1897).

ding an sich

Ding an sich is a philosophical term. It denotes the intrinsic nature of an entity, shorn of any properties which we are aware of only via the perception of the senses – an object apprehended, in other words, solely by thought or intuition, rather than by sight, hearing, touch, taste or smell. In German it means literally 'thing in itself', and indeed *thing-in-itself* has been used as a term in English since the late 18th century. It was originated by the German philosopher and metaphysician Immanuel Kant (1724–1804), and English borrowed it in the mid-19th century.

Directoire

The *Directoire*, or in English the *Directory*, was an executive body which constituted the government of France during the First Republic, 1795–99. It consisted of five men, known as 'directors', who were elected by a so-called 'Council of Ancients' (men over 40 years of age) and a 'council of Five Hundred'. English uses French *Directoire* as an adjective in two distinct modes. First, denoting a style of women's dress characteristic of this period, influenced by ancient Greek and Roman models and typified by diaphanously thin dresses with a waistline just under the bust. *Directoire knickers* are elasticated knickers that reach to the knee. Second, denoting the French neoclassical style of furniture, objets d'art, and interior decoration typical of this period.

dirigisme

Dirigisme is a mainly derogatory term for a policy of strict central control, allowing for no initiative below top level. It was originally and remains mainly a political term, denoting state control of all economic and social matters, but it is used more widely too: 'linguistic *dirigisme*, standards of correctness in a constantly evolving language' (*Archivum Linguisticum*, 1951). English acquired it from French in the middle of the 20th century, and sometimes anglicizes it to *dirigism*. The derived adjectives *dirigiste* and *dirigistic* are also used.

disjecta membra

The *disjecta membra* of something are its 'scattered fragments'. The expression is an alteration of a phrase of Horace, the Roman poet: *disjecti membra poetae* 'the limbs of a dismembered poet' (*disjectus* is an adjective formed from the past participle of the Latin verb *disicere* 'throw apart, scatter, disperse'). It has been used in English since the early 18th century, now mainly in the sense 'extracts taken from the writings of somebody'.

distingué

Distingué means 'distinguished', but in the very specific sense 'having an air of distinction, having an aristocratic or refined demeanour, stylish'. In French it originated as an adjectival use of the past participle of *distinguer* 'distinguish', and English borrowed it at the beginning of the 19th century. Use of English *distinguished* in the same sense dates back to the mid-18th century.

distrait

French *distrait* 'absent-minded, inattentive' is an adjectival use of the past participle of the verb *distraire* 'distract, divert' (which is of course closely related to English *distract*). English has borrowed it twice. The first time was in the 14th century, but within about a hundred years it had died out, and it did not reappear until the mid-18th century. To its original sense 'absent-minded' has been added latterly 'mildly agitated or worried', presumably under the influence of another near relative, *distraught* (which comes from Latin *distractus*).

dolce far niente

Dolce far niente sums up for English-speakers the proverbial sun-dappled indolence of the south. It means in Italian literally 'sweet doing nothing' (Italian *fare* 'do, make' is the equivalent of French *faire*), and English uses it to express the notion of the pleasures of inactivity: 'It is there ... that the dolce far niente of a summer evening is most heavenly' (H. W. Longfellow, 1830). Its English career began at the beginning of the 19th century.

Italian *dolce* (which is related to English *dulcet*) is also used in English as a musical direction, meaning 'in a soft smooth way'. (See also **la dolce vita**.)

doli capax

Latin *doli capax* means literally 'capable of grief' (late Latin *dolus* 'pain, grief' is the source of English *doleful* and of French *deuil* 'mourning'). It is used as a legal term denoting that a person is capable of distinguishing between right and wrong, and can therefore be said to have had an evil intention when committing a crime. It is typically applied to someone no longer legally categorized as an infant. It is first recorded in English in the late 17th century, as is its opposite, *doli incapax*.

donnée

Donnée is a nominalization of the feminine past participle of French *donner* 'give', and so denotes literally 'that which is given'. It is used for a basic proposition accepted as true for the purpose of argument or further elaboration; for the fundamental idea or motif of a story; and, in the plural, for information assembled (like the parallel Latin *data*). English has taken the term over in the first two of these uses. It is first recorded in the 1870s, in the writings of Henry James (in the same decade his brother, the philosopher William James, introduced the loan translation *given* into English). The inauthentic masculine form *donné* is sometimes used.

doppelgänger

Strictly speaking, a *doppelgänger* is a ghostly duplicate of a living person, a wraith who follows him or her around. That is the import of German *doppelgänger*, which literally means 'double-goer, double-walker'. English adopted it in the early 19th century, in its original sense, but latterly it has come to be used much more commonly for 'someone who looks exactly like someone else' (presumably owing to the similarity to English *double*). To begin with, it was often partially anglicized to *double-ganger*. In the 20th century *doppelgänger* has been the norm, but even this is commonly pronounced, and indeed written *doppelganger*.

dos-à-dos

French *dos-à-dos* means literally 'back to back'. *Dos* is descended from Latin *dorsum* 'back', which also lies behind English *dorsal* and *doss*. The phrase began to appear in English as an adverb in the early 19th century, used particularly in the contexts of dancing and of the placement of furniture, and before the end of the century we find it being employed as a noun, designating a type of back-to-back seating (as on public transport). But its best-known incarnation in English is in the naturalized form *do-se-do*, or *do-si-do*, dating from the 1920s, which refers to a sort of square dance in which the dancers circle around back to back.

double entendre

In *double entendre*, English has preserved a French expression that has long since gone out of use in its native France. In early modern French it was used in the sense 'double meaning, ambiguity' (*entendre* was a noun use of the verb *entendre* 'mean'), and English took it over in the late 17th century. However, since then French has abandoned it in favour of *double entente* (which has actually been sporadically used in English as a more 'correct' form since the late 19th century). Both *double entendre* and *double entente* usually carry the connotation of a possible risqué or indecent meaning that underlies the innocent surface meaning ('No *double entendres*, which you sparks allow, / To make the ladies look – they know not how', John Dryden, *Love Triumphant*, 1694).

doyen

Someone who is described as the *doyen* of a particular group of people or area of activity is viewed as its most distinguished member or representative by virtue of seniority, experience, and often also excellence (as in 'John Gielgud, the doyen of English actors'). The word was borrowed from French in the late 17th century, and was followed around the end of the 19th century by the feminine form *doyenne*. Its original and still current literal meaning there is 'dean', and indeed ultimately *doyen* and English *dean* are the same word. Both are descended via late Latin *decanus* from Greek *dekānos*, which meant originally 'leader of a group of ten'. *Dean* entered English in the 14th century through Anglo-Norman *deen*, whose Old French source *deien* was the ancestor of modern French *doyen*.

dramatis personae

The *dramatis personae* of a play are the characters who appear in it. The term in Latin means literally 'people of the drama, characters of the drama', and began to be used in English in the early 18th century. In its original sense it still takes a plural verb, but latterly it has come to designate more commonly a 'list of characters in a play, printed at the front of its published text', and in this role it is treated as a singular noun.

droit de seigneur

Proverbially, in medieval times the lord of the manor had the right to deflower the newly-married wife of any of his feudal underlings on her wedding night, pre-empting the husband. This right is designated in French the *droit de seigneur* or *droit du seigneur* 'the lord's right' (French *seigneur* designates 'lord', or more specifically 'feudal lord of the manor', and is related to English *senior*). English took the term over, in both forms, in the 19th century; present-day English usage tends to prefer *de* to *du*. Latterly it has frequently been employed metaphorically to denote any excessive claim imposed on a subordinate.

duce

Italian *duce* 'leader' is a direct descendant of Latin *dux* 'leader', which also gave English *duke*. It was adopted as a title by the fascist leader Benito Mussolini (1883–1945) when he came to power in 1922. Straightaway the word began to appear in English texts (the title often given in its full form *Il Duce* 'The Leader'), and it has remained a common way of referring to Mussolini ever since. In the 1930s there was some tendency to generalize *duce* as a term for any 'fascist dictator', and since then it has occasionally been used broadly for other Italian leaders (such as Garibaldi).

duende

Spanish *duende* means 'imp, goblin, ghost', but it is also used metaphorically for the demon of inspiration that fires a dancer to a frenzy. It is that sense that provided the main impetus for the introduction of the term into English in the 20th century, but it is also used more generally for 'frenzied artistic inspiration' ('Roy Campbell [the poet] had this "*duende*",' Edith Sitwell, 1960).

duma

The *Duma* (or *Douma*) was the Russian parliament set up by
Czar Nicholas II in 1906 and finally dissolved following the
Bolshevik Revolution of 1917. It was established following the
1905 Revolution, so as to introduce some semblance of demo-
cracy into Russia. Its full name was *Gosudárstvennaya Dúma*
'national legislative assembly'. Russian *dúma* 'elective municipal
council' (first recorded in English in 1870) was borrowed originally from Gothic *dōms* 'judgment', a relative of English *deem*
and *doom*.

dummkopf

German *dummkopf* means literally 'dumb-head'. *Dumm* is related
to English *dumb*, and *kopf* 'head' originally denoted 'drinking
cup', and has links with English *cup*. The term is used as an
insult, equivalent to English *blockhead, idiot*. It began to filter
into English in the 1830s (the first record of its use in English is
in the works of the Germanophile Thomas Carlyle), and it has
been sporadically used since then, sometimes in the partially
anglicized form *dumbkopf*. In American English and also in
Scottish English the translation *dumbhead* enjoyed some currency in the late 19th and early 20th century. But in fact the
very earliest intimations of the word in English go back to early
19th-century America, from where there is an isolated record of
the form *dom cop*. This is in Washington Irving's *A History of
New York* (1809), an account of the early Dutch settlers of New
York written under the pseudonym 'Diedrich Knickerbocker',
and was presumably inspired by *domkop*, the Dutch equivalent
of *dummkopf*

E

eau de cologne

Eau de cologne is a toilet water consisting of alcohol and various fragrant essential oils, originally made in Cologne, Germany. The term in French means literally 'water of Cologne', and is first recorded in English at the beginning of the 19th century. In general usage it is now usually abbreviated to *cologne*.

Several other French terms have come into English containing *eau* 'water' (a descendant of Latin *aqua*). *Eau de Javel* denotes a solution of potassium hypochlorite or sodium hypochlorite in water, used as a bleach or disinfectant, and commemorates Javel, now a suburb of Paris, where the solution was first made. *Eau de nil*, literally 'Nile water', is a term for a pale green liquid which supposedly resembles the colour of the river Nile. *Eau de Portugal*, also a sort of perfume, contains an essential oil called 'essence of Portugal'.

echt

German *echt* means 'real, genuine'. It began to infiltrate English in the early years of the 20th century (Bernard Shaw is the first on record as using it), and it has made a niche for itself as an imprimatur of authenticity or typicality. It is often prefixed adverbially to an adjective of nationality ('folk dances with an *echt*-Russian feeling') or placed before the name of a writer, artist, etc to suggest that something is definitely the work of, or is typical of the person ('lyrical passages that are *echt*-Chopin'). But it is occasionally to be found predicatively: ' "Are you married?" he asked ... "I see your ring, but is that camouflage or *echt*?" ' (Nicholas Freeling, *Love in Amsterdam*, 1962).

éclat

French *éclat* means literally 'splinter of wood', 'clap of thunder', and also 'explosion' (it is a derivative of the verb *éclater* 'burst, explode', which is of Germanic origin and distantly related to English *slit*). But it is also used figuratively for 'brilliance, dazzling effect' and for 'scandal', and it was in those two senses that English originally acquired it in the late 17th century. They have now died out, having been gradually replaced since the mid-18th century by 'conspicuously brilliant success' and 'great acclaim'. There are sporadic examples from the 18th and 19th centuries of the use of *éclat* in English as a verb, meaning 'become or make known'.

écorché

The *écorché* transports the anatomist's dissecting room into the artist's studio. It is a picture or model of the body or of a body part with the skin stripped away, so as to show the muscles and other structures underneath. From the 16th century onwards such models of human bodies (and occasionally also of horses) formed part of the essential equipment of artists' workshops, as aids to composition. Amongst the best-known of *écorché* drawings are those of Leonardo da Vinci. The word is a noun use of the past participle of French *écorcher* 'skin, flay', and came into English in the mid-19th century.

editio princeps, plural editiones principes

Latin *editio princeps* means 'first edition', and it is used by bibliographers, literary scholars, etc to designate usually not so much first editions of new books as the first printed versions of ancient texts that formerly existed only in manuscript (one might for instance talk of an '*editio princeps* of Ovid'). The term, which is a modern Latin coinage, first appeared in English at the beginning of the 19th century.

effendi

Effendi has made its way into English via stories and accounts of the Near and Middle East. It represents Turkish *efendi* 'master', which is used as a polite term of address to a man, roughly equivalent to English *sir*. This is descended from Greek *authentēs* 'lord, master' (pronounced 'afthendis'), which is also the ancestor of English *authentic*. Its use in English dates back to the early 17th century.

eheu fugaces

Eheu fugaces are the opening words of number 14 in the second book of odes of the Latin poet Horace. The first sentence is *Eheu fugaces, Postume, Postume, labuntur anni, nec pietas moram rugis et instanti senectae afferet indomitaeque morti* 'Alas the fleeing years slip away, Postumus, Postumus [a personal name], nor will moral behaviour bring a delay to wrinkles and iminent old age and unconquerable death'. The subject of the ode as a whole is the certainty of death, and its first two words are used in English as an abbreviated tag regretting the brevity of human existence.

élan

Élan connotes 'flair', 'flamboyance', 'dash'. English acquired the word in the late 19th century from French, where it retains its original literal meaning 'dash, rush, bound'. It was derived in the Old French period from the verb *eslancer* (in modern French *élancer*) 'throw out', which in turn was based on the verb *lancer*, etymologically 'throw a lance'.

The term *élan vital*, literally 'vital impetus', was coined by the French philosopher Henri Bergson (1859–1941). He used it to denote the creative force that shapes growth and evolution within an individual organism and within nature at large. It is first recorded in English in the early 20th century.

el dorado

The original *El Dorado* was a legendary kingdom (or city) in South America, or more specifically in Amazonia, which was believed by the Spanish in the 16th and 17th centuries to be a source of fabulous wealth in gold and jewels (the term means in Spanish literally 'the gilded one'). It was introduced to English by Sir Walter Raleigh, who in 1596 wrote a treatise entitled *Discoverie of Guiana, with a relation of the Great and Golden Citie of Manoa (which the Spaniards call El Dorado)*. It is now widely used metaphorically for any place or set of circumstances which offers the opportunity of acquiring fabulous wealth.

embarras de richesse

If you have more money than you know what to do with, you have an *embarras de richesse*. The term was borrowed into English from French (where it means literally 'embarrassment of wealth') in the mid-18th century. It appears to have originated as the title of a book, *L'embarras des richesses* (1726), by the Abbé d'Allainval. In modern usage its application is mainly metaphorical, denoting in general 'too much of a good thing'.

A parallel French phrase used in English is *embarras de choix*, which denotes the awkward situation of having too many possibilities to choose from.

English occasionally uses the vernacular *embarrassment* in similar contexts: 'happy anticipations, happy memories, an embarrassment of happiness' (Martin Amis, *London Fields*, 1989).

embonpoint

There are few better ways of disguising unpleasant reality than by clothing it in the decent obscurity of a foreign language, and *embonpoint* is a case in point. It is a French word in origin, based on the phrase *en bon poir.t* 'in good condition', and it means 'plumpness, stoutness'. English seized on it gratefully in the mid-18th century as a delicate euphemism for 'corpulence', and nowadays its associations are particularly with a 'fat abdomen'.

embourgeoisement

The term *embourgeoisement* denotes the process of becoming bourgeois, by which members of the working class are assimilated into the middle class. Rising incomes enable the realization of aspirations towards a modest gentility, and imperceptibly the term *working class* becomes an anachronism. *Embourgeoisement* is part of the impedimenta of Marxian terminology, and was introduced into English from French in the 1930s. In the 1980s it enjoyed a particular currency in slighting references to the changing policies of the British Labour Party, designed to recapture the *nouveau bourgeois* vote from the Tories. A related term sometimes encountered is *embourgeoisification*, a blend of *embourgeoisement* and the synonymous *bourgeoisification*.

embusqué

An *embusqué* is, in plain terms, a column-dodger, someone who evades military service that would otherwise be compulsory by taking some job in government service that confers exemption. The word was borrowed into English during World War 1 from French, where it is a noun use of the past participle of the verb *embusquer*. This literally means 'lie in ambush' (indeed it is related to English *ambush*), but it passed metaphorically by way of 'lie in hiding' to 'shirk active service'.

emeritus

Someone who is designated *emeritus* holds his or her post on an honorary basis, having formerly occupied it as a full-time salaried employee. The word is the past participle of the Latin verb *emereri* 'earn by service' (a relative of English *merit*), and in Roman times was chiefly applied to a soldier who had served his time and been honourably discharged. English took it over in the early 19th century, and uses it mainly as a title for professors who have retired, as in 'Ronald Smith, emeritus professor (*or* professor emeritus) of history'. It is also used as a noun, denoting someone who holds such a title (in which case its plural is *emeriti*). Occasionally in the past the anglicized form *emerited* has been employed, referring, as in Latin, to retired soldiers and sailors. John Evelyn in his *Diary* (1681) mentions a 'Royal Hospital for emerited souldiers'.

éminence grise

The original *éminence grise* was a French Franciscan friar, François le Clerc du Tremblay (1577–1638), known as Père Joseph, who from 1611 was the secretary of Cardinal Richelieu, the powerful French statesman. He was held to wield shadowy but extensive influence (particulary in ensuring the participation of France in the Thirty Years' War). He received the nickname *éminence grise*, *éminence* being the title given to cardinals in French and *grise* 'grey' being the colour of the habit worn by Franciscans. It was inspired by *éminence rouge* 'red eminence', the nickname of his master Richelieu, whose cardinal's habit was red. The term is first recorded in English in the 1830s, but it does not seem to have been until about 100 years later that it began to be used as a general expression meaning 'someone exerting power through their influence over a superior'.

en bloc

French *en bloc* means literally 'in a block', hence 'as a whole, all together' (French *bloc* has given English both *block* and *bloc*). English started to use it in the middle of the 19th century, generally with the implication of taking something wholesale, as a single undifferentiated unit, rather than piecemeal. Its standard grammatical role is as an adverbial phrase, as in its native French, but English also occasionally employs it as an adjective ('a mere *en bloc* rendering', *English Studies* XLVII, 1966).

en brosse

En brosse is a coiffeur's term, introduced into English from French around the turn of the 20th century. Literally· 'in (the style of) a brush' (*brosse* is the source of English *brush*), it denotes hair cut very short so that it stands up stiffly, rather like the bristles of a brush – a crewcut, in other words.

enchanté

English uses French *enchanté* 'enchanted' as part of its vocabulary of polite social interchange. It serves as a rather high-falutin alternative to *pleased to meet you* when one is introduced to someone. It is the past participle of the French verb *enchanter*. The vernacular *enchanted* is somewhat less pretentious.

en clair

En clair was introduced into English from French by cryptographers and cipher experts. Literally 'in clear', it denotes that a message has been sent in ordinary language, not in code. It is recorded as being in use in English towards the end of the 19th century.

en famille

If one dines with people *en famille*, one takes an intimate meal with them in their own house, without other outside guests. The French expression (literally 'in the family') is first recorded in English in the early 18th century, and continues in use to this day for 'as one of the family' ('a quiet luncheon *en famille*, and a nap in an olive grove', C. D. Eby, *The Siege of the Alcázar*, 1965). It often carries connotations of 'lack of ceremony'.

enfant terrible

Originally, an *enfant terrible* (in French a 'terrible child') was a child which embarrassed its parents by behaving badly, making excessively frank remarks in front of their friends, etc. It was used in that sense in English as long ago as the 1850s ('the *enfant terrible*, young Alfred, announcing to all the company at dessert, that Ethel was in love with Clive', William Thackeray, *The Newcomes*, 1854), and it retains the meaning 'little terror' in French. But in English it is now used only in the extended sense 'someone (not necessarily young) who causes embarrassment to other members of a group by unconventional behaviour, outrageous statements, etc' (as in 'Michael Foot, once the *enfant terrible* of the Labour Party'). It often carries undertones of admiration for the *enfant terrible*'s daring and outspokenness.

Other French terms incorporating *enfant* that are sporadically used in English include *enfant gâté*, literally 'spoiled child', which denotes someone who is excessively indulged, and *enfants perdus* 'lost children', which is applied to soldiers sent on a mission that will almost certainly result in death.

en fête

French *en fête* means literally 'in festival'. English borrowed the noun *fête* from French in the 18th century, and its Old French ancestor *feste* was responsible for English *feast*. The phrase is used to denote that someone or something is in a suitable condition for festivities: that a person has on his or her best party clothes, that a town is decked out in bunting, that everyone is dancing and singing and celebrating. English acquired it around the middle of the 19th century.

enfleurage

Enfleurage is a term of the perfumer's trade. It denotes a process by which fragrant essential oils are extracted from flowers. The petals, etc are brought into contact with a small amount of an odourless fat, which absorbs the essential oil. This is then extracted with a solvent. It is an old process, for which originally purified lard or olive oil was used. The word *enfleurage* is French, and its use in English goes back to the mid-19th century; the loan translation *enflowering* is of slightly later date.

engagé

Someone who is *engagé* has a deep commitment to a political ideology, artistic philosophy, etc – is not, in other words, simply on a self-indulgent ego trip. *Engagé* is a word of the second half of the 20th century, borrowed from French in the years following World War 2. It originated as the past participle of French *engager* 'engage'. It is generally used of writers, painters, and other practitioners of the arts.

en garde

French *en garde* is a fencing term, a call by a fencer to his or her opponent to take up a posture of defence in readiness for a match. English uses it not just as an exclamation but also as an adjective, denoting a fencer who has taken up such a defensive stance. (It presumably lies behind the vernacular *on guard*, which dates back to the late 16th century.)

en masse

French *en masse* denotes 'all together in a mass', rather than singly or individually (as 'I don't mind his relations in ones and twos, but *en masse* I really can't handle them'). Its use in English dates back to the beginning of the 19th century (when it was sometimes partially anglicized to *en mass*).

ennui

English has been using the French word *ennui* since the mid-18th century, but its closest assciations are perhaps with more recent times. The concept of a world-weary listlessness brought about by a lack of any ideas or activities capable of engaging one's intellect is a product essentially of the Romantic movement, and its encapsulation in the term *ennui* has particular links with the French poet Charles Baudelaire (1821–67): *Tes yeux sont la citerne où boivent mes ennuis* 'Your eyes are the tank from which my tedium drinks' ('Sed non satiata', *Spleen et idéal*, 1857). The word goes back ultimately to the Latin phrase *mihi in odio est* 'it is hateful to me'. In Vulgar Latin, *in odio* was lexicalized as *inodio*, which in Old French became *anui* or *enui*. This passed into English in the 13th century, and has since evolved into *annoy*, while in French *enui* developed into *ennui*.

en passant

French *en passant* means literally 'in passing', and English uses it in two particular ways. It was originally borrowed in the mid-17th century as a general term meaning 'by the way, incidentally', and that remains its most familiar use. But then at the beginning of the 19th century it began to emerge as a chess term: to take an opponent's pawn *en passant* is to capture a pawn that has made an initial advance of two squares by moving one's own pawn forward to one of the squares next to it (from which it would have been able to capture the enemy pawn in the conventional diagonal manner had it only advanced by one square).

en plein

French *en plein* means literally 'in full'. English uses it chiefly as a term in roulette and similar gambling games to denote a bet that is placed entirely on a single number or on a single side (eg red). It contrasts with *à cheval*, which refers to a bet placed on two numbers. Its history as an English term dates back to the late 19th century.

Other idiomatic French phrases incorporating *en plein* to have been sporadically used in English include *en plein air* 'in the open air' and *en plein jour* 'in broad daylight'.

en prise

En prise is a piece of chess terminology, borrowed from French in the early 19th century. Literally 'in capture', it denotes that a piece is in a position where it is exposed to capture – for example, if one moved a pawn into a line diagonal to an opponent's bishop, it would be *en prise*. A semi-anglicized version of the expression, *in prise*, is recorded in *Chess made Easy* (1750), but it does not seem to have caught on.

en route

French *en route* 'on the way' is now well established in English, having first crossed the Channel in the mid-18th century. English construes it with *from* and *to* ('We met him *en route* to London'), or with *for* ('We were *en route* for New York'). In American English in the 20th century the tendency has developed to spell it as one word: *enroute*. One usage that has not come with it from French into English is an exclamatory or exhortatory one, urging people to be on their way.

The noun *route* itself was originally borrowed from French in the 13th century, and made sporadic appearances in the language from then onwards, but it did not become a fixture (in its French spelling *route*) until the early 18th century. It goes back ultimately to Vulgar Latin *via rupta*, literally 'broken way', hence metaphorically 'beaten track'.

en suite

A hotel bedroom that has a 'bathroom *en suite*', or an '*en suite* bathroom', has a bathroom next to it as part of an integrated and interconnected set of rooms, with a door leading directly from one to the other: you do not have to go out of the bedroom door and down the corridor to find it. English borrowed the term from French (where it means literally 'in sequence') at the end of the 18th century, but it came first in the sense 'in agreement, blending in', now obsolete: 'The decorations ... were not even *en suite* with the polish of the owner's mind' (Agnes Bennett, *The Beggar Girl*, 1797). The current meaning made its first appearance in the early 19th century. It is now sometimes spelled *ensuite* (not to be confused with French *ensuite* 'afterwards'), and in attributive use it is often hyphenated: 'The warlord sleeps in a huge four-poster bed under a canopy of red silk with an en-suite swimming pool' (*Today*, 21 January 1991).

entente

French *entente* means literally 'understanding', and it is used in the concrete sense of an 'agreement between nations' that falls short of being a fully fledged alliance. English took it over in the mid-19th century as part of the international language of diplomacy. Its commonest role is probably as part of the term *entente cordiale* 'friendly *entente*', which is of roughly equal antiquity in English. This is applied specifically to the agreement reached between the governments of Britain and France in April 1904. The two countries were colonial rivals, particularly in Africa, but with the looming threat of Germany they could not afford to be enemies and, partly thanks to the conciliatory efforts of Edward VII, they decided to put aside their differences, with Britain recognizing France's colonial interests in Morocco, and France recognizing Britain's in Egypt.

en tout cas

French *en tout cas* means literally 'in all cases', and the underlying implication of this is 'in any emergency' – which led to its use as a noun for a 'sunshade which can also in case of rain be used as an umbrella'. English used the term in the second half of the 19th century and the first half of the 20th century, but it has now more or less passed into history. However, *En-Tout-Cas* remains familiar to English speakers as the tradename for a type of all-weather surface used for lawn-tennis courts. It was registered in Britain in 1928.

entrée

English has borrowed French *entrée* (literally 'entry') three times. It first crossed the Channel in the 13th century, and in that guise has been thoroughly anglicized as *entry*. The next acquisition came towards the end of the 18th century. This was again with the meaning 'entry', but in the restricted sense 'entry into a place, group, etc of restricted (and often privileged) access', which soon evolved into 'access to such a place or privilege'. The final borrowing, in the early 19th century, was a culinary one. In former times in elaborate French banquets there was an intermediate course called the *relevé* (literally 'remove'). The course which followed this was therefore known as the *entrée*. By the time the term reached English it was being used for a course intermediate between the fish and the roast (consisting, perhaps, of a soufflé, a pasta dish, or caviare). As meals became less complicated it came to be applied to a dish served before a main course, and nowadays it is passing out of use in British English (in American English it is used for a 'main course').

entre nous

English started employing French *entre nous* as long ago as the late 17th century. Literally 'between us', it is used for 'confidentially, in private'. In modern usage it frequently occurs in the phrase 'strictly *entre nous*'. The vernacular English *between* has itself been used to denote confidentiality since earliest times, and provides synonyms for *entre nous* in *between ourselves* and *between you and me* (or the ungrammatical *you and I*).

eo ipso

Eo ipso is very closely synonymous with *ipso facto*: it is used to suggest that a consequence follows logically and necessarily from a set of premises, that one thing implies another (as in 'To insult their flag is *eo ipso* to insult their nation'). It is the ablative case of Latin *id ipsum*, and means literally 'by that thing itself, by that fact alone'. Its use in English (which dates back to the late 17th century) is mainly restricted to technical contexts in philosophy, logic, etc.

épatant

It was probably the currency of the expression *épater les bourgeois* in English that led to the adoption of the adjective *épatant*, meaning 'astonishing, shocking' – particularly in the context of startling the conventional with some outrageous act. It is an adjectival use of the present participle of French *épater* 'flabbergast', and is first recorded in English in the 1920s.

épater les bourgeois

If you do something to *épater les bourgeois*, you do it to disconcert the prim and proper. The expression is most commonly used in the context of artistic productions which defy convention, and outrage the sense of propriety or morality of the man in the street. The phrase in French means literally 'shock the middle class' (*épater* is roughly equivalent to English *flabbergast*), and appears to be a cut-down version of 'Je les ai épaté, les bourgeois', 'I have astounded them, the middle class', an assertion attributed to one Alexandre Privat d'Anglemont (died 1859). Its first recorded use in English is in the dedication to Bernard Shaw's *Man and Superman* (1903), and it is now firmly enough established to permit some variations: 'Clearly determined to *épater les haut-bourgeois*, Gosling deployed his unique arsenal of irritating vocal mannerisms' (*The Sunday Times*, 20 January 1991).

épris

The French reflexive verb *s'éprendre* means 'fall in love', and its past participle *épris* is used adjectivally to signify 'in love'. English writers began to use it towards the end of the 18th century. In French it is construed with *de* 'of', and this usage is sometimes echoed in English ('Mr Ventry is *épris* of Nicola', Cyril Hare, *When the Wind Blows*, 1949), but English also uses *with*, on the model of *in love with*. In the appropriate circumstances English employs the feminine form *éprise* as well.

erratum, plural errata

Erratum denotes an error, typographical or factual, in a book or other printed material. Its commonest use is in the plural form *errata*, heading a list of such errors that have been discovered too late to be corrected before publication, but the singular is also quite frequent in attributive usage in the term *erratum slip*, signifying a small piece of paper inserted into a newly published book at the last moment giving details of a mistake or mistakes. The word is a noun use of the neuter past participle of Latin *errare* 'wander, stray'. It began to be used in English in the late 16th century. The plural *errata* is sometimes treated as if it were a singular, although this is disapproved of by purists.

ersatz

German *ersatz* means 'replacement, substitute' (it is a derivative of the verb *ersetzen* 'replace'). It is used attributively in compounds such as *ersatzblei* 'replacement lead (for a propelling pencil)' and *ersatzschauspieler* 'understudy for an actor', and it was in this quasi-adjectival role that it began to be used in English in the late 19th century. Its connotations of a second-rate substitute for the real thing apparently began to emerge in the 1920s, but were probably cemented during World War 2, a period which had to come to terms with many dubious replacements for scarce commodities (roasted grain, for instance, or even roasted acorns were used to make '*ersatz* coffee').

esprit de corps

The French expression *esprit de corps* made its debut in English in the late 19th century, in good time for the rise of the great public schools of Victorian England, one of whose major preoccupations was the instilling of 'team spirit' into their pupils. It was by no means a male preserve, though; one of the earliest references to it in print, in Jane Austen's *Mansfield Park* (1814), has Mary Crawford saying to her married sister Mrs Grant (who had just spoken up for married people) 'Well done, sister! I admire your *esprit du corps* [sic]. When I am a wife, I mean to be just as staunch myself'. The French term means literally 'spirit of a group of people, corporate feeling', and denotes the feelings of solidarity, loyalty and shared purpose that keep a group of people together and motivate each member to act in the interests of all.

esprit de l'escalier

French *esprit de l'escalier*, or *esprit d'escalier*, means literally 'staircase wit', and denotes a witty, devastatingly appropriate or clinching riposte which one does not think of until the opportunity to use it has passed. The notion underlying the metaphor, which is attributed to the French philosopher Denis Diderot (1713–84) in his *Paradoxe sur le Comédien*, is of someone thinking of a bright remark when leaving down the stairs. English has been using the expression since at least the early 20th century, and it has also inspired a range of vernacular terms – direct translations, such as *staircase wit* and *spirit of the staircase*, and also adaptations, including *bravery of the staircase*, *staircase thought* and *staircase afterthought*.

estaminet

French *estaminet* denotes a 'small café or bar'; it may come from Walloon dialect *staminet* 'manger', but the origins of that are unknown. English writers began using it in the early 19th century, and its role in the language ever since has been to suggest small and often rather seedy or shabby bistros or bars in French towns.

et al

Et al is an abbreviation of Latin *et alii* 'and others'. It is used in English to avoid giving a complete and possibly over-lengthy list of all items. A particular application is in identifying and giving a reference to a book which has multiple authors, when for brevity often the name of only the main author, or the alphabetically first name, is given, followed by *et al*, as in 'Cameron, A., *et al.*, eds (1970). *Computers and Old English Concordances.* Toronto: Toronto University Press'. It is recorded in Samuel Fallows's *Handbook of Abbreviations and Contractions* (1883), but it does not seem to have come into common use in academic references until the 20th century.

et hoc genus omne

Latin *et hoc genus omne* means 'and all this sort of thing'. Its use was inspired probably by a passage in Horace's *Satire* I, 2: *Ambubaiarum collegia, pharmacopolae, mendici, mimae, balatrones, hoc genus omne maestum ac sollicitum est cantoris morte Tigellus* 'The tribe of *ambubaiae* ['Syrian girls in Rome who supported themselves by their music and immorality', Lewis & Short, *Latin Dictionary*], sellers of quack remedies, beggars, actors, jesters, and all this sort of people are sad and worried at the death of Tigellus the singer'. English took to using the phrase in the mid-18th century as a sort of up-market alternative to *etc* – often with derogatory connotations of 'all that common sort of riffraff'. *Et id genus omne* 'and all that sort of thing' is sometimes used instead.

et tu, Brute

Legend has it that when Brutus added his stab to the assassins' blows that killed Julius Caesar in 44 BC, Caesar cried out *Et tu, Brute!* 'And you, Brutus!' – an allusion to his surprise that even Brutus, whom he had pardoned and made governer of Cisalpine Gaul, had joined in the conspiracy against him (*Brute* is the vocative case of Latin *Brutus*). It is not clear how much truth there is in the legend, although the Roman historian Suetonius did record 'Some have written that as Marcus Brutus came running upon him, he said "*Kai su, teknon*", "and you, my son"' (in Philemon Holland's 1606 translation). It was Shakespeare who introduced *Et tu, Brute* into the English language: Caesar's last words after being stabbed (*Julius Caesar* III. i) are '*Et tu, Brute?* Then fall, Caesar!' Shakespeare may have got it from the lost Latin play *Caesar Interfectus*. It has come to be used generally in English to denote surprise and dismay that a supposed friend has joined in a conspiracy against one.

eureka

The Greek mathematician Archimedes (c 287–212 BC) was commissioned by King Hiero II of Syracuse to find out whether his new gold crown had had some silver surreptitiously mixed into it by its maker. He wasn't sure how to go about this, so he took to his bath to ponder the problem. According to Plutarch he filled the bath to overflowing, and it was this that suddenly gave him the idea that if the crown were pure gold, it would displace more water when immersed than if it were made of gold and silver. Excited at his discovery, he ran out of the house shouting *heurēka!* 'I have found!' (the perfect tense of Greek *heuriskein* 'find'). There are isolated examples of its use as a Greek word (complete with Greek characters) in English from the 16th century, but it was not until the mid-18th century that it began to be naturalized as an English cry of triumph at a discovery.

ewigkeit

German *ewigkeit* means 'eternity' (*ewig* 'eternal' is distantly related to English *age* and *ay* 'ever'). It began to put in an appearance in English in the late 19th century, usually used (semi-)facetiously in the sense 'the next world to which the dead and defunct are dispatched'. In particular it is used in such contexts as 'vanish into the *ewigkeit*', 'evaporate into the *ewig-keit*', etc, where it might be roughly translated as 'thin air'.

ex cathedra

Latin *cathedra* meant 'seat' (its metamorphosis into English *cathedral* came about because a 'cathedral church' is one that contains the bishop's 'seat' or throne). So a remark that is made '*ex cathedra*' is literally made 'from the seat'. In practice, *cathedra* is being used here metaphorically in the sense of 'seat of authority, source of authority', and *ex cathedra* is used of pronouncements that are made with full and solemn authority, and are therefore decisive and incontrovertible: 'Gibbon ... called the first person singular "the most disgusting of pronouns". Braudel, on the other hand, is almost naive in its introduction: nobody ever spoke more unassumingly or more unashamedly *ex cathedra*. Magisterially modest, he recommends "tolerance"' (*The Sunday Times*, 30 December 1990). It is often applied specifically to judgments given by the pope on matters of morals or dogma, which are held by Roman Catholics to be infallible and not open to question. It has probably been used in English since at least the 17th century, to judge from the short-lived derived verb *excathedrate* 'condemn authoritatively', which dates from then.

exceptis excipiendis

Exceptis excipiendis means 'with all appropriate exceptions made, leaving out everything which is to be left out'. *Exceptis* is the ablative plural of the past participle of Latin *excipere* 'leave out, except'; *excipiendis* is the ablative plural of its gerundive (a form expressing that which is to be done); and so literally the phrase (which is of post-classical origin) denotes 'with things excepted that are to be excepted'. Its use in English dates from the late 19th century.

excursus

An *excursus* is a digression in which the writer or speaker goes off at a tangent, dealing in some detail with a topic not central to the main theme. The word was first used in English, at the beginning of the 19th century, by editors of classical texts, who applied it specifically to a lengthy disquisition on a textual point too complex or important to be handled in a conventional brief note. They adhered to its original Latin plural form, *excursus*, but this has long since been superseded by the anglicized *excursuses*. Etymologically, the Latin word denotes a 'running out'. It is a derivative of the verb *excurrere* 'run out', which has also given English *excursion*.

exeat

In many British public schools, pupils need written permission to leave the school premises. This permission is known as an *exeat*. The word is a noun use of the third-person present subjunctive singular of *exīre* 'go out', and means literally 'let him/her go out'. It was originally used in English as long ago as the 15th century, as a stage direction, equivalent to present-day *exit* (the plural form *exeunt* was employed when more than one character had to leave the stage). Its modern application dates from the early 18th century. It is also used for 'permission given by a bishop for a clergyman to leave a diocese', and until recently the public-school type *exeat* extended its grip into the older English universities.

exempli gratia

Exempli gratia is one of the commonest Latin loan-expressions in English, but it is usually found in its abbreviated form *eg*. It means literally 'for the sake of example'. *Gratia* 'in favour of, on account of, for the sake of' is a prepositional use of the noun *gratia* 'favour', source of English *grace*; it takes the genitive case. In classical Latin, the usual way of expressing the notion of 'for instance' was *exempli causa* (which is occasionally recorded in English from the mid-16th century), but the synonymous *exempli gratia* was used at that time too, and this moved into English in the mid-17th century. The abbreviation *eg* dates from around the same time.

exemplum, plural exempla

English *example* comes, via Old French *example*, from Latin *exemplum*, and the language acquired the Latin word again in its original form in the late 19th century. It is sometimes used in a general sense, as a synonym of *example*, but its more usual role is to denote a story which illustrates a moral point or expounds a moral argument, particularly as used in medieval sermons.

ex gratia

An '*ex gratia* payment' is one that is made as a favour, without any legal obligation. The term is often encountered· in cases where someone has suffered as a result of another's actions or negligence, and the offending party offers the sufferer an '*ex gratia* sum' to try to show kindness and concern without admitting legal liability. It means literally in Latin 'from favour' (Latin *grātia* 'favour' is the source of English *grace* and *gratis*). It is first encountered in English as a legal term in the 18th century, but it does not seem to have passed into general usage until the 20th century.

ex hypothesi

Latin *ex hypothesi* means 'from the hypothesis', and is used to introduce a conjectural statement advanced for the sake of argument (as in 'If *ex hypothesi* the world is flat, we will fall off the edge of it'). It is a modern Latin coinage, introduced into English at the beginning of the 17th century. (*Hypothesis*, incidentally, is a Latinization of Greek *hupothesis*, which was derived from the verb *hupotithena* 'propose, suppose'.)

ex libris

Those who have, or like to think they have, a superior collection of fine books often choose to put their own personal mark on the items of their library by pasting a decorative bookplate in the front of each volume, on which appears the legend *ex libris* followed by their name (the grander sort generally show the owner's coat of arms). Latin *ex libris* means literally 'out of the books', that is, 'from the library of ...'. It is sometimes abbreviated to *ex lib*. English has used the term since at least the late 19th century as a noun, to designate the bookplate itself, and a derivative *ex-librist* has even been coined from it, denoting someone whose hobby is collecting such bookplates.

ex nihilo

Latin *ex nihilo* means 'out of nothing' (*nihil* may originally have been a compound word formed from the negative prefix *ne-* and *hīlum* 'small thing of no importance, trifle'). It has been used in English since the 16th century, chiefly in the context of 'creating something out of nothing', and often with explicit reference to the Latin proverb *ex nihilo nihil fit*. This corresponds to English 'Nothing comes of nothing', and goes back ultimately to Greek *ouden ek oudenos genoito* (recorded in a fragment by Alcaeus, the 6th-century BC lyric poet).

ex officio

Someone who has membership of a body *ex officio* has it by virtue of the office or position he or she holds. For example, if the chief executive of a public authority is *ex officio* a member of the board of that authority (or is an *ex officio* member of it), then whoever holds that post is automatically a member of the board, and does not have to be specifically appointed to it. The Latin phrase, which means literally 'from office, by virtue of office', was first used in English legal terminology as long ago as the early 16th century, but at that time it was in a rather different sense, now defunct: it was applied to particular sorts of oaths or lawsuits. Its present-day usage does not seem to have emerged until the 18th century.

ex parte

An *ex parte* injunction is one made on behalf of one side only in legal proceedings. The Latin phrase means literally 'from (one) part, from (one) side', and has been used in English legal terminology since the 17th century to denote that an application of some sort comes from only one of the parties to a case. In the 19th century it developed a more general meaning, 'one-sided, partisan', but this has never gained very wide currency.

ex pede Herculem

The Greek mathematician and philosopher Pythagoras is said to have used the measurements of Hercules's foot to calculate his height. And so the Latin expression *ex pede Herculem* 'Hercules from his foot' came to be used to express the idea of estimating the extent of the whole of something from a small or relatively trivial part of it. Its career in English dates back to the mid-17th century. A synonymous alternative sometimes encountered is *ex ungue leonem* 'the lion from its claw'.

experimentum crucis

An *experimentum crucis* is literally a 'crucial experiment'. The term is used for the putting of a range of hypotheses to the test, in such a way as will prove conclusively which, if any, is correct. It is a modern Latin coinage, and this use of *crucis* (which is the genitive form of *crux* 'cross') does not correspond to anything in classical Latin. Its seeds are said to have been sown by the English philosopher Francis Bacon, who in the early 17th century used the term *instantia crucis* 'crucial instance' to denote a case which finally proves one hypothesis and disproves all others; he explained *crux* in this context as being a metaphorical extension of the word's application to a signpost at a crossroads. *Experimentum crucis* was used by Robert Boyle and Isaac Newton (the first record of it in an English text is in Newton's 1672 treatise on light and colours), and it sometimes occurs in the translated form *crucial experiment*. It led to the general use of English *crucial* for 'decisive' and eventually, in the 20th century, for 'very important'.

experto crede

In Virgil's *Aeneid*, the Greek warrior Diomede tells of the prowess of Aeneas in battle from first-hand knowledge: '*experto credite*', he says, 'trust my experience when I tell how mightily he springs up behind his high-held shield'. Latin *experto credite* means literally 'believe the person who has experienced'. *Experto* is the dative form of the past participle of the Latin verb *experiri* 'test by experience'; *credere* 'believe' takes an object in the dative. English has used the phrase since the 16th century (more commonly with the singular imperative form *crede* than the plural *credite*) to denote 'I've experienced this myself, so believe what I say about it'.

ex post facto

Medieval Latin *ex postfacto* meant literally 'from a thing done afterwards' (*postfacto* was the neuter ablative singular form of *postfactus*, past participle of an assumed verb **postfacere* 'do afterwards'). English started to use the phrase in the 17th century, but (presumably under the influence of **post factum**) took to splitting up the past participle into *post facto*, as if *post* were a preposition and *facto* a noun. The term means 'formulated or applied retrospectively or retroactively', and is used especially with reference to laws.

ex silentio

If a conclusion is drawn *ex silentio*, it is reached for lack of any evidence to the contrary. In Latin literally 'from silence', the term is often used in the expression *argumentum ex silentio* 'argument from silence'. Such assumptions are of course by their very nature contingent, and liable to be blown out of the water by a single scrap of concrete evidence.

ex voto

Latin *ex voto* means literally 'in accordance with a vow' (English *vow* itself comes ultimately from Latin *votum*). English has used it since the early 19th century as an adjective, relating to such things as offerings, inscriptions, etc, denoting something made in fulfilment of a vow – equivalent to the native *votive*. By the 1830s it was being employed as a noun too, in the sense of 'votive offering'.

F

facetiae

Facetiae is a euphemism of librarians and the bookselling trade. It is a code-word used in catalogues to disguise pornography, the lexical equivalent of a plain brown-paper cover ('He puts to the end of his catalogue ... two pages that he calls "Facetiae" ... indecent books, indeed', Henry Mayhew, *London Labour and the London Poor*, 1851). It originated as the plural of Latin *facētia* 'jest' (a relative of English *facetious*), and to begin with was employed in English much as in Latin, for 'humorous remarks, witticisms'. This usage dates back to the early 16th century, but it seems to have died out by the end of the 19th century, having been pushed aside (for reasons that are not altogether clear) by the present-day 'pornography' sense.

facile princeps

Latin *facile princeps* means literally 'easily first (man)'. *Princeps* was both an adjective, meaning 'first', and a noun, 'first man, leader, chief', and it lies behind English *prince* and *principal*. English began to use the phrase in the early 19th century as a noun denoting someone who is generally acknowledged to be the leader in his or her field: 'Dr M. R. James ... is, with the exception of Vernon Lee, of all writers of ghost stories to-day *facile princeps*' (Montague Summers, *The Supernatural Omnibus*, 1931).

facilis descensus Averni

In Virgil's *Aeneid*, Aeneas begs to be allowed to descend into the Underworld, to see again his dead father Anchises face to face. But the Sybil warns him *Facilis descensus Averni: noctes atque dies patet atri ianua Ditis; sed revocare gradum superasque evadere ad auras, hoc opus, hic labor est* 'The descent to Avernus is easy: night and day the door of gloomy Dis [Pluto, god of the Underworld] stands open; but to retrace the steps and escape back to upper airs – that is the task and that is the toil'. Avernus was a lake near Naples, thought to be an entrance to the Underworld; its modern name is Lago di Averno. Since the 17th century English has used the phrase *facilis descensus Averni* to express the ease with which one can fall into evil ways; it is sometimes shortened to simply *facilis descensus*.

façon de parler

If a remark is passed off as 'merely a *façon de parler*', it is dismissed as a formulaic phrase or a figure of speech, not intended to be taken literally. Use of the French term in English texts dates from the early 19th century, but its influence may have been felt in the language much earlier in providing the basis of the vernacular expression *manner of speaking*, which is a direct translation of it: 'To turn the other cheek is a manner of speaking and not to be understood as the words sound' (William Tindale, *An Exposition upon the Fifth, Sixth, and Seventh Chapters of Matthew*, 1532).

fait accompli

A *fait accompli* is something that has already been done or settled, and therefore cannot be changed. The term is generally used in the context of an act which has a direct and often unwelcome effect on a person, but which that person does not find out about until after it has been done, so that he or she cannot reverse it or do much to mitigate its effects. It means in French literally 'accomplished fact', and began to be used in English around the middle of the 19th century. It is often to be found in the expression 'present someone with a *fait accompli*'.

famille

The French word *famille* 'family' is used in a range of technical terms designating different sorts of Chinese porcelain. It is qualified by various colour adjectives: *famille jaune* denotes porcelain whose main background colour is yellow; *famille noire* porcelain whose main background colour is black; *famille rose* porcelain with a design whose main colour is pink; and *famille verte* porcelain with a design whose main colour is green. Use of the various terms in English dates back to the 1870s.

farceur

French *farceur* denotes a 'joker', a 'wag', someone who is always telling funny stories or playing practical jokes. When English began to use the word, in the early 19th century, it was in this sense. It was not until the end of the century that the meaning we are most familiar with today, 'performer in or writer of farces', began to emerge.

farouche

English borrowed the adjective *farouche* from French as long ago as the mid-18th century, but it still retains an outlandish air. It denotes a mixture of shyness and unsociability, but its comparative unfamiliarity seems often to lead those who do attempt to use it into error. In particular, a passing similarity to *louche* sometimes causes it to be used for 'disreputable'. Its ultimate source is medieval Latin *forasticus*, a derivative of Latin *foras* 'out of doors' (the semantic progression is 'out of doors', 'in outside places', 'in wild remote places, not characterized by human contact', 'wild', 'shy and unsociable').

fartlek

The word *fartlek* is a Swedish contribution to English. It denotes a sort of athletics training, used particularly by long- and middle-distance runners, which involves running across country with alternate jogging and sprinting. The Swedish word is a compound formed from *fart* 'speed' and *lek* 'play' (a relative of Northern English dialect *lake* 'play'), and came into English in the early 1950s. The vernacular synonym is *interval training*.

fata morgana

A *fata morgana* is much the same as a *mirage* – something one thinks one sees, but which has no objective reality – but whereas a mirage is the result of atmospheric conditions, a *fata morgana* is attributed to witchcraft. The term is the Italian equivalent of *Morgan le Fay* (*fay* is an old word for 'someone with magical powers', and is related to *fairy*). In Arthurian legend, Morgan le Fay was the half-sister of King Arthur, but she is also portrayed as a sorceress, and in some versions of the story she tries to bring about Arthur's death. It seems that the Normans considered her home to be in Calabria, in the southwest tip of Italy, which led to her name being attached to a mirage which appeared in the nearby Straits of Messina, held to be the work of sorcery. The earliest evidence of the use of the term in English dates from the beginning of the 19th century.

fatwa

Arabic *fatwā* denotes a formal legal opinion delivered by an Islamic religious leader. It is derived from the verb *aftā* 'give a legal decision', whose active past participle *muftī* has given English *mufti* 'Muslim legal expert'. It made occasional appearances in English from the 17th century in the guise *fetwa*, but the seeds of its recent reintroduction, as *fatwa* or *fatwah*, were sown in 1988, when Salman Rushdie published his novel *The Satanic Verses*. This contained several passages that were taken by many Muslims as blasphemous, and caused a great furore in the Muslim community in Britain and worldwide. The brouhaha culminated in the issuing of a fatwa by the Ayatollah Khomeini, spiritual leader of Iran, on 14 February 1989, which decreed that Rushdie was subject to the penalty of death for his presumption. The novelist was forced to go into hiding, lest anyone should try to carry out the late Ayatollah's sentence.

faute de mieux

French *faute* (a relative of English *fault*) means primarily 'lack, need, want', and is used in the construction *faute de* 'for lack of, lacking'. *Faute de mieux* hence denotes 'for lack of anything better', with the underlying sense of putting up with something mediocre because nothing of adequate quality is available: 'At seven o'clock, up came a *cotelette pannée – faute de mieux*, I swallowed the composition' (Edward Bulwer-Lytton, *Pelham*, 1828). Use of the expression in English dates from the mid-18th century.

faux ami

The term *faux ami*, literally in French 'false friend', denotes a word or other linguistic form in a foreign language that is superficially identical with or similar to a form in one's own language, but in fact is different in meaning. The similarity is often close enough, semantically as well as formally, to mislead learners of the foreign language into using the *faux ami* inappropriately – hence the name, with its suggestions of treacherous plausibility. For instance, French *actuel* means 'current, of the present time', but is often rendered into English by beginners as *actual*. A more extreme example is German *gift*, which means not 'present' but 'poison'.

faux-naïf

A *faux-naïf* is someone who pretends to be unsophisticated, innocent, etc, but underneath the ingenuous exterior knows perfectly well what's what. English borrowed the expression from French (where it means literally 'falsely naive') in the early 20th century, and uses it as an adjective as well as a noun – in both cases usually with at least a tinge of disparagement. (*Naive* itself, incidentally, was acquired from French in the 17th century, and has now become more or less naturalized. Some people, however, still like to spell it *naïve*, and there are even a few adherents of the original French masculine form *naïf*.)

faux pas

To commit a *faux pas* is to make a terrible social blunder, the memory of which makes one's hands go clammy – for example, addressing someone by the wrong name, or forgetting their name. The term was acquired from French, where it means literally 'false step', in the second half of the 17th century, and at first was often used for a literal 'false step' – a 'trip' or 'fall'. Gradually the figurative sense took over completely, and in the 19th century it was frequently given a more specific application still – to a 'woman's fall from virtue'. In the past the translation *false step* has been used in its stead.

felix culpa

The *Exultet*, the Roman Catholic hymn sung on the Saturday before Easter Sunday, contains the line *O felix culpa, quae talem ac tantum meruit habere Redemptorem* 'Oh happy fault, which has deserved to have such and so great a Redeemer'. The words *felix culpa* 'happy fault' were St Augustine's allusion to original sin, which ultimately had the fortunate consequence of bringing Christ to earth to redeem mankind. The term is used allusively in English for any wrongdoing which has a paradoxically beneficial outcome.

felo de se, plural felones de se or felos de se

Felo de se is a legal term for someone who commits suicide. It means literally 'felon of oneself, one who commits a crime against himself/herself'. It is first recorded in Anglo-Latin legal texts of the 13th century, but it does not start to appear in English until the 17th century. (At first it was often anglicized, partially to *felon de se* or wholly to *felon of oneself*, but these forms did not survive long.) Since the 18th century it has also been used for the 'act of suicide' itself. The etymology of Anglo-Latin *felo* is uncertain. Like English *felon*, which comes via Old French, its source was medieval Latin *fello*, but the origins of that are not known.

femme fatale

A *femme fatale* (in French literally 'fatal woman') is a woman who is so provocatively sexy that she leads her poor male conquests unresistingly into compromising situations. The term connotes a mysterious allure, and perpetuates the age-old myth of the siren-female entrapping the guileless male. The first recorded use of it in English dates from the early 20th century, in one of Bernard Shaw's letters, where he refers to seeing 'a *Femme Fatale* who was a fine figure of a woman' (1912).

ferae naturae

Latin *ferae naturae* means literally 'of wild nature', and it is used in English to designate wild as opposed to domesticated animals. It dates back to the mid-17th century, but now survives mainly as a legal term. It is scarcely any longer available, as it was in Dryden's day, as a source of metaphor: 'Women are not comprised in our laws of friendship: they are *ferae naturae*' (John Dryden, *An Evening's Love*, 1668).

festina lente

It was the Roman historian Suetonius, in his *Divus Augustus*, who encapsulated this piece of advice to the rash in the words *festina lente* 'make haste slowly' (although he probably based it on an earlier Greek model *Speude bradeōs*). Records of its use in English as a maxim go back to the 16th century, and by the middle of the 18th century we begin to find evidence of its anglicized form *Make haste slowly* (the earliest known use of which is in Benjamin Franklin's *Poor Richard's Almanack*, 1744). Latin *festinare* 'hurry' has also given English the short-lived and now obsolete *festinate* 'hasten, accelerate' and *festination*.

festschrift

When professors and other distinguished scholars retire, their colleagues often mark the occasion and pay tribute to a fine record of achievement by contributing to a volume of essays and papers dedicated to the retiree. This is likely to contain contributions to the dedicatee's field of study (in some cases, perhaps, papers that have not been able to find a home elsewhere), and may well also include an account of his or her career and a bibliography of publications. The concept of such a book originated in Germany, and English uses the German name for it, *festschrift*, which means literally 'festival-writing'. The first volume to which it is known to have been applied in English is the *English Miscellany* (1901) presented to the philologist and literary scholar F. J. Furnivall, which was subtitled a 'Festschrift'.

fête champêtre

French *fête champêtre* means literally 'rustic festival'. The term refers to a sort of outdoor party popular with the 18th-century upper crust, a grand picnic in a picturesque rural setting. It first appeared in English towards the end of that century, and has continued to crop up sporadically ever since: 'The battue system [of shooting parties with beaters] developed into the sort of fête champêtre, with hot lunch, champagne, and liveried attendants' (Stephen Dowell, *A History of Taxation and Taxes in England*, 1884). Today, however, it is mainly encountered as an art-historical term applied to an early 18th-century genre of painting which features figures, typically engaged in dalliance, in a pastoral setting. Its most famous exponent was the French painter Jean-Antoine Watteau (1684–1721), and its influence lived on in the works of Boucher and Fragonard. Synonymous with *fête champêtre* in this context is *fête galante*, literally 'elegant festival'.

feu de joie

French *feu de joie* (literally 'fire of joy') has had a long and varied career in English. In its original sense of 'bonfire' it first appeared as long ago as the early 17th century (it was frequently applied specifically to fires used as beacons). This has long since died out, but from the early 18th century it began to be replaced by a new use: it refers to a fusillade of musketry fired as a salute, in which each soldier in turn discharges his gun, giving a continuous effect. From the 1930s it has also been used for a sort of firework which mimics the effect of the multiple-musket salute.

fidus Achates

One of Aeneas's companions on his journey from Troy to Italy was Achates. In Virgil's *Aeneid*, Aeneas is often pictured as going into perilous situations accompanied only by Achates, and in Book 6 his friend is described as the 'faithful Achates', *fidus Achates*. English has used the Latin expression sporadically since the early 17th century for a 'loyal follower', often with somewhat negative connotations of a 'henchman willing to carry out orders unthinkingly'. (Achates is also credited, in the *Iliad*, with killing Protesilaus, commander of the Thessalian forces attacking Troy.)

fille de joie

The concept of the prostitute naturally attracts euphemisms, and *fille de joie* is one of them. In French literally 'girl of joy, girl of pleasure', it made its first appearance in English as long ago as the beginning of the 18th century.

film noir

Film noir (in French literally 'black film') originated as a term in French movie criticism denoting a film whose mood is pessimistic and cynical and whose visual impact is sombre. In the English-speaking cinema, it is applied particularly to a genre of films produced in the USA in the 1940s and early 1950s. Shot in grainy monochrome which highlighted the contrast of black and white, these films dealt mainly with the seedy underworld of small- and medium-time crime in US cities. With a low-key narrative style and a laid-back cynical hero (eg Philip Marlowe in *The Big Sleep*), they seemed to inhabit an appropriately night-time world. Use of the term *film noir* in English dates from at least the late 1950s, and in recent years *noir* has come to be employed on its own to refer to such films and their style ('corny 40s venetian blinds and noir voice-overs. Worth seeing once – to dream about the film it could have been', *City Limits*, 15 August 1985). The derivative *noirish* has even been recorded.

fin de siècle

French *fin de siècle* means literally 'end of the century' (*siècle* is descended from Latin *saeculum* 'generation, age', which also produced English *secular*). But it refers not to any century, but specifically to the end of the 19th century in Western culture. The 1890s were viewed at the time, and later, as a decade of world-weary decadence and overblown sophistication whose epitome amongst writers and artists was perhaps Oscar Wilde. English was quick off the mark in acquiring the term *fin de siècle* from French, the earliest known record of it dating from 1890.

flâneur

French *flâner* means 'stroll around idly or aimlessly', and its derivative *flâneur* has come to denote an 'idler' or 'loafer', 'someone who passes his time in aimless amusement'. English began to use the word in the mid-19th century, and it has also taken over the related *flânerie* 'idling, lounging'. It has even, semi-facetiously, coined a verb from it, variously *flâné* or *flane*: 'In Paris, in London I have been a happy flâneur; I have flânéd in New York and Washington and most of the great cities of Europe' (H. G. Wells, *Apropos of Dolores*, 1938). The ultimate source of the French word is Old Norse *flana* 'wander about'.

floruit

Floruit is a term which writers of potted biographies have recourse to when the exact dates of birth and death of their subject are not known. For example, an entry for the Anglo-Saxon poet Caedmon in a biographical dictionary might say '*floruit* 670'. This would mean that Caedmon lived in the second half of the 7th century, and that the years around 670 were probably his most productive period, but that we do not know precisely when he was born and when he died. *Floruit* means literally 'he or she flourished' (it is the third-person singular past tense of Latin *florere* 'bloom, flourish', source of English *flourish*), and it has been used in English since the early 19th century. There are sporadic examples of its being turned into a English noun, denoting 'period when someone flourished'.

Another form of Latin *florere* used in English is the third-person singular present subjunctive *floreat*, 'may he, she, or it flourish'. It invokes success on a particular individual or institution, and is mainly found in mottoes and slogans. The best known in Britain is probably *Floreat Etona*.

folie à deux

French *folie à deux* means literally 'madness relating to two (people)'. It denotes a psychiatric condition in which certain symptoms of mental illness (eg delusions) coexist simultaneously in two people who are closely connected or related (eg husband and wife or brother and sister). The first record of its use in English dates from 1913.

folie de grandeur

People suffering from *folie de grandeur* have what in the vernacular would be called 'delusions of grandeur': they think they are more magnificent, of higher rank or station, more powerful, richer, etc than they really are, and often act on these mistaken megalomaniac assumptions. The French term means literally 'madness of grandeur', and is first recorded in English in J. S. Billings's *Medical Dictionary* (1890).

fons et origo

If something is described as the *fons et origo* of something, it is regarded as the source from which it originally sprang, its starting point and cause. Latin *fons* 'spring, fountain' lies behind English *font* and *fountain*, and of course *origo* is the origin of English *origin*. Earliest examples of the use of this phrase in English date from the beginning of the 19th century. To start with it was restricted to the expression *fons et origo mali* 'source and origin of evil', but by the second half of the century it had branched out into wider contexts.

force de frappe

The *force de frappe* is the French equivalent of the 'independent nuclear deterrent': a delivery system capable of launching a nuclear attack on an enemy. It was a key element in President de Gaulle's strategy for rebuilding France's pride and self-respect when he came to power in the late 1950s – an independent French nuclear capability that would earn it a place amongst the top nations, without being tied to America's coat-tails. Essentially it has consisted of Mirage IV aircraft carrying nuclear bombs. The term *force de frappe*, which means literally 'strike force', first appeared in English in 1962.

force majeure

If one of the parties to a contract is unable to fulfil its obligations under the contract because of some intervention by a non-foreseeable event (such as a civil war), it is liable to declare *force majeure*, thereby avoiding the penalties it would otherwise have incurred. French *force majeure* means literally 'superior force', and it has been used as a legal term in English, particularly in commercial law and insurance, since the middle of the 19th century. It also serves as a more general term, denoting 'irresistible force': 'One cannot be a respected and highly respectable Civil Servant for twenty years without learning to bow to the *force majeure* of public opinion' (G. Mitchell, *The Man who Grew Tomatoes*, 1959).

fourgon

A *fourgon* is a large covered wagon, used typically for carrying luggage, supplies, etc. English took the word over from French in the middle of the 19th century. It goes back to Old French *furgon* 'poker', a derivative of the verb *furgier* 'search', which was descended ultimately from Latin *fūr* 'thief' (source of English *ferret*).

franc tireur

French *franc tireur* means literally 'free shooter' – that is, someone armed with a gun who is not part of the regular military forces. The term was originally applied to unofficial military units formed during the French Revolution. They still existed at the time of the Franco-Prussian War, and took an active part in the fighting. At first, not being part of the French Army, their members were liable to be shot if captured by the Prussians. Since then the term has broadened out to denote generally 'irregular soldier or guerilla' and also 'sniper'. The first record of it in English dates from 1808.

friseur

A *friseur* is an up-market hairdresser. The term was borrowed from French in the middle of the 18th century, and for a time seems to have been in fairly common usage, but by 1898 the *Oxford English Dictionary* was describing it as 'now rare'. This suggests a word on its way out, but confounding predictions, *friseur* has remained a part of the language, albeit in a small way. Etymologically it denotes a 'curler' of hair: it is a derivative of the verb *friser* 'curl', which in the 19th century gave English *frizz*.

frisson

French *frisson* means 'shiver', including the very literal sort of shiver you get from being too cold; but it is in the very special sense of the sort of (pleasurable) tingle you get up and down your spine in moments of great excitement, suspense or danger that English has adopted the word. There are sporadic examples of it in English from the late 18th century (Horace Walpole is the first writer on record as using it, in 1777), but it was not until the beginning of the 20th century that it became at all common: 'I'm not sure [Oscar Wilde] would envy Orton's freedom of expression: his own art relied on the frisson of an erotic *samizdat*' (*The Sunday Times*, 9 December 1990).

führer

It was Benito Mussolini who set the fashion amongst fascist dictators of giving themselves a title with the simple gran-diloquence of 'the Leader'. In 1934, a year after he came to power in Germany, Adolf Hitler followed the example of *il Duce*, calling himself *der Führer* (his full title was *Führer und Reichskanzler* 'leader and imperial chancellor'). *Führer* is a derivative of the German verb *führen*, which is related to English *fare*. It has been used in English since 1934, its first vowel often spelled *ue* rather than *ü*, and it was soon adapted as an insulting term for anyone bossily asserting authority.

G

galère

French *galère* means literally 'galley'. It appears to be connected in some way with English *galley*, although the precise nature of the relationship is not clear, and the words' ultimate origin is unknown. In Molière's *Les Fourberies de Scapin*, Scapin tells Géronte that his son Léandre has been lured into a Turkish galley and is being held to ransom. Géronte exclaims (no fewer than seven times) *Mais que diable allait-il faire dans cette galère?* 'But what the devil was he going to do in that galley?' The force of his question is 'What on earth was he doing there, why did he go there, why did he get mixed up in that situation?' And, inspired by this passage, *galère* has come to be used for a 'group of people with whom one gets mixed up, coterie', particularly an unsavoury one. It was this sense in which English borrowed the word in the mid-18th century. English has also, since the mid-19th century, occasionally used *galley* itself in a translated version of Géronte's question, 'What are you doing in that galley?', meaning 'Why are you associating with that crowd of people?' More recently the contexts in which it occurs have led to *galère* being used for an 'unpleasant situation'. (See also **vogue la galère**.)

gamin

French *gamin* means 'young street urchin'. It is not entirely clear where it came from, but it may be an adaptation of German *gammel* 'ne'er-do-well', which in turn is connected with English *game*. English has used the word sporadically since the mid-19th century, but it is the feminine form *gamine* that has really made an impact on the language in the 20th century. It denotes a slim boyish young woman with a pert and teasing manner, and is often used attributively to characterize the sort of hairstyle thought to be typical of such girls – very short. English has also used the French derivative *gaminerie* to refer to the behaviour or attributes of a *gamin* or *gamine*.

garçon

The archetypal English use of French *garçon* is to hail a waiter in a French or French-style restaurant (a practice usually heartily disliked by the waiters). But that is far from being the only or even the main sense of the word in French. There it denotes chiefly 'boy'. Ultimately it is probably of Germanic origin. Its career as an English word began in the late 18th century, and took a new pathway in the mid-20th century when it started to be used also to denote a style of short boyish haircut for women. Also occasionally used in English is the derivative *garçonnière*, which refers to a bachelor's apartment.

gastarbeiter

A *gastarbeiter* is an immigrant worker, especially in a German-speaking country. The term means literally 'guest-worker' in German, which has a genteel sound, but the reality is less romantic. It is typically used to refer to Turkish, Yugoslav or Italian workers drawn to West Germany in the post-World War 2 period by the promise of employment (menial by German standards) and money to send back to their hard-up families back home. Their presence in Germany often created social problems. Use of the word in English dates from 1964.

gaudeamus

Gaudeamus is the first word of a medieval German students' song, *Gaudeamus igitur, juvenes dum sumus* 'Let us therefore rejoice while we are young'. *Gaudeamus* is the first person plural present subjunctive of Latin *gaudēre* 'rejoice', which has also given English *gaudy*. In the 19th century English used the word as a noun, denoting jollifications held by university students, with much singing of hearty songs and perhaps the odd tankard of beer. The song itself is best known from its incorporation into Brahms's *Academic Festival Overture* (1881).

gauleiter

The German term *gauleiter* was coined to denote a political official in charge of a local district under the Nazi regime (German *gau* means 'administrative district', and *leiter* is the equivalent of English *leader*). It first found its way into English around 1936 and, gauleiters being proverbial for their overbearing dictatorial ways within their modest fiefdoms, it was not long before it was being applied metaphorically to any petty tyrant: 'two bullies, gauleiters almost, from whom everyone fled in terror' (L. P. Hartley, *The Boat*, 1949).

gegenschein

Gegenschein is a faint glowing spot that can be seen in the night sky in a position opposite to that of the sun. It is part of the zodiacal light, sunlight reflected from dust particles in space. The term is a German one, meaning literally 'against-light, opposite light'. It seems originally to have been used by Alexander von Humboldt at the beginning of the 19th century, but the man credited with introducing it as a technical term is T. J. C. A. Brorsen in 1854. It has been used in English since the 1880s, and is sometimes translated as *counterglow*.

gemütlich

German *gemütlich* is an adjective of approval whose nearest English equivalent is perhaps *cosy*, but which covers a range of other attributes including comfort, congeniality, cheerfulness and easy-goingness. It is not surprising, given her German connections, that Queen Victoria was amongst the first to use it in English; her letters and the pages of her journal are dotted with examples of it ('The view was so beautiful over the dear hills; the day so fine; the whole so *gemüthlich*', *Journal*, 11 October 1852). It has since established a niche for itself in the language, usually either denoting aspects of comfortable respectable German middle-class life-style, interior decoration, etc regarded by some as suffocating or kitschy, or suggesting a general 'naiceness'. English has also taken over the abstract noun *gemütlichkeit* for the 'quality of being *gemütlich*'.

gendarme

A *gendarme* in France and other French-speaking countries is, in strict terms, a member of the national police force which is regarded as a branch of the armed services, and whose duties include internal defence, the guarding of frontiers, traffic control, and general police work in country areas. The term is a singular formed from the plural *gens d'armes*, literally 'men of arms', and originally denoted a mounted trooper in the French army. English began to use it in this earliest sense as long ago as the mid-16th century, but its modern application began to emerge around the end of the 18th century. In current English usage it commonly refers loosely to any French policeman, and it is even used jocularly for any 'policeman' in general. English also uses the derivative *gendarmerie*, both as a collective term for the police force consisting of *gendarmes*, and for the headquarters of the *gendarmes*.

genius loci

Latin *genius loci* means literally 'genius of place'. *Genius* originally denoted a 'tutelary deity', so the basic sense of the expression is of a god who watches over and protects a particular place. Virgil records in the *Aeneid* that when Aeneas arrived with his comrades in Latium, he 'offered prayer to the spirit of the place'. English-speakers were evidently familiar with the phrase from at least the late Middle Ages, to judge from partially translated versions dating from the early 16th century: 'If that every man's shrewd desire be as his God and Genius in that place' (Gavin Douglas, *Aeneid*, 1513). But the first known examples of the complete Latin phrase in English, from the late 18th century, reveal a different sense of Latin *genius*: 'spirit, atmosphere'. English now uses the expression in both guises, with the preponderance of usage probably going to 'characteristic atmosphere that pervades a particular place'.

gestalt

Gestalt is a psychological term which denotes a configuration that can be apprehended only as the sum of its parts: a common example given is a tune, which can be analysed into a series of individual notes, but can be fully appreciated only as an indivisible whole. It is a specialized application of the German word *gestalt*, which means literally 'form, shape', and was introduced in 1890 by Christian von Ehrenfels. It came into English in the 1920s in the phrase *gestalt psychology*, the name of a psychological school of thought (founded in Germany by Wolfgang Köhler and Kurt Koffka) which holds that mental phenomena are arranged in the form of gestalts. For example, learning is viewed as the internalizing of an entire situation (often partly by intuition) rather than as an aggregate of piecemeal responses to individual stimuli. The term *gestalt* is now also used in other fields, such as philosophy and literary criticism.

gesundheit

German *gesundheit* means literally 'health' (*gesund* 'healthy' is related to English *sound*). It is traditionally uttered as an exclamation when someone sneezes (much like English *bless you!*), as if to drive away the illness of which the sneeze is a symptom. Evidence from the second decade of the 20th century suggests that it had already by then found its way into English, through German immigrants in the USA.

glasnost

Russian *glasnost* means literally 'publicity' (it is a derivative of *glas* 'voice'), but it was not until the mid-1980s that Mikhail Gorbachev's use of the term to denote greater openness in Soviet affairs propelled it into the English language. It was soon well enough established for the derivative adjectives *glasnostian* and *glasnostic* to be formed from it, and for it to be applied figuratively over a wide range of contexts: 'Being able to see the chef at work is not regarded as a gimmick, but as a basic right of the customer. This kind of gastronomic glasnost is a rarity over here' (*The Sunday Times*, 20 January 1991). Its original reference was to President Gorbachev's initiative to dissipate traditional Soviet secrecy, and make information widely available both to Soviet citizens and to the rest of the world – an initiative that by the early 1990s was looking distinctly dog-eared. (*Glasnost* was actually used for 'freedom of information' by Lenin, but at that time it did not make it into English.)

gnōthi seauton

Greek *gnōthi seauton* meant 'know thyself'. It was one of two precepts carved in the stone of the temple of Delphi, site of the supreme oracle of ancient Greece (the other was *mēden agan* 'nothing in excess'). Its mingling of simplicity and profundity has commended it to later ages (Juvenal in his *Satires* noted 'From the gods comes the saying, "Know thyself"'), and English has adopted it as a proverbial maxim, either in the original Greek, in the Latin form *nosce te ipsum*, or translated as *know thyself*.

go

Go is a Japanese board game. It actually originated in China (where it is known as *Wei-ch'i*) well before the time of Christ, but it is Japan that has popularized it in the Western world. It is played on a board with 361 holes in an intersecting grid. One player has 181 small black stones which fit into the holes and the other has 180 small white stones (Japanese *go* means literally 'small stone'). The purpose of the game is to gain territory on the board by the placement of one's stones. The players take it in turn to put down one stone. The term *go* began to be used in English in the late 19th century.

götterdämmerung

German *götterdämmerung* means 'twilight of the gods' (*dämmerung* 'twilight' is distantly related to English *dim*). Richard Wagner used it as the title of the last opera in his 'Ring' cycle, first produced in 1876. It tells of the deaths of Siegfried and Brynhilde and the return of the magic ring, the fulcrum of the entire tetralogy, to its original owners, the Rhine maidens. English took the word over in the early 20th century, mainly under the influence of Wagner's opera, to denote the downfall of any once powerful system.

goût

English has been using *goût* since the late 16th century, but it has always remained a conscious Frenchism. Its ultimate source is Latin *gustus* 'taste', which is distantly related to English *choose* and has also given English *disgusting, gustatory* and *gusto*. Its usage covers the same range of senses as the vernacular *taste*, from the literal 'flavour of food' through 'liking, fondness' (the earliest recorded meaning) to 'artistic appreciation'. A related French word also occasionally encountered in English is *goûter*, a noun use of the verb *goûter* 'taste', which denotes the French equivalent of 'afternoon tea'. (See also **chacun à son goût**.)

goy, plural goys or goyim

Hebrew *gōy* means 'nation, people'. It passed into Yiddish as an often derogatory term for someone of non-Jewish race, a Gentile, and from there it got taken over by English in the middle of the 19th century. The feminine form *goyah* 'female Gentile' has also occasionally been used in English (the more familiar term is **shiksa**).

grande dame

As a complimentary term for a lady, *grande dame* is rather two-edged. It implies pre-eminence in a field ('Pamela Vandyke Price, *grande dame* of wine writers'), but there is no getting away from the fact that, like its nearest masculine equivalent, *grand old man*, it does suggest a certain advancement in years. Literally in French 'great lady', it was introduced into English as long ago as the mid-18th century, but for most of its career in the language it has been used much as in French, to denote a lady of high social rank and perhaps exaggeratedly dignified bearing. Its application to a 'woman held to be the most distinguished member of a profession or other group' appears to be a comparatively recent development.

Grand Guignol

Guignol was the main character in a late 18th-century form of French puppet theatre. He was rather similar to the English Mr Punch, and indeed the plays in which he took the starring role resembled Punch and Judy shows, in featuring scenes of extravagant violence and mayhem. In 1897 the Grand Guignol theatre opened in Montmartre, Paris, named after Guignol, and it quickly gained a reputation for putting on plays of a highly sensational nature. The aim was to make the audience shriek with horror and come back for more, and to this end the director is even reputed to have invented an artificial blood that congealed, for added verisimilitude on stage. By the beginning of the 20th century the name *Grand Guignol* was being used generically for this sort of macabre drama, and in 1908 it made its first recorded appearance in English.

grand mal

The term *grand mal* (in French literally 'large illness') denotes the more severe of the two forms of epilepsy, in which convulsions affect the whole body. It begins with the patient falling to the ground unconscious: all muscles go into spasm, including the breathing muscles, so that the skin turns blue. Then the body starts to shake, and the tongue may be bitten. The seizure ends with the patient either coming round or falling asleep. The expression *grand mal* apparently began to be used in English in the 1840s. Alternative terms are *major epilepsy*, and in technical use *tonic-clonic fit*. (See also **petit mal**.)

grand prix

The original *Grand Prix* was a French horse race. Established in 1863, it was run annually in June at the Longchamps racecourse in Paris, its field limited to three-year-olds. Its full name was the *Grand Prix de Paris* 'Great Prize of Paris', but it was often referred to simply as the *Grand Prix*. (*Prix* is the modern descendant of the Old French word that has given English *prize* – and *price*.) Then when the sport of motor racing began to get under way at the beginning of the 20th century, the term *grand prix* was applied to important races. As early as 1906 it became institutionalized as the name of a class of race for high-performance cars held on various tracks around the world, which in 1950 formed the basis of the newly constituted World Drivers' Championship.

grand seigneur

French *grand seigneur* means 'great lord', and English has used it since the late 19th century to denote someone of haughtily aristocratic demeanour, who lords it over his supposed inferiors. Very often, plain *seigneur* suffices to encapsulate the meaning: '"Yes, yes, yes"', said Ukridge with testy impatience, quite the seigneur resenting interference from an underling' (P. G. Wodehouse, *Ukridge*, 1924). Between the 16th and 19th centuries the equivalent Italian term, *Grand Signior*, was used in English as the title of the Sultan of Turkey.

grand siècle

The epithet *grand siècle* is applied to the 17th century as a period in French art, literature, etc, and particularly to the reign of Louis XIV, the 'Sun King' – 1643 to 1715. It means literally 'grand century', and his was indeed a brilliant reign, centred on the sumptuous court of Versailles. It was the Augustan age in French literature: its great figures were the dramatists Racine, Molière and Corneille and the prose writers Descartes and Pascal. The leading painters of the time were Poussin, Claude and La Tour, and Lully was court composer to Louis XIV. English began to use the term *grand siècle* in the early 18th century, and occasionally employs it metaphorically to refer to any period of outstanding excellence.

gran turismo

Italian *gran turismo* means literally 'great touring' – that is, 'touring on a grand scale' – and was applied in the 1920s to a large powerful car, typically open and with a folding top, designed to carry five or more people over long distances at relatively high speed. English called such cars *tourers* or (especially in the USA) *touring cars*, and by the time *gran turismo* (or more usually its abbreviation *GT*) began to take a foothold in the language in the 1960s it was being used rather more loosely as a marketing name for a souped-up version of a standard production saloon, with a sporty trim, wire-look wheels, and a more powerful engine.

gratis

Gratis has been around in the English language for a considerable time – since at least the late 15th century, in fact – but it still has a slightly alien feel, has never entirely thrown off its Latinity. It is a contracted version of *gratiis*, the ablative plural of *gratia* 'kindness, favour', which meant literally 'out of kindness'. The notion of doing something simply as an act of kindness led on naturally to 'expecting no payment' – whence the use of *gratis* in English for 'free of charge'. From the 16th to the 19th century it also had the meaning 'gratuitously, without justification', but this usage has now died out.

gravitas

Latin *gravitās* 'weight' is the source of English *gravity* (a 16th-century introduction, either anglicized direct from Latin or borrowed from French *gravité*). But in the 20th century it has been readopted in its original form, to denote a metaphorical sort of 'weight' – weightiness of demeanour, the avoidance of all unseemly frivolity or levity, verging sometimes on a pompous solemnity: '*Gravitas*, the heavy tread of moral earnestness, becomes a bore if it is not accompanied by the light step of intelligence' (*The Listener*, 20 March 1969).

gringo

Gringo is a Mexican-Spanish contribution to English, which appeared in the USA in the middle of the 19th century. It is used by Spanish-speakers or people of Spanish descent in the Americas to refer slightingly to English-speakers. At first its take-up in the language was slow (*Harper's Magazine* in 1884 had to explain the word to its readers as 'a term of ridicule and obloquy applied to Americans throughout all Mexico'), but in the 20th century its frequent appearance in stories and films of the Wild West has made it increasingly familiar. In metropolitan Spanish, *gringo* means generally 'foreigner' (albeit with special reference to Americans and Britons), and carries overtones of incomprehensible 'foreign' speech – *hablar en gringo* is the Spanish equivalent of English 'talk double-Dutch'. It is thought that it is an alteration of *griego* 'Greek', in the metaphorical sense 'foreigner, stranger', which in turn goes back to Latin *graecus*.

grosso modo

Grosso modo is an Italian contribution to English, first recorded in the mid-20th century. Literally 'big way, coarse way', it is used adverbially to denote 'approximately, roughly'. It is sometimes explicitly contrasted with *sensu stricto* 'in a strict sense'.

gulag

Russian *Gulag* is an acronym, based on the initial letters of *Glavnoye Upravleniye Ispravitelno-Trudovykh Lagerei* 'Main Administration for Corrective Labour Camps'. This is the title of the department of the Soviet security service set up in 1930 to administer prisons and forced-labour camps. It was probably the publication in 1973 of the first volume of Alexander Solzhenitsyn's *The Gulag Archipelago*, an exposé of the labour camps and the treatment of political prisoners there, that provided the impetus for the adoption of *gulag* by English as a generic term for such camps.

guru

Hindi *gurū* denotes a spiritual guide or leader, one who in the Hindu and Sikh religions acts as a personal mentor to his disciples. The word is descended from Sanskrit *guru*, which was originally an adjective signifying 'heavy', hence metaphorically 'venerable'. Apart from an isolated example in the 17th century, it was the 19th century that saw the introduction of the word into English – at first usually spelled *gooroo*. But it was the 1960s that really saw *guru* take off as an English term, thanks to a sudden explosion of interest in Eastern mystical religions. Suddenly it seemed that anyone who aspired to be the brains behind a particular movement, or who was looked to to provide its guiding principles, was accorded the epithet *guru* ('Wolfgang Puck, the California superchef and restaurant design guru', *The Sunday Times*, 20 January 1991). Another legacy of that decade was the so-called *guru jacket*, a men's jacket with a high button-up collar inspired by oriental styles.

H

habeas corpus

The principle of *habeas corpus* goes back a long way in English
law, although it was not enshrined in statute until the Habeas
Corpus Act of 1679. It maintains the right of the subject to
protection from unlawful imprisonment. People who believe
themselves to be held illegally can apply to the High Court for
a writ of *habeas corpus*. Their legal representative is allowed to
interrupt any other proceedings with the cry 'My Lord, I have
a matter concerning the liberty of the subject!' when making
the application, since so grave an issue is at stake, and the judge
may then direct that the person be brought before him, so that
a judgment can be made on the legality of the detention. Latin
habeas corpus means literally 'you should have the body'. It is
short for *habeas corpus ad subjiciendum* 'you should have [ie
produce or cause to appear] the body [ie the person concerned]
to undergo [ie to undergo whatever judgment the court may
award]', the first words of the writ.

haiku, plural haiku

A *haiku* is a Japanese poem consisting of only three lines, containing respectively five, seven, and five syllables. The genre
appeared in the 16th century, and was popularized by the poet
Basho in the 17th century. Spare to the point of starkness, haiku
traditionally take an image from the natural world (eg the flight
of a crane) and leave it suspended in the mind, like a raindrop
at the tip of a leaf, so that its subtle allusions may work on the
imagination. The Japanese term *haiku* is a compound, formed
from *hai* 'amusement' and *ku* 'sentence, verse'. It is first recorded
in English at the end of the 19th century. A *hokku* was originally
the opening half-line of a linked series of haiku, but the term is
now used synonymously with *haiku*. *Haiku* should not be confused
with *tanka*, which denotes a five-line Japanese poem of five,
seven, five, seven, and five syllables respectively (it is a compound of Japanese *tan* 'short' and *ka* 'song').

hajj

The *hajj* (or *hadj*) is the pilgrimage to Mecca that all devout Muslims are required to make at least once in their lives if they are physically able to do so. When there, they visit various holy places, and in particular the Kaaba, a cube-shaped building in the centre of the great mosque which according to tradition was built by Abraham and Ishmael. The pilgrims walk round the Kaaba several times, and kiss the Black Stone, which is supposed to have been brought to Abraham by the archangel Gabriel. The Arabic word *hajj* means literally 'pilgrimage', and has been used in English since at least the early 18th century. From it is derived *hajji* (or *hadji*) 'pilgrim', denoting someone who has made this pilgrimage to Mecca, which goes back even further in English, to the 17th century.

haka

The *haka* is familiar to anyone who has seen a New Zealand national sports team preparing for action on the field. The word is a Maori one, and originally denoted a Maori war dance accompanied by chanting. English first used it in that sense as long ago as the 1830s, but it was not until about 100 years later that we find evidence of its sporting application. The *haka* is used particularly by the All Blacks rugby union team, symbolically to put the fear of God into their opponents: they gather round in a semicircle on the field, chanting and stamping rhythmically and with inceasing vigour, and finally jumping into the air with an explosive shout.

hakenkreuz

Hakenkreuz is the German for 'swastika' (it means literally 'hooked cross'). Use of the symbol by the Nazis led to the introduction of the German term into English in the early 1930s.

Halacha

Hebrew *hālākāh* means literally 'that which one walks by', hence 'way' (it is a derivative of the verb *hālāk* 'walk'). It came to be used for a 'legal decision regarding a matter for which there is no precedent in Jewish law', and English took it over in this sense in the mid-19th century. It is also used more broadly for a 'Jewish religious law', and it is additionally applied to that part of the Talmud which deals with legal matters, interpreting the laws and the scriptures. A Hebrew judge is termed a *Hal-achist*.

halal

The adjective *halal*, or *hallal*, denotes meat that comes from an animal killed in strict accordance with Muslim law. Various stipulations apply, one of the most salient being that the animal must have had its throat cut. The word is borrowed from Arabic *halāl*, which means literally 'lawful', but in fact when it first came into English, in the middle of the 19th century, it was used as a verb, in the sense 'slaughter in accordance with Muslim law'. Nowadays that is seldom encountered, and the word is most familiar as an adjective, or as a noun denoting meat produced in this way.

hapax legomenon, plural hapax legomena

Hapax legomenon is a linguistic term mainly encountered in the field of textual criticism – particularly in the editing of classical texts. It means in Greek literally '(thing) said only once', and in its broadest use it refers to a word or word form that has been recorded only once, is known to have existed from only one example. In practice, however, textual scholars generally relate it to the writings of a particular author, or to some other corpus of literature (eg '*Ælwiht* "monster" is amongst the *hapax legomena* in *Beowulf*'). Its use in English dates back to the beginning of the 19th century. In the trade it is often abbreviated to *hapax*. It should not be confused with *nonce word* or *nonce form*, which also denotes a word that occurs only once, but is usually used of more modern formations, and often suggests a word coined deliberately for a specific occasion.

haut

French *haut*, a relative of English *haughty*, means literally 'high', but it is also used (rather like English *higher*) to denote the more exalted grades of a particular undertaking, profession, etc. Many terms incorporating it have made their way into English, including *haute bourgeoisie* 'upper middle class', *haute coiffure* 'up-market hairdressing', *haute politique* 'high politics', **haute couture, haute cuisine, haute école**, and **haut monde**. The great majority use the feminine form *haute*, and it may be that *haute* is beginning to take on an independent life of its own in English in this sense: 'The world of *haute* Waspdom in which

Bush was raised believed in clear and definite rules of behaviour' (*The Sunday Times*, 6 January 1991).

haute couture

French *couture* means literally 'sewing, needlework, tailoring' (it is descended from Vulgar Latin *consūtūra, a noun formed from the past participle of Latin *consuere* 'sew together'). So *haute couture* is 'higher tailoring' – dressmaking as practised at the stratospheric level of the high-fashion Parisian houses (Dior, Chanel, Balmain, etc) for those with deep enough pockets. The term began to be used in English around the beginning of the 20th century, and it is quite often abbreviated to simply *couture* (as in 'the leading *couture* houses'). At around the same time English acquired *couturier*, in the sense 'male fashion designer' (the feminine form *couturière* was borrowed about a century before with the more humble meaning 'dressmaker').

haute cuisine

The term *haute cuisine* denotes cookery of the very highest quality, especially as practised by the top (French) hotel and restaurant chefs. It is often used specifically with reference to the very elaborate style of cuisine evolved in the 19th and early 20th century by the likes of Carême and Escoffier – with its myriad sauces, laden with butter and cream, its passion for luxurious and expensive ingredients such as truffles and foie gras, its labour-intensive set-piece dishes, and its desserts constructed like baroque castles – the sort of food against which the **nouvelle cuisine** rebelled in the second half of the 20th century. It began to make its appearance in English in the 1920s.

haute école

Haute école is an equestrian term. It denotes the most advanced form of dressage, in which the horse is taught to do very intricate manoeuvres, including turns and leaps. The most famous exponents of it are the Spanish Riding School in Vienna and the Cadre Noir of the French Cavalry School at Saumur. English acquired the term, which means in French literally 'high school', in the mid-19th century. It is sometimes also used in music, to denote a highly refined and expert style of playing.

haut monde

Haut monde, in French literally 'high world', denotes 'high society, fashionable society', as composed of the top people in the land – the aristocracy and those on its fringes, the very wealthy, the best families, and so on, or at least those of them that care for being thought fashionable. Used in English since the mid-19th century, it often contrasts implicitly with *beau monde*, which perhaps lays rather more stress on 'fashionability' at the expense of 'aristocracy'.

havdallah

The *havdallah*, or *habdallah*, is a Jewish religious ceremony celebrating the end of the sabbath or other holy day. It features blessings over wine, candles, and spices. English acquired the word as long ago as the early 18th century from Hebrew *hab-dālāh*, which means literally 'separation, division'. An alternative form of the word, influenced by Yiddish, is *havdoloh*.

heimisch

German *heimisch* corresponds morphologically to English *homy*. Semantically it has a rather wider range, but it is with its 'homy' connotations – cosiness, comfort, unpretentiousness, etc – that it has become an English word. It originally entered the language in the USA, at some point in the 20th century, and frequent spellings like *haimisch* and *heymish* suggest that it came via Yiddish rather than direct from German. English has also created the derivative *heimischness*.

heldentenor

A *heldentenor* is a tenor singer with a large powerful voice that can easily penetrate to the furthest reaches of an opera auditorium, suitable for singing weighty tenor roles (as in many of Wagner's operas). The term means literally in German 'hero-tenor', and began to be used in English in the 1920s. Older opera buffs are wont to complain that there are no true *heldentenors* any more, and look back nostalgically to the days of the great Wagnerian tenor Lauritz Melchior (1890–1973). The corresponding Italian term for such a singer is *tenore robusto*. A tenor with a lighter style of voice is termed a *lyric tenor*.

herrenvolk

German *herrenvolk* means literally 'master people, master race'. *Volk* is first cousin to English *folk*, while *herr* is etymologically a title of respect accorded to those with venerably grey hair, and is related to English *hoary*. The word was applied particularly to the German people as being, in Nazi racial theory, superior to all other ethnic groups and destined to rule over them, and as such made frequent appearances in English in the 1940s. It survives in its original application, and also in the broader sense of any racial group arrogantly asserting superiority over another. The translated version *master race* also dates from the 1940s.

heurige, plural heurigen

The Austrian German adjective *heurig* means 'of this year' (it is descended from the prehistoric Germanic demonstrative **hiu-* which also lies behind German *heute* 'today'). It is used particularly of wine produced in the current year: *heuriger wein* is wine of the year, a crisp, fruity, deceptively powerful white wine, typically produced from the Grüner Veltliner grape, the Austrian equivalent of Beaujolais nouveau (the official date when *wein* becomes *heuriger* is 11 November). The word *heurige* is also used as a noun, to denote such wine; and the taverns in Vienna's suburbs that serve such wine, typically made from the landlord's own vineyards, are termed *heurigen* too. English began to use the word in the 1930s, but it did not become widely known until the 1960s, with the growth of Austria as a holiday venue.

hic jacet

Latin *hic jacet*, literally 'here lies', may be found carved on old gravestones, as the first words of the epitaph, followed by the name of the deceased who lies underneath. It is sometimes abbreviated to *H. J.* Modern lapidary terminology tends to the vernacular *here lies*. Between the 17th and the 19th centuries English occasionally used *hic jacet* as a noun, meaning 'epitaph, memorial inscription': in Shakespeare's *All's well that ends well*, Parolles says 'I would have that drum or another, or *hic jacet*.'

hoi polloi

Greek *hoi polloi* has had a chequered career in English, both
semantically and syntactically. It means literally 'the many' (*hoi*
is the plural of *ho*, the definite article, and *polloi* is the plural of
polus 'many', from which English gets the prefix *poly-*), and
hence by extension 'the masses'. English started to take it up
seriously in the early 19th century, and uses it mainly as a
dismissive or derisive term for the common people, viewed from
the vantage-point of the well-off and privileged. However
(perhaps because of some subconscious association with *hoity-
toity*), some tendency is apparent to use the term as if it meant
almost exactly the opposite, 'upper-class people, toffs'. English-
speakers have also had some trouble with *hoi*: not realizing that
it is the definite article, they prefix it with the redundant English
the: 'the *hoi polloi*'.

hombre

Spanish *hombre* is the equivalent of French *homme*, Italian *uomo*,
etc – all descended from Latin *homō* 'man' (a relative of English
human). It began to infiltrate English via American-Spanish in
the mid-19th century. To begin with it was usually used for
Spanish-speaker or a man of Spanish descent, but as it became
more firmly ensconced in the language, and more widely dis-
seminated through the medium of Wild West stories, it broadened out in meaning to simply 'man'. It is particularly common
in the phrase *tough hombre*, first recorded in 1940, which suggests
the strong silent brave hero of modern American legend.

homme moyen sensuel

French *homme moyen sensuel* means literally 'average sensual
man', and denotes a person with normal appetites and desires,
neither lost in the realms of rarefied intellect nor entirely given
over to mindless self-indulgence. English has been using it sporadically since the late 19th century, occasionally varying it with
the translated version *average sensual man* ('Samuel Pepys's day-
by-day record of how the average sensual man comports himself'
Aldous Huxley, *Themes and Variations*, 1950). Variations on the
theme of *homme moyen sensuel* to have been used in English
include *homme lettré moyen* 'average literate man' and *homme
moyen cynique* 'average cynical man'.

homo sapiens

Homo sapiens was coined as the scientific name of the human species by the Swedish biologist Linnaeus, and first appeared in the tenth edition (1758) of his *Systema naturae*, a systematic description of all animals by genus and species. By the end of the 18th century it was coming into general scientific use in English. It means in Latin literally 'wise man' (Latin *sapiens*, source of English *sapient*, is an adjectival use of the present participle of the verb *sapere* 'taste', hence 'have good taste', and by metaphorical extension 'be wise'). Latin names of other (now extinct) species of hominids include *homo erectus* 'upright man' and *homo habilis* 'handy man'.

honnête homme

French *honnête homme*, literally 'honest man', denotes a 'gentleman' – a man of innate dignity, natural decency, politeness, honour, etc. The term was sporadically used in English in the 17th and 18th centuries, but it did not make a significant impact on the language until the 20th century. In particular, literary critics and others began to employ it to refer to the archetypal 17th-century gentleman of the Augustan age.

honoris causa

Latin *honoris causa* means 'for the sake of honour', and was used sporadically in English from the 17th century to denote something done as a mark of honour. Its real establishment in the language, however, dates from the late 19th century, when it began to be used to designate honorary university degrees, conferred not in recognition of passing exams or preparing a research thesis but to honour the achievements of a person in a particular field (as in 'Dame Ann Smith, D Litt *honoris causa*'). Such degrees conferred on distinguished scholars, statesmen, etc are generally doctorates, but honorary masters degrees are presented to people who have given long service to a university.

hors concours

Something that is *hors concours* is literally 'out of the competition', and the term is often used to mean just that – 'not entered for a contest'. However, it also came to have the connotation of 'being so superior that it would be superfluous to compete with others', and its commonest use in English is in the sense 'best by far, unequalled'. It was borrowed from French in the late 19th century.

hors de combat

Someone or something *hors de combat* is 'out of the fight' – either literally, or figuratively, in the sense 'not in a position to participate'. The French term originated in the notion of injury incurred by a soldier or damage sustained by a naval ship that precluded taking any further part in a battle. It began to be used in English in the mid-18th century.

hors d'oeuvre

French *hors d'oeuvre* means literally 'outside the work' (see **oeuvre**). It has a range of specialized senses, including 'out of alignment' and (of a precious stone) 'unmounted', but it is the use of the phrase as a noun denoting a foodstuff that has propelled it into widespread international usage. It denotes either a small snack, such as a canapé, a small piece of cheese on a stick, a peanut or two, etc, served with drinks at a cocktail party or as an appetizer before a meal; or any of a range of small dishes, such as cold meats, melon, salad (but not soup) served as the first course of a meal. English originally took the expression over in the early 18th century in the sense 'outside of the ordinary course of events', but by the middle of the century the culinary sense was establishing itself. In French, the word is unchanged in the plural, but English usually adds *-s*: *hors d'oeuvres*.

hwyl

Welsh *hwyl* means basically 'mood', but it is applied specifically to the sort of Celtic fervour that grips Welsh orators, poets, and indeed rugby crowds. It can also be used as a form of farewell, roughly equivalent to English 'best of luck!', but it is as a word for Welsh emotional ardour that it has infiltrated English. The earliest record of it in an English text is in the 1 March.1899 edition of the *The Daily News*. It is pronounced /'hu:ɪl/.

I

ibidem

Latin *ibidem* means literally 'in the same place' (it was originally a compound, formed from the adverb *ibi* 'there' and the demonstrative suffix *-dem*). It was the terminology of bibliography that introduced it to English in the mid-17th century. It is used in footnotes and the like after a reference, to indicate that the same book, chapter, passage, etc has been cited previously, thereby avoiding any necessity to repeat all the bibliographical details. For example, a reference to 'J. Smith, *History of Germany*, 1978, p 117' might be followed a few lines later by 'Smith, *ibidem*, p 63'. It is commonly abbreviated to *ibid*, and sometimes to *ib*. (See also **idem**.)

id

Latin *id* means simply 'it', and we owe its presence in English to psychoanalytic theory. It was the German psychologist Georg Groddeck who first applied the term 'it' (German *es*) to the impersonal part of the mind, associated with instinctual impulses. He appears to have adapted the usage from the philosopher Nietzsche, for whom *es* encompassed the notion of the impersonal in human nature, that which is beyond individual control or choice. Groddeck was using the term in the second decade of the 20th century, and in 1923 published *Das Buch vom Es* ('The Book of the It'). In the same year appeared Sigmund Freud's *Das Ich und das Es* ('The I and the It'). Freud had adopted Groddeck's term, and applied it to his own theory of the division of the psyche into an impersonal instinctive portion (the 'It') and a conscious portion (the 'I'). It appears to have been Joan Riviere in her translation of Freud's work into English in the mid-1920s who introduced the term *id* for German *es*.

idée fixe

If someone has an *idée fixe* about something, they are obsessed by it. Literally in French 'fixed idea' (the adjective *fixe* is descended from *fixus*, the past participle of Latin *figere* 'fasten'), the term denotes a notion that becomes permanently entrenched in one's mind, a fixation that cannot be shaken off, a view of things from which (although perhaps irrational or at variance with reality) one cannot be dissuaded. It may take over to such an extent as to dominate one's behaviour. The term seems to have made its first appearance in English in the translated form *fixed idea* in the 1820s, but the original French *idée fixe* was not long in following.

idée reçue

French *idée reçue* means literally 'received idea', that is, an opinion or view that is generally accepted, without question. The implication behind the term is often of an uncritical acceptance of something which is out of date or which, on deeper inquiry, might be found to be invalid. It is a comparatively recent introduction to English, dating from between the two world wars, and no examples of the translated version *received idea* are on record from before the 1950s, but the use of *received* to mean 'generally accepted' dates back at least to the 15th century ('Suidas followeth the common received opinion, that the Salamander quencheth the fire,' Edward Topsell, *The historie of serpents*, 1608).

idem

Latin *idem* meant 'the same, the identical one' (English *identity* comes ultimately from a Latin abstract noun based on it). It has been used in English since the 15th century as a sort of verbal equivalent to the ditto sign, to avoid repeating something already referred to – at first mainly to avoid repeating definitions for synonymous words in glosses, dictionaries, and the like, latterly as part of the apparatus of references, footnotes, etc in scholarly books. It is commonly abbreviated to *id*. (See also **ibidem**.)

ignotum per ignotius

Latin *ignotum per ignotius* means literally 'the unknown by means of the more unknown' (*ignotius* is the neuter accusative comparative form of *ignotus* 'unknown'). It is used in English as a noun signifying an explanation that is even more abstruse and involved than the difficulty it purports to explain, and leads to even more confusion: 'He even goes so far ... as to explain an Egyptian *chiaoush* as being analogous to an Indian *chobdav*, which to some readers may be a case of *ignotum per ignotius*' (*The*

Times Literary Supplement, 30 July 1931). It has a long history in English, going right back to Chaucer's *Canon's Yeoman's Tale* in the 1380s. A parallel Latin expression also used in English is *obscurum per obscurius*, literally 'the obscure by means of the more obscure'.

ikebana

Ikebana is the Japanese art of flower arranging. It is a highly formalized art, aiming for an effect that is at once simple, balanced and naturalistic. It dates back to the 6th century, when it was used as part of the preparation for Buddhist ceremonies. There are a range of different styles (eg *shoka*, an 18th-century form based on three branches arranged asymetrically). Other natural objects, such as stones, are sometimes used in the arrangements. *Ikebana* is a compound word, formed from the verb *ikeru* 'keep alive, arrange' and *hana* 'flower'. It began to appear in English around the turn of the 20th century.

in absentia

The kinds of things that one can have done to one *in absentia* include having an academic degree conferred upon one and being tried and sentenced in a court of law. The term is applied to occasions which would conventionally require one's presence, but which can proceed quite satisfactorily (if slightly irregularly) in one's absence (Latin *in absentia* means literally 'in absence'). Its use in English dates from the late 19th century.

in aeternum

Latin *in aeternum* means 'into eternity'. *Aeternus* 'eternal' is a derivative of *aevum* 'age', from which English gets *age* and *medieval*. English occasionally uses the phrase (perhaps inspired by its appearances in liturgical texts, such as the *Te Deum*) to mean 'forever, eternally'.

inamorato

A girl's *inamorato* is her 'sweetheart', and conversely a young man's *inamorata* is his 'girlfriend'. The two words, masculine and feminine, were borrowed into English around the end of the 16th century from Italian, where they are noun uses of the past participle of *inamorare* 'charm, enamour'. In modern Italian the word has moved on orthographically to *innamorare*, but English continues to use forms with a single *n*. The words carry connotations of temporary infatuation rather than permanent attachment.

in camera

Latin *in camera* means literally 'in the room' (*camera* is the ancestor of English *chamber*); but its connotations are 'behind closed doors, not in public'. In particular it is used in English as a legal term to denote that proceedings are conducted either privately in a judge's chambers rather than in open court, or in a closed session of court to which the public, journalists, etc are not admitted. Such a course may be adopted in various circumstances – when matters of national security are adjudged to be at stake, for instance, or in certain matrimonial cases (it happens in criminal cases only very exceptionally, as when a young child is involved). The term has also come to be used more widely for any proceedings held in closed session or in (unwarrantable) secrecy.

incommunicado

If someone is 'held *incommunicado*', they are detained in such a way that they are unable to communicate with others. They are deprived of the right to speak or get messages to people in the outside world, including legal representatives, and they may well be locked up in solitary confinement. The term *incommunicado* does not invariably have such gloomy connotations, however ('The captain was in the lavatory, and temporarily *incommunicado*'); indeed, it is often used to suggest a voluntary withdrawal from tiresome society. Orthographically, it is a partial anglicization of *incomunicado*, the past participle of Spanish *incomunicar* 'prevent from communicating'. Its use in English dates from the mid-19th century.

incunabulum, plural incunabula

An *incunabulum* is a book printed before 1501 (for example, a book printed by Caxton). The term was coined by German bibliographers, and introduced into English in the mid-19th century. It was based on the Latin neuter plural noun *incunabula*, which meant literally 'swaddling-clothes', and hence by extension 'infancy' (the reference is to the 'infancy' of the art of printing). This in turn went back ultimately to *cunae* 'cradle'. In English, *incunabulum* is sometimes anglicized to *incunable*. One who collects such books is termed an *incunabulist*. English also uses the plural *incunabula* to denote the 'earliest stages in the development of something' ('The Gospel is silent respecting the incunabula of the Master's life', James Martineau, *Essays, Reviews and Addresses*, 1864); indeed, that is the earliest recorded application of the word in English, from the 1820s.

in extenso

Latin *in extenso* is used in English to make greater claims than the vernacular *extensively*; it is employed, particularly in contexts relating to the quoting or reporting of material, to denote 'at full length, in full' ('Nearly every section is quoted *in extenso*' *Modern Law Review* XXVIII, 1965). Its career in English dates back to the early 19th century.

in extremis

Latin *in extremis* means literally 'in the last', and has been used in English since at least the 16th century to denote the 'final moments of life': 'The Master of the Rolls . . . tumbled out of his chair last Sunday at church, and is, they say, *in extremis*' (G. Williams, 1764). However, over the centuries, the connotations of the 'agonies of death' and the association with English *extreme* have gradually pulled the meaning of *in extremis* away from 'death' towards 'in extremity, in dire straits, in serious difficulties'. In modern English it is often used virtually synonymously with 'if the worst comes to the worst'.

in flagrante delicto

In flagrante delicto spread from legal terminology into the general language. In Latin it means literally 'with the crime blazing' (*flagrante* is a form of the present participle of *flagrare* 'burn, blaze' and *delictum* 'crime' is related to English *delinquent*), and it is used to refer to the discovery or capture of a person in the very act of committing a crime – 'red-handed', in other words. In 20th-century colloquial usage it often applied (semi-)humorously to the discovery of someone, particularly a spouse, in an act of illicit sexual intercourse. It is common to find it abbreviated to *in flagrante* ('He'd surprised his wife *in flagrante* with the milkman').

infra dig

Infra dig is short for Latin *infra dignitatem* 'below dignity' (Latin *infra* 'below' is related to English *inferior*). It is not clear where the phrase *infra dignitatem* came from (it occurs in one of the essays in William Hazlitt's *Table Talk*, 1822), but the first instance on record of its shortened form *infra dig* is in *Redgauntlet* (1824) by Sir Walter Scott, that inveterate introducer of new words and reviver of old. It denotes something that is 'beneath one's dignity', something that it would be undignified to do, not consistent with one's social position or rank. Latin *infra* has itself been used in English since the late 19th century as part of the terminology of textual reference, to denote something that appears later on in a text.

ingénue

An *ingénue* is an innocent or naive young woman, inexperienced in the ways of the world and of men. The word is a nominalization of the feminine form of French *ingénu* 'guileless' (a relative of English *ingenuous*), and it came into English in the mid-19th century (the first record of it is in William Thackeray's *Vanity Fair*, 1848). It is often used in theatrical contexts to refer to actresses who play the role of artless young things, and to such roles themselves. In common with other French borrowings containing nasalized vowels (see **lingerie**), *ingénue* has sometimes proved too much for English-speakers, and it is not uncommon to hear it pronounced something like *onjenue*.

in loco parentis

A guardian looking after a child whose parents are absent, or a teacher who has responsibility for a child while he or she is at school, is said to be *in loco parentis*. This means in Latin literally 'in place of a parent' (*locus* 'plaсе' has given English *local*, and *parens* 'parent' was a noun use of the present participle of *parere* 'give birth'). The term has been used in English since the late 18th century.

in medias res

It was the Roman poet Horace, in his *Ars poetica*, who launched the term *in medias res*, literally 'into the midst of things'. Describing Homer's ploy of starting a story in the middle, he wrote *Semper ad eventum festinat et in medias res non secus ac notas auditorem rapit* 'He ever hastens to the issue, and hurries his hearers into the midst of things as if they knew it before'. Homer had a reputation for this technique in classical times: the Roman rhetorician Quintilian wrote *Ubi ab initiis incipiendum, ubi more Homerico e mediis vel ultimis?* 'When should one start from the beginning, when, in Homeric fashion, from the middle or the end?' English has been using the phrase since the late 18th century, often in the expression 'plunge *in medias res*' – suggesting a headlong impetuousness to begin.

in memoriam

Latin *in memoriam* 'in memory' commonly appears on grave-stones, preceding the name of the deceased and invoking his or her memory. Its most famous use in English, however, is in the title of Tennyson's poem *In Memoriam A H H*, written between 1833 and 1850. This is an extended elegy for his friend Arthur Hallam, who died at the age of 22, which enjoyed great success when it appeared. Amongst its most celebrated lines are "Tis better to have loved and lost than never to have loved at all', 'Nature, red in tooth and claw', and 'Ring out, wild bells, to the wild sky … Ring out the old, ring in the new, ring, happy bells, across the snow; the year is going, let him go; ring out the false, ring in the true'. Inspired by it, for a time in the second half of the 19th century *in memoriam* was used as a noun, for a 'memorial poem or other piece of writing'.

in nomine

In nomine (in Latin literally 'in the name') is a musical term, denoting various types of contrapuntal composition charac-teristic of the 16th and 17th centuries. Their common features are that they were generally written for a consort of viols (although there are also *in nomines* for keyboard instruments and for the lute), and that they were based on a melody derived from the Vespers antiphon *Gloria Tibi Trinitas Aequalis*. They constitute the earliest known musical form that is not either church music or dance music. One of the first composers, if not the originator, of the *in nomine* was John Taverner (?1495–1545), and it may be that the term was inspired by *In Nomine Domini*, the first words of the Benedictus in Taverner's setting of the Mass, which is identical with his *In Nomine*. Purcell revived the form in the 17th century.

in perpetuum

English uses Latin *in perpetuum* (literally 'into the everlasting') as a learned alternative to the native *in perpetuity*. The latter goes back at least to the 15th century, and in fact was probably based on the Latin expression, although there is no evidence of *in perpetuum* in English texts before the mid-17th century (and even thereafter it was far from common). Alternative versions of the vernacular phrase which have now largely fallen by the wayside include *for perpetuity* and *to perpetuity*.

in personam

In personam is a legal term. In Latin literally 'against the person', it is used in English to denote that legal proceedings have been instituted against a person (in the broadest sense of that term in law, including an organization) rather than against a thing. It is contrasted with **in rem**.

in petto

If a new cardinal in the Roman Catholic Church has been selected by the pope but the public announcement of his appointment has been delayed, his name is said to be *in petto*. Literally in Italian 'in the breast, in the chest', this denotes metaphorically that the pope is still keeping it to himself, hugging it as it were to his breast. The pope may do this if he feels for any reason that the time is not opportune to reveal the cardinal's identity (perhaps because it would endanger his life, for example). The practice was introduced by Paul III (1468–1549). Use of the term in English dates back to the late 17th century, and at first it was used fairly broadly for 'in secret'; it is only in more recent times that usage has become concentrated on the ecclesiastical sense. The synonymous Latin *in pectore* is sometimes also encountered.

in posse

To say that something exists *in posse* is to say that it potentially exists, it could exist. The Latin phrase means literally 'in possibility' (*posse* is a noun use of the verb *posse* 'be able,' which evolved in medieval Latin). From the Latin texts of the schoolmen it passed into English apparently in the 16th century. It is frequently used together with *in esse* 'in being', to point up a contrast between that which actually exists and that which only has a potential to exist. The same idea is sometimes expressed by *in potentia*: 'The egg ... is a chicken in *potentia*' (Ben Jonson, *The Alchemist*, 1610).

in proprie persona

Latin *in propria persona* means 'in one's own person', that is, 'in person, personally'. It is used in English (frequently as a legal term) to denote that one does something oneself, in person, rather than through a representative or by some remote means of communication such as a letter. It began its career in English in the mid-17th century.

in re

Latin *in re* means literally 'in the thing, in the affair', and hence by extension 'concerning the matter'. It made its way into English via legal terminology, in which it came to be used prepositionally to denote 'in the case of' (particularly in connection with actions for bankruptcy). From there it spread out into the general language, meaning 'in connection with, with regard to'. It has never been particularly common, but it has spawned the abbreviated version *re*. This proliferated originally in commercial language ('Re your communication of the 21st inst'), and has always inspired the opprobrium of writers on usage, who regard it as at once pompous and petit bourgeois. It apparently began to burgeon after World War 1. *In re* is also used as a technical term in metaphysics, denoting universals which have real existence, and which are not just mental constructs.

in rem

In rem, in Latin literally 'into the thing, against the thing', is a legal term denoting judicial proceedings that are instituted against a thing rather than against a person. 'Thing' in this context can cover anything that is not legally a person: property, for instance, a right, or a status. The term is often explicitly contrasted with **in personam**.

inshallah

Inshallah is an exclamation used by Arabic-speakers to defer to the will of God when referring to future plans, hopes, etc – roughly the equivalent of **deo volente** or, more secularly, *touch wood*. The word is an English conflation of Arabic *in šā' Allah* 'if Allah wills'. It has been used in English since the mid-19th century, mainly in passages representing the speech of Arabs.

in situ

Latin *in situ* means literally 'in place' (*situ* is the ablative of *situs* 'place', source of English *site* and *situate*). English uses it, and has done since the mid-18th century, for 'still in its original place, not removed elsewhere or lost'. Since the early 20th century there have been sporadic instances of its being used adjectivally: 'The Department of the Environment ... has responsibility for *in situ* historical monuments in England' (*Nature*, 24 December 1971).

in statu pupillari

Someone who is *in statu pupillari* is literally 'in the status of a pupil' (the classical Latin diminutive *pupillus* meant 'little boy', but it has given English *pupil*). The term has been used in English since the mid-19th century to designate someone who is under the tutelage of another. Specifically, in the regulations of many English universities it denotes a member of the university who has not gained the degree of master: that is, an undergraduate or the holder of a bachelor's degree.

inter alia

Latin *inter alia* means 'among other things'. *Alia* is the neuter accusative plural of *alius* 'other', which has also given English *alias, alibi*, and *alien* and is related to *alter* and *else*. The phrase is used, as an alternative to the vernacular *among others*, to denote that one or a few examples are being selected from several possibilities. The first record of it dates from the mid-17th century. Also occasionally used in English is *inter alios* 'among other people'.

inter se

Inter se denotes interaction within a group, excluding outsiders. In Latin it means literally 'among themselves', and English apparently began to take it up in the mid-19th century: 'the "little wars" which Spaniards wage *inter se*' (Richard Ford, *A Hand-book for Travellers in Spain*, 1845).

in toto

English took to using Latin *in toto* around the end of the 18th century. The phrase is found only once in classical times, and that in the sense 'on the whole, in general'; the Romans used *in totum* to express the notion of 'in total, altogether'. However, it is in this latter meaning that English has adopted the expression. The first known record of it is in a letter from George Washington dating from 1798, in which he writes of rejecting a group of items '*in toto*'.

in vacuo

Latin *in vacuo* means 'in a vacuum', and it was in its literal physical sense that English first began to use it, in the mid-17th century. Experimenters might refer, for instance, to 'igniting a substance *in vacuo*'. That original sense continues in use, but it seems to be only relatively recently that it has been joined (and probably overtaken in frequency) by the metaphorical 'in isolation, without considering other relevant data' – as in 'attempting to solve the problem *in vacuo*'.

in vino veritas

In vino veritas is a proverbial warning to those who overindulge in alcohol, that the drink may loosen their tongue and they may say something that in a sober state they would have kept quiet about. In Latin literally 'in wine (there is) truth', its use as a proverb in English dates back to the late 16th century. Its model was perhaps a line of Pliny's, *Vulgoque veritas iam attributa vino est* 'Now truth is commonly said to be in wine' (*Natural History*), but evidently the sentiment was commonplace well before he wrote it.

in vitro

Latin *in vitro* means literally 'in glass' (*vitrum* 'glass' has given English *vitreous*, so named because of its glassy appearance, and also *vitriol* of its sulphates). It was coined in English at the end of the 19th century as a term denoting the carrying out of biological experiments, such as growing microorganisms, in pieces of laboratory equipment like test tubes and Petri dishes (which are made of glass), rather than in living organisms. At first it was used only adverbially, but over the decades it has increasingly been pressed into service as an adjective. In recent times its most familiar application has been to the fertilization of human eggs outside the mother's body ('*in vitro* fertilization'). The corresponding term for biological procedures carried out within a living organism is *in vivo*, literally 'in a living body'.

ipse dixit

Disciples of the Greek mathematician Pythagoras were wont, when repeating sayings of their master, to emphasize their authenticity and authority with the phrase *autos epha* 'he himself said (it)'. Translated into Latin this became *ipse dixit*, which English began to use in the 16th century as both a phrase and a noun denoting an 'assertion made on the grounds solely of the authority of a particular person, without any objective proof'. It may connote incontrovertibility ('To all his views on "scenery" she listened with reverence: he said of "Arthur's seat" that he was sure the Acropolis could not be finer. That he had never seen the Acropolis did not matter: *ipse dixit*', E. F. Benson, *As We Were*, 1930); but the ironic implication is often that the authority invoked, however distinguished, is not sufficient to secure credence. It is now also used more broadly, for a 'dogmatic and arbitrary pronouncement'. In the 19th century the derivative *ipse-dixitism* was coined, denoting the making of such pronouncements.

ipsissima verba

Latin *ipsissima verba* means 'the very words themselves, precisely the words' (*ipsissimus* is the superlative form of *ipse* 'just, precisely, itself'). The expression is used as a noun in English to denote the exact words used by someone, quoted verbatim, or when referring to an original document. The first records of it date from the early 19th century. The ablative form *ipsissimis verbis* is occasionally encountered too, as an adverbial phrase meaning 'in those very words, verbatim'.

ipso facto

The Latin ablative phrase *ipso facto* means literally 'by the fact itself'. English has used it since the 16th century to denote the logical or practical necessity by which one thing follows from another – as in 'By renouncing their religion, they *ipso facto* gave up their legal rights'. This signifies that the very fact that they renounced their religion meant that they also lost their legal rights.

ipso jure

Latin *ipso jure* means 'by the law itself'. Its force is that the due process of the law, if followed through to the strict letter, will inevitably produce a particular result. It occurs in the *Institutes* of the 2nd-century AD Roman jurist Gaius. The first intimation of its introduction into English is its appearance as an entry in the first edition of *Webster's New International Dictionary* (1909).

irredenta

An *irredenta* is an area containing a population ethnically related to that of another country, which seeks to gain or regain political control over it. Thus Germany in the 1930s regarded the Sudetenland as an *irredenta*, as it contained a large German-speaking population, and seized it from Czechoslovakia. The term is of Italian origin, and is short for *Italia irredenta*, literally 'unredeemed Italy'. This phrase was used by Italian nationalists in the late 19th century to refer to areas which they thought belonged by right to Italy and should be reclaimed, such as Trieste, Istria, and Corsica. *Irredenta* is the feminine form of *irredento* 'unredeemed', which comes ultimately from Latin *redemptus*. The first appearance of the word in English was in the guise of its derivatives, *irredentism* and *irredentist*. They at first referred specifically to Italy, but have since broadened out considerably, even being used vaguely for 'one who wishes for the recovery of what has been lost': 'The articles ... are largely mischief-making, designed to amuse the irredentist Thatcher supporters who wrote them' (*The Observer*, 20 January 1991). *Irredenta* itself arrived in the early 20th century, and is sometimes used (quasi-Italian) as a post-nominal adjective (as in 'Rumania *irredenta*').

J

jacquerie

The original *Jacquerie* was a revolt in which in 1358 the French peasantry, driven to desperation by famine, plague, and the ravages of the Hundred Years' War, rose up against the nobility. It was summarily suppressed. Its designation was derived from the French name *Jacques*, which was used as a generic term for a 'peasant'. The word was first used in English as long ago as the early 16th century, but it does not seem to have been until the 19th century that it began to enjoy some vogue as a general term for a 'peasants' revolt'. In former centuries it was often anglicized to *jacquery*, but now the French form has become firmly re-established.

j'adoube

Like that other subtle and sometimes devious activity, international diplomacy, chess gets much of its terminology from French. *J'adoube* means literally 'I adjust'. It is a formulaic expression used by a player who wishes to touch a piece that he does not actually intend to move – failure to give this or a similar warning would mean, under the 'touch and move' law, that the piece once touched would have to be played. The rule also applies to touching an opponent's piece – indeed the first reference to it in an English text, in J. H. Sarratt's *A Treatise on the Game of Chess* (1808), is in such a context: 'If a player *touch* one of his adversary's pieces, without saying "*J'adoube*", he may be compelled to take it'.

The original, and now historical, sense of *adouber* in French is 'equip a knight', and it also means 'make someone a knight', which gives away its link with English *dub*. Its other current sense is 'repair a ship', and it means 'adjust' only in the context of chess.

jalousie

A *jalousie* is a slatted window shutter that lets in fresh air and filtered light but keeps out the rain. It is typical of more southerly climes than Britain's, and English did not begin to use the word with any regularity until the early 19th century. It was borrowed from French, where it means literally 'jealousy' (and indeed English *jealousy* was acquired from its Old French ancestor). Its application to the shutter (which probably originated in and spread from Italian *gelosia*) may refer to the fact that you can see through the horizontal slats without being seen, as a jealous husband might when keeping watch on a wife about whom he harboured suspicions. (In the 17th, 18th and early 19th centuries English used the term *jealous glass* for the sort of translucent glass used in bathroom windows.)

je m'en fiche

French *ficher* is related to, and in some respects the equivalent of, English *fix*. It is used in a range of relatively mild exclamations and imprecations, including *fichez-moi la paix!* 'shut up!', *va te faire fiche!* 'go to hell!', and *je m'en fiche!* 'I couldn't care less!'. The last has been sporadically used in English since the late 19th century, generally in French contexts, and English has also employed the derivative *je-m'en-fichisme* for an 'attitude of cynical indifference'. Similar in meaning but rather ruder is *je m'en fous*, based on the verb *foutre* 'shove, stuff, fuck', which began to appear in English in the early 20th century. It too has been followed by its derivative *je-m'en-foutisme*.

je ne sais quoi

In French, *je ne sais quoi* means literally 'I do not know what'. It is used in a wide range of contexts suggesting lack of definite knowledge: for example, *un je ne sais quoi de déplaisant* 'something indefinably unpleasant', *Un je ne sais quoi nous a écrit* 'Someone or other has written to us'. When English speakers began to use it, in the 17th century, its application seems to have been equally broad; Thomas Blount, for one, in his *Glossographia* (1656), identifies it as an affected term for a pretended illness: '*Je-ne-scay-quoi*, four French words, contracted as it were into one, and signifies *I know not what*, we use to say they are troubled with the *Je-ne-scay-quoy*, that faign themselves sick out of niceness but know not where their own grief lies, or what ayls them'. Nowadays, however, its use is restricted to a 'certain indefinable but admirable quality or characteristic'.

165

jeu d'esprit

Jeu d'esprit – in French literally 'play of wit' – denotes a 'witty sally', a 'witticism', and also a 'lightweight, typically brief literary piece characterized by wittiness'. The term was introduced into English in the early 18th century, but has never become fully anglicized; its still-perceived Frenchness seems to lend it an extra tinge of lightness and frivolity. Other terms containing *jeu* (which is distantly related to *jocose, joke* and *juggler*, and provides the first syllable of *jeopardy*) have been taken over by English at various times. These include *jeu de mots* 'play on words, pun', *jeu de paume*, literally 'palm (of the hand) game', an early form of tennis, and *jeu de théâtre* 'stage trick'.

jeune fille

A *jeune fille* is a young unmarried woman, a girl from the time when she reaches sexual maturity to roughly (the term is not chronologically precise) her early twenties. English borrowed the term from French at the beginning of the 19th century, but it did not really start to come into its own in the language until the 20th century, when it took on a role as an adjective, denoting a girlish romanticism and naivety.

jeune premier

Jeune premier is the role aging actors cling to most tenaciously, often beyond the bounds of seemliness or even plausibility. It is that of the young(ish) actor who plays juvenile leads. The term was borrowed from French (where it means literally 'first young man') in the mid-19th century, and frequently in its subsequent career has been pressed into service metaphorically for a 'vigorously youthful leading male figure': 'Lord Rosebery ... was the *jeune premier* of that generation' (letter from Mrs Belloc Lowndes, 1946). For the leading part for a young actress, the equivalent feminine form is *jeune première*.

jeunesse dorée

French *jeunesse dorée* means literally 'gilded youth'. It originated as an epithet for a group of wealthy young men of good family who in 1794 helped to bring about the fall of Robespierre and the ending of the Reign of Terror, in which over a thousand 'opponents of the Revolution' were guillotined. By the 1830s its application had broadened out considerably, and it was being used (usually somewhat patronizingly or deprecatingly) for the fashionable, wealthy, sophisticated, privileged youngsters within a society (originally young men, but now it is a unisex term). As well as adopting it unaltered, English has also translated *jeunesse dorée* into the vernacular, to begin with as *gilt youth*, but now generally as *gilded youth*.

jihad

A *jihad* is a holy war undertaken by Muslims against unbelievers. Its largest and most far-reaching manifestation was the advance of Muslim armies from Arabia through the Middle East and North Africa in the 7th and 8th centuries AD, carrying out their religious duty of bringing Islam to the infidels of those areas. They later spread further into Africa and into Spain, and eventually their activities provoked a Christian response in the form of the Crusades. The Arabic word *jihād* means literally 'conflict, struggle'. English acquired it in the 1860s, and has occasionally used it additionally as a general term for a 'concerted action taken against something with religious fervour' – in other words, a 'crusade': 'An economical government bargained to abolish the deer. So the edict went forth, and a "Jihad" against the deer was proclaimed' (*19th Century*, 1886).

joie de vivre

Joie de vivre, literally in French 'joy of living', was borrowed into English, appropriately enough, in the middle of the Belle Époque, on the threshold of the Naughty Nineties: the first record of it in an English text dates from 1889. It did not take long for it to establish itself firmly in the language. *Joie* is of course ultimately the same word as English *joy*, which was acquired from Old French in the 13th century. Their common source is Latin *gaudium* 'joy', which also produced the English noun *gaudy* 'university dinner for former students' and probably the adjective *gaudy* 'garish' (although not all etymologists are agreed on this).

jolie laide

A *jolie laide* is a woman who, while not conforming to the conventional image of feminine beauty, is nevertheless sexually attractive. It is of a piece with the stereotyped reputation of the French for expertise and discrimination in sexual matters that they should have provided the straitlaced English with a term conveying the relatively sophisticated notion that features which might be termed ugly can actually be a sexual turn-on: the expression means literally 'pretty ugly'. It crossed the Channel at the end of the 19th century. Five hundred or more years earlier, Old French *jolif*, the ancestor of modern *joli*, had given English *jolly*.

Jugendstil

Jugendstil is the German term corresponding to *art nouveau*: it denotes a style of late 19th-century decorative art characterized by long curling sinuous lines and stylized natural forms. Amongst the leading exponents of *Jugendstil* were the illustrator Otto Eckmann and the sculptor and designer Hermann Obrist. It apparently took its name from *Die Jugend* 'Youth', a magazine which first appeared in 1896: so *Jugendstil* literally means '"Youth" style'.

Junker

The Junkers were a class of Prussian land-owning aristocracy. From small beginnings they rose until by the 15th century they held large areas of land and wielded considerable political and commercial power and influence (the first recorded reference to them in English dates from 1554). Under the patronage of Frederick the Great and later of Bismarck, they gained a reputation for being arrogant, militaristic, and extremely reactionary, and eventually this began to emerge in the metaphorical use of the word *Junker* in English: 'The Junker is by no means peculiar to Prussia ... Lord Cromer is a Junker' (G. B. Shaw, *What I really wrote about the War*, 1930). It originated as a compound word, formed in Middle High German from *junc* 'young' and *herre* 'lord' (the ancestor of modern German *Herr* 'Mr'). The Dutch equivalent, *jonker*, is the ultimate source of *Yonkers*, the name of a city in New York state.

jus

Latin *jūs* 'law' has given English *jury, just, justice*, etc and also lies behind *injury* and *judge*. But in addition to that, it forms the basis of a number of Latin terms used in English to denote various sorts or bodies of law. Among them are *jus canonicum* 'canon law', law governing church affairs; *jus civile* 'civil law', particularly as it existed in ancient Rome; *jus cogens* 'compelling law', any of the basic principles of international law which cannot be contracted out of; *jus divinum* 'divine law'; *jus gentium* 'law of nations', the concept in Roman law of those provisions which are shared by the legal codes of all countries, but later broadened to denote a common and agreed international legal framework; *jus naturale* 'natural law', originally in Roman law a system of justice based on innate ideas of right and wrong, but later used synonymously with *jus gentium*: *jus primae noctis* 'law of the first night', the right of a feudal overlord to deflower a woman on her wedding night (see **droit de seigneur**); *jus sanguinis* 'law of blood', the principle that a person's nationality is the same as his parents'; and *jus soli* 'law of soil', the principle that a person's nationality is that of the country he was born in.

jusqu'au bout

French *jusqu'au bout* means 'to the very end, to the bitter end' (*bout* 'end' is related to the English verbs *butt* and *beat*). English acquired it in the very specific context of World War 1, when it was used to refer to the policy of pursuing the war to a successful conclusion (as opposed to reaching an agreement to stop fighting with neither side the clear victor). People who advocated this policy were termed *jusqu'auboutistes*, their point of view *jusqu'auboutisme*. Since then the phrase and its derivatives have receded from general use, but they still crop up occasionally in broader contexts.

juste milieu

Juste milieu is the French way of saying 'happy medium'. Literally 'right middle course', it started to infiltrate English in the early 19th century. To begin with it was apparently used, as in French, to denote something intermediate between two extremes, with no overtones of praise or blame; but more recently there seems to have been a tendency (inspired by the closeness of French *juste* and English *just*) to apply it approvingly to a 'judicious and moderate avoidence of extremes', and even to the 'correct rejection of false extremes'.

K

kaffeeklatsch

When Americans get together for a *kaffeeklatsch*, they are having a good gossip. The word was borrowed from German where it means literally 'coffee-gossip' – conjuring up a picture of friends sitting round a café table putting the world to rights over a cup of coffee. It is first recorded in English in Anna Randall-Diehl's *Two thousand words and their definitions; not in Webster's Dictionary* (1888). These days the coffee element is optional, the essential point of the kaffeeklatsch being the gossip. The semi-Anglicized version *coffeeklatsch* is sometimes encountered, as is the simple *klatsch* on its own.

kamerad

Kamerad is one of those words – like *achtung* and *schweinehund* – which in pulp World War 1 and 2 fiction pepper the speech of German soldiers, supposedly lending verisimilitude to their remarks. It was originally borrowed into German from French *camarade* 'comrade', but it came to be used in the military as an exclamation meaning essentially 'Let's be friends! I don't want to fight you', and hence 'I surrender!' English writers seized on it during World War 1 for their portrayal of the enemy; the first record of it in English comes in an October 1914 issue of the *Illustrated London News*.

kamikaze

Kamikazes – Japanese suicide pilots who deliberately crashed their aircraft, loaded down with explosives, on to Allied, and especially US warships – appeared on the World War 2 scene towards the end of the war in the Pacific. As events began to turn against Japan, the desperate expedient of piloting these flying bombs at the enemy was resorted to. The first such attack was at the battle of Leyte Gulf, in 1944, and in the attack on Okinawa in 1945 twenty-one US warships were sunk by the kamikazes. The term in Japanese means literally 'divine wind', and is a re-application of an epithet originally used in 1281 for a typhoon which overwhelmed Kublai Khan's invading naval forces.

It was in the early 1960s that the word's metaphorical possibilities began to be explored in English, and it is now widely used to suggest a reckless tendency to self-destruction. It has also been adopted into the terminology of surfing, denoting a deliberate fall from the board, or wipe-out.

kanaka

It was in the mid-19th century that the word *kanaka* began to establish itself in English. It was introduced by voyagers in the north central Pacific, who encountered it in the Hawaiian Islands. In the Hawaiian language it means simply 'person' (it is related to Samoan, Tongan, and Maori *tangata*, which also means 'person'), but English adopted it as a term for a 'South Sea islander'. In the late 19th century it was also used specifically for a Pacific islander who was forcibly transported to Australia and put to work in the sugar plantations of Queensland. It is still used in Australian English for a South Pacific islander, but in its native Hawaii it is applied in English specifically to someone born in those islands, as opposed to an incomer.

kapellmeister

In Germany in former times, especially the 18th century, a *kapelle* was the musical establishment attached to the court of a prince, consisting of an orchestra and usually also a choir. The person who was in charge of the *kapelle*, and who conducted its musicians, was the *kapellmeister*. English has used the term since the early 19th century, and has also given some currency to the compound *kapellmeistermusik*, a derogatory expression denoting the sort of technically correct but uninspired music that kapellmeisters supposedly write for their players and singers to perform.

kaputt

English acquired *kaputt* (also spelled *kaput*) from German, in the sense 'completely destroyed, done for, washed up, or dead', at the end of the 19th century, but its antecedents are rather convoluted. Its ultimate source is French *capot*, a term in the card game piquet which denotes a clean sweep of all the tricks (English borrowed it in this sense in the 17th century). It is not known where *capot* itself came from, though a connection with

French dialect *capoter* 'castrate' has been suggested, but it could also be the same word as French *capot* 'hooded cloak' (a relative of English *cape*), in which case its underlying meaning would be analogous to English 'be hoodwinked'. *Être capot* is to 'fail to win any tricks', and hence colloquially to 'be done, be finished', and it is this metaphorical sense that found its way via German into English.

karaoke

Karaoke is a Japanese phenomenon that in the 1990s is beginning to achieve some popularity in Britain. In bars, clubs, etc members of the public take it in turns to come up and sing a solo, to the accompaniment of a band or (more usually) a recorded backing. Many such places have special *karaoke* jukeboxes that provide the instrumental support. This custom is called *karaoke* (in Japanese it means literally 'empty orchestra').

karezza

The term *karezza* was introduced into English by Dr A. B. Stockham in a book of the same name (1896). Adapting it from Italian *carezza* 'caress', he used it to denote a form of sexual intercourse in which the man avoids orgasm and ejaculation. Technically it is the same as *coitus reservatus* (see **coitus interruptus**), but Dr Stockham evidently intended the term to convey higher things. He viewed this suppression of base gratification by will-power as in some way permeating the (married) relationship between the sexual partners, and promoting a more profound union. Aldous Huxley was a later advocate of *karezza*.

karma

In Hinduism and Buddhism, karma is the force produced by a person's actions during his or her life, which determines what will happen to that person in succeeding reincarnations. English took the word *karma* over in the early 19th century from Sanskrit, where it encapsulates the notions of 'action' and 'effect', of making one's fate by one's own deeds. 'Action' and 'effect' are the literal meanings of the word, which is a derivative of the verb *karoti* 'he makes, he does'. For much of the word's career in English it remained a rather out-of-the-way term in comparative religion, but the explosion of interest in Eastern mysticism in the 1960s gave it a new lease of life in the more general sense of 'fate, destiny'.

kasher

Kasher is a verb which means essentially 'make kosher': for example, if you *kasher* meat, you remove surplus blood from it in the way prescribed by rabbinic law; and if you *kasher* a knife, a bowl, etc, you clean it thoroughly, getting rid of any non-kosher substances with which it may have been in contact. The word is borrowed from Hebrew, where it was originally an adjective, *kāshēr*, meaning 'right, proper'; via Yiddish it has also given English *kosher*.

kashrut

Kashrut, or *kashruth*, is the body of Jewish laws relating to ritual purity. The term is applied particularly to those laws which relate to the preparation and eating of food: they cover the way in which animals are slaughtered, the removal of surplus blood from meat, the rigid separation of food containing milk or milk products (*milchik*) from food containing meat or meat products (*fleishik*), and the forbidding of certain foodstuffs (eg pork). *Kashrut* is a Hebrew word, meaning literally 'appropriateness, fitness'; it first appeared in English at the beginning of the 20th century.

katzenjammer

German *katzenjammer*, literally 'cats' wailing, caterwaul', is used metaphorically for a 'hangover'. By the middle of the 19th century German immigrants had introduced the term to American English, and it was not long before a further figurative extension took it to 'confused uproar'. In 1897 the cartoonist Rudolph Dirks introduced a comic strip into the *New York Journal* entitled 'Those Katzenjammer Kids', which centred on the mischievous exploits of Hans and Fritz. This inspired the use of *Katzenjammer kids* or *Katzenjammer children* in American English to denote any naughty or noisy children.

khalukah

In former times, Jews around the world would make financial contributions in order to support Jews still living in Palestine. The practice continued until the 1940s, when the establishment of the state of Israel rendered it no longer relevant. The distribution of these funds was termed *khalukah*. The word is a derivative of the Hebrew verb *hālaq* 'distribute', and it first appeared in English towards the end of the 19th century.

kia ora

Kia ora is a Maori salutation, meaning literally 'be well!', which is used in New Zealand English as a greeting, to wish someone good luck, etc. In Britain it became known as the brand name of a range of fruit squashes and other soft drinks.

kibbutz, plural kibbutzes or kibbutzim

The first kibbutzim (to use the original Hebrew plural) were set up in Palestine between the two World Wars, and since the formation of the state of Israel have become a major feature of the national economy. They are collective agricultural settlements, communally administered, in which the land is either owned or leased by the members. Children all live together rather than with their parents. The word *kibbutz* is an adaptation of modern Hebrew *qibbūs* 'gathering', which in turn goes back to ancient Hebrew *qibbūtz*, a derivative of the verb *qibbētz* 'he gathers'. It is first recorded in English in 1931. Someone who belongs to a kibbutz is termed a *kibbutznik*.

kibitzer

A kibitzer is someone who looks on and gives unwanted advice, much to the irritation of the person advised. The word was introduced to American English in the 1920s from Yiddish: *American Speech* in 1928 noted that 'The trade journal ... devotes an editorial ... to the "kibbitzer". It defines "kibbitzing" as a slang expression used to indicate the act of offering gratuitous advice by an outsider.' It is a derivative of the verb *kibitzen* (from which English gets *kibitz*), which in turn came from German *kiebitzen* 'be an onlooker'. This was formed from the noun *kiebitz*, whose main and original meaning is 'lapwing', but which came to be used metaphorically for 'someone who looks over others' shoulders as they are playing cards and interferes in what they are doing'.

kinder, kirche, küche

Kinder, kirche, küche, literally 'children, church, kitchen', was the formula prescribed in Nazi Germany for the wives and mothers of the Fatherland; woman's place was firmly in the home, giving birth to and bringing up children, seeing to their spiritual welfare, and preparing food for the rest of the household. The phrase found its way into English in the 1930s, in slighting references to Germany, but it survived World War 2, and it has remained in the language as a way of referring to outdated views of women's place in society.

kitsch

Kitsch, a collective insult denoting decorative objects in poor or trashy taste but with pretensions to art, was acquired from German. The first record of its use in English comes from the mid-1920s, and it crops up sporadically thereafter, but it seems not to have been until the 1960s that it moved from being a fairly recherché foreignism to wider use as a term for the vulgarly sentimental in art (that is when the derivative adjective *kitschy* first appeared). The German word *kitsch*, which means 'rubbish' in general as well as 'trashy art', is derived from *kitschen*, a verb of unknown origin with the sense 'cobble together in a slapdash way'.

kolkhoz

A *kolkhoz*, or *kolkhos*, is a collective farm in the Soviet Union, a farm which is owned and run by the community. The term is short for Russian *kollektivnoe khozyaistvo* 'collective farm', and began to appear in English as early as 1921, soon after the setting up of the first *kolkhozes* in post-Revolutionary Russia.

kommandatura

German *kommandatur*, an acquisition ultimately from French, denotes a 'command post', the 'headquarters of the commander of an army'. There is some evidence of its use in English in the 1930s, but it was in the post-World War 2 period that it came into its own in English, in the slightly altered form *kommandatura*, as a word for the headquarters of the military government of a city, particularly in the context of cold-war central Europe.

konditorei

German *konditor* 'person who makes and sells pastries, cakes, sweets, etc' comes ultimately from Latin *condīre* 'preserve, pickle' (source also of English *condiment*). The establishment where a *konditor* sells his wares is called a *konditorei*, and English adopted the term in the early 20th century for referring to such shops-cum-cafés in Germany and Austria. It also refers to the pastries and other goodies themselves.

kulak

Kulak has been a term tinged with contempt in Russia for over a century. In pre-Revolutionary times kulaks were peasants or villagers who had made money and thus exercised a resented control over the affairs of their community. Their meanness, and the usuriousness of their interest rates when they lent to their neighbours, became a byword, and earned them their name; for *kulak* means literally 'fist' in Russian, and so by metaphorical extension came to be used for a 'tight-fisted person'. The word was originally borrowed into Russian from Turkic *kul* 'hand'. It is related to Turkish *kol* 'arm'. English acquired it in the 1870s.

After the Revolution the concept of the kulak was for a time regarded with favour by the new state. Lenin's New Economic Policy wanted to foster private enterprise in agriculture, and wealthy peasants were a good advertisement for this. But in 1927 everything changed. Stalin collectivized the land and imposed heavy taxes on the kulaks. They naturally opposed this, but Stalin set about their liquidation.

kulturkampf

Kulturkampf is the name given to an extended struggle in the late 19th century between the Prussian secular state, largely in the person of Bismarck, and the Roman Catholic Church for the control of various social institutions. Hitherto the Church had had a tight grip on areas such as education and marriage, and was accustomed to interfere generally in politics, but a series of laws passed in the 1870s and 1880s took these matters out of its hands. Many felt, though, that the pendulum had swung too far in the opposite direction, and by 1887 outrage at the persecution of priests forced Bismarck to reinstate the Church's rights. The German term *kulturkampf* means literally 'culture struggle' (*kampf* as in *Mein kampf* 'My struggle', the title of Adolf Hitler's book of political philosophizing), but *kultur* is being used here in the sense 'system of beliefs', not with any artistic connotations, so the underlying force of the term is 'conflict of beliefs'.

kvetch

To *kvetch* in American slang is to 'complain annoyingly or persistently': 'The Beatles ... came along in the middle of a wave of *kvetching* – songs constantly stressing the negative'

(*Holiday*, July 1965). The word is another adoption from
Yiddish, whose German antecedent in this case is *quetschen*
'crush, press, squeeze'. It is also used as a noun, meaning
'someone who is always complaining or whingeing'.

L

lacrimae rerum

In the *Aeneid*, Virgil describes how Aeneas in the temple of Juno at Carthage sees a picture of the fighting in the Trojan War, which prompts him to say *En Priamus. Sunt hic etiam sua praemia laudi; sunt lacrimae rerum et mentem mortalis tangunt. Solve metus; feret haec aliquam tibi fama salutem*, 'Look, there is Priam! Even here high merit has its due; there are tears in the very nature of things and men's affairs touch the heart. Dispel all fear; this knowledge of you will bring salvation'. The import of *lacrimae rerum*, literally 'tears of things', is 'sorrow is part of the scheme of things', and the phrase has come to be used allusively in English since the mid-19th century (sometimes in the fuller form *sunt lacrimae rerum*).

la dolce vita

In Italian literally 'the sweet life', *la dolce vita* began to make an impact on English, as a generic term for an indolently self-indulgent lifestyle, in the early 1960s, as a direct result of the *succès de scandale* of the Italian film *La dolce vita*. Directed by Federico Fellini, this tells the story of a journalist's experiences in the fleshpots of modern Roman high society, ending up with a rather half-hearted orgy. It won the Grand Prix at the 1960 Venice Film Festival. It ensured that the expression *la dolce vita* has overtones not just of luxury but also of licentiousness. In English the vernacular definite article is often substituted for the Italian *la*, or even dispensed with altogether: 'A totally alien way of life – a dolce vita of Bicester, 1970 style' (*The Times*, 14 October 1970). Italian *dolce*, incidentally, is distantly related to English *dulcet*.

laissez-faire

Laissez-faire has two distinct meanings in English. The more specific, and longer established, denotes the principle that governments should not interfere in the economic affairs of a country, but allow people to carry on their business, trade, etc as they see fit. The phrase seems to have originated in the motto of the 18th-century French free-traders, *laissez faire et laissez passer*, which may have been coined by the economist Gournay. This means literally 'allow to do and allow to pass', and the purport of the first element, *laissez faire*, is 'let people do whatever they like'. English adopted it in the early 19th century, and already by then it was being used in the broader sense of 'refraining from interfering in the affairs of others' – with distinctly derogatory undertones of 'lack of necessary rigorous supervision' and 'indifference': 'the *laissez faire* system of apathy' (C. H. Phipps, *The English in Italy*, 1825). The standard form of the word contains the French imperative plural, *laissez*, but it is not uncommon, in British English, to find this replaced by the infinitive, *laisser*.

Other French expressions containing *laisser* 'let, allow' to have been borrowed by English are *laissez-aller* 'lack of restraint', literally 'let go', adopted in the mid-19th century, and *laissez-passer* 'permit, pass', a more recent introduction.

langlauf

The German term *langlauf* denotes a 'cross-country skiing race' (it literally means 'long run'). It was introduced into English in the 1920s by Arnold Lunn, a pioneer of skiing in Britain, and has since caught on as the name of an event that features in the Winter Olympics, over distances of 30 and 50 kilometres. Competitors use much lighter, thinner skis than downhill skiers, and for much of the course have to make their way under their own power, without benefit of gravity. An alternative term sometimes used is *ski-loping*.

langue d'oc

Langue d'oc is the Romance language that during the Middle Ages was spoken in the southern part of France, approximately below a northern boundary formed by the river Loire. It survives today in Provençal and its two subvarieties Mistralien and Occitan, and in the name of the Languedoc, an area of southern France between the Rhône and the Pyrenees. The etymological import of the term *langue d'oc* is 'language in which the word for "yes" is *oc*' (*oc* is descended from Latin *hoc* 'this'). It is explicitly contrasted with *langue d'oïl*, literally 'language in which the word for "yes" is *oïl*', which denotes the Romance language formerly spoken in northern France, from which modern French has evolved. *Oïl* comes from Latin *hoc ille*, which was short for *hoc ille fecit* 'this he did', and is the source of modern French *oui*. Both terms were in use in English by the beginning of the 18th century.

lapsus linguae

Latin *lapsus linguae* means literally 'slip of the tongue' (*lapsus* is of course the source of English *lapse*). It has been used sporadically in English since the 17th century: 'What have I done besides a little lapsus linguae?' (John Dryden, *Sir Martin Mar-all*, 1667). But it has never succeeded in ousting the native English *slip of the tongue*, which is the technical term now used in linguistics. Other expressions incorporating Latin *lapsus* to have enjoyed some currency in English include *lapsus calami* 'slip of the pen' (Latin *calamus* means literally 'reed', and is distantly related to English *haulm* 'stalks'), *lapsus memoriae* 'lapse of memory', and *lapsus pennae* 'slip of the pen'.

laudator temporis acti

The Roman poet Horace in his *Ars poetica* wrote of the old person who is *difficilis, querulus, laudator temporis acti se puero, castigator, censorque minorum* 'testy, grumbling, a praiser of time past when he himself was a boy, a critic and censor of the new generation'. The first writer of English on record as using the phrase *laudator temporis acti* is Jonathan Swift, in a letter of 1736, and it has remained in the language ever since as a derogatory term for someone who is always going on about how good the 'good old days' were. English also uses Latin *delator temporis acti* for one who denounces time past.

l'chaim

L'chaim is a Jewish toast. In Hebrew it means literally 'to life!' It started appearing in English texts, initially in the USA, between the two world wars. There is still a certain amount of variability in its spelling – alternative versions include *lechayim*, *lechaim*, and *lehaim* – but in all cases the pronunciation is /ləˈxaɪm/, rhyming with *rhyme*. The word is also used as a noun, denoting a small drink used in toasting someone.

lebensraum

In German, *lebensraum* means literally 'life space' (*raum* is a relative of English *room*, which originally meant 'space'). The earliest examples of its use in English, which date from the beginning of the 20th century, show it being employed as a term in psychology, denoting a person's environment as it affects them mentally (in this sense it was often replaced by the literal English equivalent, *life-space*). But by the 1930s a far different application was taking hold. For Germans it denoted chiefly the concept of territory sufficiently large to encompass the aspirations of their race, and the theory was given substance by Hitler, whose enforced acquisitions of land, particularly in the east (including the attempted takeover of Russia in 1941–2), were undertaken in the name of *lebensraum*. From this a new metaphorical meaning began to spring up in English – a general 'elbow-room', 'space for action': 'Music, manuscripts, and her little daughter's toys compete amiably for *lebensraum*' (*The Guardian*, 14 March 1960).

lederhosen

Lederhosen, short leather trousers usually held up with braces, are the archetypal men's wear of the Tirolean and Bavarian mountains, firmly associated with jolly, rubicund Germans performing uproarious country dances, featuring a good deal of clapping and slapping. The German term means simply 'leather trousers' (*hosen* shares a common Germanic ancestry with English *hose*), and its introduction into English dates from the period between the two world wars.

leitmotiv

Leitmotiv is Richard Wagner's leading contribution to the international vocabulary of music. He used it to denote the practice (not his invention, but certainly brought to a peak of sophistication by him) of using brief musical phrases to represent particular characters, ideas, or situations in an opera. The phrase is repeated whenever the person, situation, etc re-enters the action, and so a web of musical cross-references is built up. The German term is a compound formed from the verb *leiten* 'lead' (a relative of English *lead*) and *motiv* 'motive', which was borrowed from French *motif*. Its actual coiner appears to have been Friedrich Wilhelm Jähns, who applied it originally to the work not of Wagner but of Weber. The first recorded reference to it in English comes in Sir John Stainer's and W. A. Barrett's *Dictionary of Musical Terms* (1876). It has subsequently been partially anglicized to *leitmotive*, and completely translated as *leading motive*, but on the whole *leitmotiv* has remained the chief English form. It is now widely used in the broader metaphorical sense of 'main or recurring theme': 'It provides the *leitmotif* of German foreign policy in Spain' (Arthur Koestler, *Spanish Testament*, 1937).

lèse majesté

Originally and technically, *lèse majesté* denoted any crime against the authority of the sovereign, and in particular, treason. A borrowing from French, it goes back ultimately to Latin *laesa majestas* (itself occasionally used in English). This meant literally 'injured majesty' (*laesa* is the feminine past participle of Latin *laedere* 'harm, damage'). English acquired it in the 16th century, since when it has gradually become anglicized to *lese majesty*, a form quite commonly encountered nowadays; *lèse majesté* probably represents a more recent reborrowing from French. It has spread in meaning, too, now being used usually in the more general sense 'disrespectful action against something or someone in authority or revered': 'Dangling there, without the support of No 10, Biffen was an awful warning to his colleagues of the penalty for *lèse-majesté*' (Robert Harris, *Good and Faithful Servant*, 1990).

In French, the stem *lèse* 'harm' became quite productive of new coinages, based on *lèse majesté*: examples include *lèse-catholicité* and *lèse-société*. It has never caught on to this extent in English, but occasionally writers have used it in creating nonce-forms: 'There is scarcely an honest or independent man among them, who has not in some way or other been guilty of *Lèse-Toryism*' (General Perronet Thompson, *Exercises, Political and Others*, 1842).

lettre de cachet

In pre-Revolutionary France, a *lettre de cachet* was a letter sent under the king's seal (French *cachet* means 'seal'). In particular, the term referred to a warrant for the indefinite imprisonment without trial of someone who had incurred the monarch's displeasure. It began to appear in English in the early 18th century and has remained ever since, both as a historical term and, by extension, as a reference to any document permitting arrest, imprisonment, etc without trial.

levée en masse

Revulsion and alarm at the execution of Louis XVI in 1793 led to the formation of a coalition of European nations, including Britain, Austria, Prussia and Spain, against France. The ensuing hostilities became known as the Revolutionary Wars; they led on to the Napoleonic Wars. Under threat of attack, a Committee of Public Safety was formed, and in August 1793 Lazare Nicolas Marguerite Carnot, a member of the Committee, decreed a *levée en masse*, or 'mass mobilization', compulsorily calling up hundreds of thousands of men to defend France against the threat of invasion. English adopted the term *levée en masse* in the early 19th century, and to begin with often anglicized it to *levy in masse*. It is now used for any mass call-up of troops in response to invasion.

lied, plural lieder

German *lied* means 'song' (it is descended from Old High German *liod*, and is related to Latin *laudare* 'praise'), but it is in a rather more specialized sense that it has found its way into English. It denotes a song of the Romantic period, the late 18th and early to mid-19th centuries, which is typically a setting of a German poem for solo voice with piano accompaniment. The leading composer of such songs was Franz Schubert, but other well-known examples come from Beethoven, Schumann, Brahms and Wolf. English began to use the term in the middle of the 19th century, and it remains far more familiar in its plural form *lieder* than in the singular.

lingerie

Although now pretty well established in English (having made its debut in the early 19th century), *lingerie* is worth including in this dictionary of foreignisms for the phonetic contortions it still often precipitates when English speakers attempt it. The most salient feature of its first vowel to English ears appears to be that it is nasalized, and so in pronouncing it, English-speakers think they have done their duty in producing an approximation to any old French nasal vowel. So *lingerie*, whose first syllable in French has an unrounded front vowel, as in *vin* 'wine', in English mouths usually becomes a rounded back *o*, something like /ˈlɒnʤəri/. (See also **ingénue**.) Those with a better knowledge of what the French word actually sounds like generally attempt a short nasalized *la*, producing /ˈlãŋʤəriː/. The final syllable has fared little better. Based presumably on a perception that 'lots of French words end in an /eɪ/ sound', the pronunciation /'lɒndʒəreɪ/ is far from uncommon. *Lingerie* evidently retains an aura of 'Frenchness', reinforced by and reinforcing its application to the glamorous, frilly end of the women's underwear spectrum. In French it means 'underwear' in general, not just 'women's elegant underwear'; and etymologically it denotes 'clothing made from linen' (*linge* is French for 'linen').

lingua franca

The term *lingua franca* denotes a language used as a means of communication, particularly for purposes of trade, between people who do not understand each other's native language – for example, Swahili is widely used as a lingua franca in East Africa between people whose speech would otherwise be mutually unintelligible. It originally referred much more specifically to a sort of pidgin Italian, with elements of French, Spanish, Greek, Turkish and Arabic, spoken in Mediterranean ports between the time of the Crusades and the 18th century. In Italian it means literally 'Frankish tongue, Frankish language'. English adopted it in the second half of the 17th century.

litterae humaniores

At Oxford University, *litterae humaniores* is the name given to the study of ancient Greek and Roman history, language, literature, philosophy, etc. Literally in Latin 'more humane letters', it refers to the non-religious character of such studies, contrasting them implicitly with divinity, which in the 18th century (when the term emerged) was the other main component of university education. The vernacular equivalent, which nowadays is rather wider in application, is *the humanities*.

locum tenens

A *locum tenens* (or *locum* for short) is etymologically someone who is 'holding the place' of another – that is, someone, typically a doctor or a clergyman, who stands in temporarily for another and does that person's duties while he or she is absent for some reason. The term is a medieval Latin formation, based on Latin *locus* 'place' and *tenēns*, the present participle of *tenēre* 'hold'. It was first used in English in the mid-17th century. Formally, it is the precise equivalent of *lieutenant*, which is also made up of elements meaning 'place' and 'holding'. The abbreviated *locum* appears to date from the turn of the 20th century.

locus classicus

A *locus classicus* (in Latin literally 'classical place, classical passage') is a passage in a standard work that is frequently quoted as an authoritative source on a particular subject – and hence, by extension, a standard case or example: 'His action was successful, and the report of it is now a *locus classicus* in the law of life insurance' (*Law Times*, 1885). The term was adopted into English around the middle of the 19th century.

locus standi

In legal parlance, *locus standi* denotes the 'right to appear and be heard in court': 'An expectant occupier has a *locus standi* to apply for the renewal of a public-house licence' (*Law Times*, 1886). By extension it also refers to the right to a hearing before any body: 'The power of the Department of Trade and Industry should, of course, be discretionary, but the Panel should be given a *locus standi* with the Department' (*The Times*, 9 February 1974). But the term also has a much wider, more general meaning of 'recognized position or status with regard to something'. *Standi* is the genitive of the gerundive form of Latin *stāre* 'stand', and the phrase as a whole means literally 'place of standing'.

logos

Logos had two basic meanings in ancient Greek: 'word' and, by extension, 'reason'. Greek philosophers employed it in various extended senses. The Stoics, for example, applied it to the sort of god from whom all rationality in the universe flows; and for Heraclitus it denoted the whole rational scheme that underlies and supports the universe. Rather than attempt a translation of these subtle concepts, English writers have from the 16th century tended to adopt the word unchanged into the vernacular. The same applies to a certain extent to its theological application in Christianity. It is used in the Greek New Testament to denote Christ. In the Authorized Version this is translated as 'Word' ('In the beginning was the Word, and the Word was with God, and the Word was God' *John* 1:1), but modern New Testament scholars frequently use *Logos* to refer to the Second Person of the Trinity.

loquitur

Latin *loquitur* means 'he or she speaks' (it is the third person present singular of *loquī* 'speak, talk'). In former times it was used in English play scripts, as a stage direction beside the name of a character, denoting that it is his or her turn to speak. It was often abbreviated to *loq*.

lucus a non lucendo

Ancient (and not so ancient) grammarians often in desperation proposed etymologies that in the light of modern historical linguistics look laughably absurd. One of the culprits was the Roman rhetorician Quintilian (c.35–c.100 AD). In his *Institutio oratoria* he proposed that Latin *lucus* 'grove of trees, wood' was so named *a non lucendo* 'from not shining' – that is, from being dark (*lucendo* is a gerundial form of Latin *lucere* 'shine'). *Lucus* is indeed related to *lucere* and *lux*, but the connection appears to be that the word originally referred to a clearing in a wood, where the sunlight was able to penetrate; certainly it has nothing to do with '*not* shining'. Hence the expression *lucus a non lucendo* has come to be used as a shorthand way of referring to an absurd or paradoxical explanation of the origin of a word, and also to a name which apparently belies its application (as when a slow person is ironically called 'speedy'). Its career in English dates from the early 18th century. It is sometimes abbreviated to *lucus a non*.

luftmensch

A *luftmensch* is etymologically an 'air-person'. The word is of Yiddish origin, and was compounded of German *luft* 'air' and *mensch* 'person'. It denotes someone who is full of wonderful schemes, ideas, etc but is no good at putting them into practice. There is an isolated example of its use in English from the beginning of the 20th century, but it does not seem to have come into its own until the 1960s.

lumpenproletariat

The term *lumpenproletariat* was coined around 1850 by Karl Marx. He used it to refer to the very lowest section of the proletariat, consisting not of workers but of the outcasts of society, such as tramps, beggars, and thieves, who are characteristically poor, ill-dressed, ill-educated, etc. Etymologically it means 'proletariat dressed in rags' (German *lumpen* means 'ragged clothes'). It came into English in the 1920s, and has since broadened semantically from its original Marxian meaning, often being used as a derogatory term for the intellectually inert lower classes with no interest in improving their lot. And *lumpen* itself has become an English adjective meaning 'stupid, boorish, characteristic of the *lumpenproletariat*'.

lusus naturae

Latin *lusus naturae* means literally 'game of nature'. In the ancient world it was thought that genetic variations or mutations in new generations of plants and animals were caused by the playfulness of nature, and so this frolicsome metaphor came to be applied to what is now recognized as the result of a chance change in chromosomes or genes. English adopted the term in the 17th century, and from the start it was often used in translated form as *sport of nature*. The 19th century shortened this to *sport*. *Lusus naturae* is now used usually in non-technical contexts, for a 'freak' or 'monster'. The Latin noun *lūsus* is a derivative of the verb *lūdere* 'play', whose first-person present form *lūdo* 'I play' gave English the name of a type of board game.

lycée

In France, a *lycée* is a state secondary school, preparing students for university entry. But in a wider international context, which has since the mid-19th century found it a place in English, the word denotes a French secondary school in a foreign country, where lessons are given in French to expatriates or to international students. The French word comes via Latin *Lycēum* from Greek *Lúkeion*, which denoted the garden in Athens where Aristotle taught (*Lúkeios* was an epithet of Apollo, to whom a nearby temple was dedicated). English has also sporadically used the French derivative *lycéen* 'pupil at a lycée': 'a background of marching lycéens and charging police, not to speak of protesting schoolmasters' (*The Guardian*, 26 March 1974).

M

macho

Macho first entered English, from Mexican Spanish, as long ago as the 1920s: 'Here was I in their midst, a Macho Yankee Gringo, yet treated with consideration' (*The Nation*, 11 March 1928). At that time it retained the positive connotations of its Spanish original (which comes ultimately from Latin *masculus* 'male'): 'masculinity, virility'. It was a word of praise. It is not until the 1960s, when the rise of the Women's Movement heralded the eclipse of ostentatious manliness as socially acceptable behaviour, that we begin to see a reversal of its role into a term of abuse, denoting exaggerated and aggressive maleness. Its use proliferated in American English, and since the 1970s it has become increasingly common in British English too. The derived noun *machismo* also comes from Mexican Spanish, and indeed until recently was regarded as an unwelcome intruder by the Spanish Royal Academy, guardian of the language in Spain itself. The pronunciation closest to the Spanish original is not /mə'ʃɪzmoʊ/ or /mə'kɪzmoʊ/ but /mə'tʃɪzmoʊ/.

machzor, plural machzorim

A *machzor*, or *mahzor*, is a Jewish prayer book containing the prayers and readings specified for particular days of the Jewish year, particularly holidays and festivals. The term is an application of Hebrew *mahzor* 'cycle', and its use in English goes back to the mid-19th century.

maestro

English originally adopted *maestro* from Italian, towards the end of the 18th century, as a purely musical term, denoting an 'eminent and respected musician'. It is not until as recently as the 1930s that we begin to find records of its wider, more general use for 'someone of masterly expertise in any activity' – as in 'Stanley Matthews, the soccer maestro'. It still retains its musical connotations, of course. It is used by professional musicians as a title and term of address for distinguished conductors and soloists ('Maestro Giulini') – and not just for Italian ones

('Maestro Bernstein'). The word itself is the Italian descendant of Latin *magister* 'master', which also produced English *master* (not to mention *magisterial* and *magistrate*).

Another English borrowing involving Italian *maestro* is *maestro di capella*, literally 'master of the chapel', which denotes a 'musical director' or 'conductor'. It too is an 18th-century acquisition. English has also taken over its German equivalent, *kapellmeister*.

magnum opus, plural magna opera
Magnum opus, in Latin literally 'great work', has been used in English since at least the early 18th century. It generally denotes a particular person's artistic masterpiece, especially a literary work: 'My *magnum opus*, the "Life of Dr Johnson" ... is to be published on Monday 16th May' (James Boswell, letter to the Rev W. Temple, 1791).

Magnum is the neuter form of Latin *magnus* 'big, great'. Its use in English for a double-size wine bottle dates back to the late 18th century. In the USA it is registered as a trademark for a type of large-calibre pistol.

maharishi
Maharishi is a term of Sanskrit origin for a Hindu sage or spiritual leader, a guru. It is a compound word, formed from the adjective *māha* 'great' (a relative of Latin *magnus* 'big' and English *much*) and *rishi* 'sage'. Sporadic references to it occur in English from as long ago as the late 18th century, but it was not until the 1960s, when Eastern mysticism became suddenly trendy, that it achieved wide currency – notably as the title of the Maharishi Mahesh Yogi, founder of the Spiritual Regeneration Movement. Other Sanskrit or Hindi words incorporating *māha* to have found their way into English include *maharaja* 'great king', *mahatma* 'great soul', *Mahayana* 'great vehicle', the name of a branch of Buddhism, and also *mahout* 'elephant-driver', which was originally an honorific title, signifying literally 'great in measure'.

maillot
French *maillot* has a range of related meanings, of which the original one appears to have been 'swaddling clothes' (it is a derivative of *maille* 'band of cloth'). The notion of 'tight clothing' led in the 19th century to its application to 'tights', as worn on the stage, by gymnasts, etc, and English acquired the word in

this sense towards the end of the century. It is also used for a singlet or similar top and for a one-piece bathing costume, and English took these senses over in the 20th century.

maître d'hôtel

French *maître d'hôtel* originally meant literally 'master of the household' (in former times *hôtel* could be used for a 'large private residence'), and denoted the 'chief servant', the 'butler' or 'steward'. That was the application of the word when English first took it over as long ago as the 16th century. It was not until the late 19th century that the more familiar modern meanings began to emerge: first, a 'hotel manager', and latterly a 'manager of a hotel dining room' or a 'head waiter'. In American usage it is often abbreviated to *maître d'*. *Maître d'hôtel* butter is butter into which lemon juice and parsley have been incorporated.

malade imaginaire

Molière's play *Le Malade imaginaire* (1673) tells the story of Argan, a credulous hypochondriac who puts himself in the hands of doctors Purgon and Diafoirus. So besotted is he with the undeserved mystique of the medical profession that he even tries to marry off his daughter to the son of Diafoirus, so as to have a doctor in the family. English began to take up the phrase *malade imaginaire* in the early 19th century, and has used it sporadically ever since for a 'hypochondriac': Bernard Shaw, for instance, in the preface to his *Doctor's Dilemma* (1911), wrote of doctors who 'nurse the delusions of the *malade imaginaire*'.

mal de mer

French *mal de mer* is the equivalent of English 'seasickness', and it has made occasional guest appearances in English since the late 18th century. It is generally used as a facetious euphemism, as if making light of the discomfort and embarrassment that accompany the nausea of seasickness.

malgré lui

The French preposition *malgré* means 'in spite of' (it originated as a compound noun formed from *mal* 'bad' and *gré* 'pleasure', and meaning 'ill will'). English originally took it over in the 13th century in the Old French form *maugre*. This had largely died out by the middle of the 17th century, but at around the same time the modern form *malgré* began to put in an appearance as a foreignism. Its use in English as a freestanding preposition remains rare, but it has established a small niche for itself in the language in combination with French personal pronouns, conveying the notion of 'in spite of oneself, involuntarily'. *Malgré lui* 'in spite of himself' is probably the commonest ('He stands revealed as a moralist *malgré lui*', *Mind*, XLI, 1932), but *malgré moi*, *malgré elle*, *malgré eux*, and others have also been recorded.

mañana

In Spanish, *mañana* means, innocently enough, simply 'tomorrow'. It goes back to the Vulgar Latin expression *crās māneāna – *crās* from Latin *crās* 'tomorrow', source of English *procrastinate*, and *māneāna* 'early' from Latin *māne* 'in the morning'. But in English, the word has come to be a codeword signifying the British view of Spain as an overly easy-going country whose motto is 'Do not do today what you can put off till tomorrow'. The reputation dates back at least to the early 19th century: 'Nowhere will the stranger hear more frequently [than in Andalusia] those talismanic words which mark national character . . . the Manaña [sic]' (R. Ford, *Hand-book for Travellers in Spain*, 1845). Mexico is sometimes known as the 'Land of Mañana'.

manège

The verb *manage* was originally used mainly of the training of horses; only gradually did its now more familiar general meaning come to the fore. English got it from Italian *maneggiare*, a derivative of which provided French with the noun *manège*. English borrowed this in the mid-17th century in the sense of 'riding school', and after about 100 years the now commoner meaning 'advanced training of horses and riders' joined it.

manqué

Manqué is the past participle of the French verb *manquer* 'be missing or lacking, fail'. Adjectivally, it is used to suggest that someone has missed the opportunity of being something, that he or she could, with better luck or greater effort, have fulfilled a different destiny. Thus, to say 'C'est un peintre manqué' is to suggest that someone ought to have been a painter, since the person has the necessary skill – with perhaps the underlying feeling that there is frustration at not having made the most of this potential. English borrowed the word in the late 18th century, and retains its French adjectival position, after the noun: 'a clever, unhappy young writer *manqué*' (*The Listener*, 12 July 1962). The slang adjective *manky* 'dirty' (first recorded in the late 1950s) is related, although it is not quite clear how: one theory treats it as an alteration of the old Scottish word *mank* 'maimed, defective', influenced by *manqué*; but an alternative possibility is that it comes from Polari (an English descendant of the old Mediterranean lingua franca which still survives in a few items of male homosexual theatrical slang), which in turn got it from Italian *mancare* 'be lacking'. Either way it goes back ultimately to Latin *mancus* 'maimed', which is also the ancestor of French *manquer*.

Another derivative of the French verb *manquer* to have been acquired by English is the noun *manque*, a roulette term denoting the set of numbers between 1 and 18. It comes from the 'failure' of the ball to fall into any of the higher-numbered slots on the wheel (the numbers 19 to 36 are termed *passe*).

maquereau

French *maquereau* means 'pimp' (it is presumably the same word as *maquereau* 'mackerel', although a possible alternative source is Dutch *makelaar* 'broker'). English originally acquired it in its Old French form *maquerel* (later anglicized to *mackerel*) in the 15th century, but by the end of the 18th century it was becoming obsolete. Then at the end of the 19th century the word began to reappear in English, in its modern French guise *maquereau*. Its main use seems to be in descriptions of Continental low life.

maquillage

Maquillage is the French word for make-up or its application (it is a derivative of the verb *maquiller* 'apply make-up', which goes back to Old French *masquiller* 'stain'). English began to take it up towards the end of the 19th century.

mare clausum

In international law, a *mare clausum* is a sea that is under the jurisdiction of one particular nation, and closed to all others. Its antonym, a *mare liberum*, is a sea that is not controlled by any one nation, and is therefore open to all. The two Latin terms mean literally 'closed sea' and 'free sea', and were introduced into English in the mid-17th century, at the time of the first Dutch War. This arose out of commercial rivalry between

Britain and the Netherlands, both of whom sought to impose restrictions in favour of their trading routes and ports.

mariage blanc

In French literally a 'white marriage', a *mariage blanc* is a marriage that has never been consummated by sexual intercourse. The term seems to be a relatively recent introduction into English, dating, as far as is known, from no earlier than the 1920s; but its ability to clothe the unmentionable in delicate obscurity soon commended it: ' "The autopsy revealed that the girl was a virgin." "*Un mariage blanc?* Good Lord!" ' (Gladys Mitchell, *Spotted Hemlock*, 1958).

Other French *mariage* expressions adopted into English at one time or another include *mariage de convenance* (commoner in the translated form *marriage of convenience*), *mariage de la main gauche* 'morganatic marriage' (literally 'marriage of the left hand'), and *mariage d'inclination* 'marriage for love'.

mari complaisant

French *mari complaisant*, literally 'obliging husband', denotes a husband who (more or less) willingly acquiesces in or turns a blind eye to his wife's extra-marital activities. English began to find a use for it towards the end of the 19th century, particularly in the context of wealthy husbands of advanced years tolerating their young wives' affairs. It was conveniently to hand in the 1930s for bandying about when referring to the husband of Wallace Simpson during her pursuit of the Prince of Wales: Mrs Belloc Lowndes noted in her diary on 20 January 1937 that 'the unfortunate Mr Simpson was . . . regarded as *un mari complaisant*'.

marivaudage

Pierre Marivaux (1688–1763) was a playwright, a composer of sentimental comedies which mainly centre on the obstacles that prevent two lovers from getting together. His best-known works include *Le jeu de l'amour et du hasard* and *Les fausses confidences*. The most characteristic feature of his plays is their exhaustive analysis of sentiment, and even at the time this did not always go down well. There were those who found it prolix and affected, and they coined the term *marivaudage* as a derogatory name for it. By the 1760s this was being used in English, and since then it has broadened out to designate any over-refined analysis of sentiment or the affected language in which it is couched.

matelot

French *matelot* 'sailor' is descended from Old French *matenot* 'comrade', which itself was borrowed from Old Norse *motunautr*, literally 'meal-companion'. English acquired it as a piece of nautical slang at the beginning of the 20th century, and it remains in the language as a bright and breezy synonym for *sailor* (usually a naval rather than a merchant seaman). To begin with, its spelling was often anglicized to *matlo* or *matlow*, but these orthographic variants seem now largely to have died out. *Matelot* is also sometimes applied in English to a particular shade of deep blue. (Words for 'sailor' in other languages that come ultimately from the plural of French *matelot* include German *matrose*, Dutch *matroos*, and Swedish and Russian *matros*.)

mauvais foi

French *mauvais foi* means 'bad faith', but it was not in the conventional sense of *bad faith* ('intention to deceive') that English took it over. It was used by the existential philosopher Jean-Paul Sartre (1905–80) to denote a self-deceiving abdication of moral responsibility, as when someone tries to pretend that forces outside their control made them follow a particular course of action that in reality was embarked on of their own free will. English generally employs the translated version, *bad faith*, but *mauvais foi* is also used.

mauvais quart d'heure

A *mauvais quart d'heure* is a moment or brief period of intense embarrassment or discomfiture, of the sort which makes one go all hot and sweaty when one looks back on it later. In French the expression means literally 'bad quarter of an hour', but its metaphorical time-span is elastic: in P. C. Wren's *Beau Geste* (1924) 'at the end of ten minutes, a very *mauvais quart d'heure*, I beckoned the Sergeant-Major', whereas in 1965 *The Economist* was reporting that 'John Kennedy had his *mauvais quart d'heure* between April and June, 1961'. The first record of the term in English dates from 1864.

mauvais sujet

French *mauvais sujet* (literally 'bad subject') denotes a 'bad lot, someone who is no good'. As a piece of slang it is of long standing in the language, and its acquisition by English dates from as far

back as the end of the 18th century. It has never gained wide
currency, but sporadic examples continue to turn up: 'The
mauvais sujet – always women are attracted to him' (Agatha
Christie, *Curtain: Poirot's Last Case*, 1975).

maven

A *maven* or *mavin* (both rhyming with *raven*) is someone with
a great depth of expertise in a subject – a connoisseur. The word
is a Yiddish contribution to English, first appearing in New
York in the 1960s, and it has yet to make much impact outside
the USA. It comes ultimately from Hebrew *mevin* 'understanding'. Leo Rosten, in his *Joys of Yiddish* (1968), gives its
flavour: '*Mavin* was recently given considerable publicity in a
series of newspaper advertisements for herring tidbits. "The
Herring *Mavin* Strikes Again!" proclaimed the caption. The
picture showed an empty jar. A real advertising *mavin* must have
thought that up.'

mazel tov

Mazel tov is a Hebrew exclamation of good wishes or con-
gratulation – for example, on an impending marriage, or the
birth of a child. It has been used by Jewish speakers of English
since at least the mid-19th century, especially in the USA. It
goes back ultimately to ancient Hebrew *mazzālōth*, a plural noun
meaning 'constellations'.

mea culpa

Mea culpa, doubling in English as an admission of culpability
and an expression of repentance, originated as part of the Con-
fiteor, a Latin prayer of confession and penitence used in the
Roman Catholic Mass. In the ablative case, it means literally
'through my fault'. Sporadic examples of its use in English date
back to Chaucer's time, usually in religious contexts, but it is
only over the past 100 years or so that it has become more
widely used in the general language. Keener repentance still is
expressed by *mea maxima culpa* 'through my very great fault'.

médaillon

French *médaillon*, literally 'medallion', is used as a culinary term
to denote a piece of meat, poultry, or fish cut into a circular
shape of varying thickness. Particularly common examples are
médaillons of veal and of venison. *Médaillon* shapes can also be

made of mixed chopped vegetables and other ingredients; these are known as *médaillons composés*. The term came into English around the turn of the 20th century, and now is often substituted by the vernacular *medallion*.

memento mori

Memento mori means in Latin literally 'remember that you must die' (*memento* is the imperative form of Latin *meminisse* 'remember', and the verb *mori* means 'die'). It denotes an object, such as a skull, or some trinket or locket decorated with symbols of death, that reminds people of their mortality. In sterner days, when life was shorter, such devices were felt to serve a salutary moral purpose, preventing people from getting too carried away by transitory happiness. The first known reference to them in English comes in Shakespeare's 1 *Henry IV*: Falstaff, replying to Bardolph's assertion that his face, with its refulgent nose, does him no harm, says 'No, I'll be sworn; I make as good use of it as many a man doth of a Death's head, or a *memento mori*: I never see thy face but I think upon hell-fire and Dives that lived in purple: for there he is in his robes, burning, burning'.

The coinage *memento vivere*, literally 'remember to live', goes back to the 1920s. It denotes something that reminds one, in blacker moments, that life is not so bad after all.

ménage à trois

The term *ménage à trois* denotes an accommodation arrangement or sexual relationship in which a couple, typically a husband and wife, live together under the same roof with the lover of one of them. It was adopted from French (where it means literally 'household of three') towards the end of the 19th century, an era when the concept of 'free love' was still intellectually fashionable – indeed the first record of it in English comes in the writings of the free-thinking Bernard Shaw – but such arrangements go back, of course, far further than that. One of the best-known historical *ménages à trois* was that of Nelson with his lover Lady Hamilton and her husband (who turned a blind eye to Nelson).

mene, mene, tekel, upharsin

Mene, mene, tekel, upharsin are the words that appeared on the wall during Belshazzar's Feast, written by the 'fingers of a man's hand'. Belshazzar asked his wise men to interpret them, but they could not, so on the advice of his wife he asked Daniel, chief wise man of his father Nebuchadnezzar. Daniel told him that they meant: 'God hath numbered thy kingdom, and finished it; thou art weighed in the balance and found wanting; thy kingdom is divided' (the words are actually Aramaic, and mean literally 'numbered, numbered, weighed, divided'). The prophecy of Belshazzar's downfall was fulfilled that very night. The phrase is occasionally used allusively in English to suggest impending doom.

mensch

German *mensch* means 'person' (etymologically it is a noun use of an adjective based on Germanic **man*- 'human being'), but as adopted into Yiddish, where it is generally spelled *mensh*, it is used specifically to refer to a person who has integrity, behaves honourably, would not play a mean trick on someone (as in 'He's a real *mensch*'). It began to infiltrate English from Yiddish after World War 2, spelled either *mensch* or *mensh*, or even occasionally *mench*.

mens rea

Mens rea is a legal term which denotes 'criminal intent', a state of mind amounting to a determined purpose to commit an illegal act, which must in theory be demonstrated in court if the perpetrator of the act is to be found guilty (although in practice there are some minor offences that are crimes of absolute liability, where *mens rea* does not have to be proved, and it usually becomes a point of issue only for serious offences, such as murder). The Latin phrase literally means 'guilty mind'. The adjective *reus* 'guilty' was to begin with a noun, derived from *res* 'thing', in the sense 'legal action'. It originally meant simply 'person involved in a legal action', and only later narrowed down first to 'person accused, defendant' and then to 'guilty person, criminal'.

mens sana in corpore sano

It was the Roman author Juvenal who first enunciated the principle *mens sana in corpore sano*, in his *Satires*: *Orandum est ut sit mens sana in corpore sano. Fortem posce animum mortis terrore carentem, qui spatium vitae extremum inter munera ponet naturae* 'Your prayer must be that you may have a sound mind in a sound body. Pray for a bold spirit, free from all dread of death; that reckons the closing scene of life among nature's kindly boons'. It began to appear in English texts in the early 17th century, but it was in the 19th century that it really came into its own as a guiding maxim of the English educational system, and particularly the public schools, with their emphasis on a rigorous physical regimen (cold baths, plenty of sport, etc) underpinning the development of the intellect.

meum et tuum

Meum et tuum (literally in Latin 'mine and yours') encapsulates a principle in the law of property: 'what's mine belongs to me and what's yours belongs to you, and each party should respect the right of the other to retain and enjoy his property'. It has been used in English (with minor variations such as *meum and tuum, meum or tuum*, and *meum, tuum*) since the 16th century.

midinette

A *midinette* is a young Parisian girl who works in a humble capacity in a clothes shop or hat shop, and who has come to have an almost mythic status as the poor but beautiful shopgirl who is the sexual prey of men about town but may hope one day to be swept up and married by a handsome duke. The French word *midinette* began to appear in English at the beginning of the 20th century. It is thought that it may be a compound formed from *midi* 'midday' and *dinette* 'light meal' – a reference to the fact that shopgirls only had time for a snack at lunchtime.

miles gloriosus, plural milites gloriosi

Miles gloriosus is the title of a play by the Roman dramatist Plautus which tells the story of a boastful, swaggering soldier called Pyrgopolynices (Latin *miles gloriosus* means 'boastful soldier'). The braggart soldier was a stock character in ancient Greek comedy, which Plautus did much to introduce into Roman drama, and he reappears in Shakespeare's Falstaff and Pistol. Use of the expression *miles gloriosus* in English, mainly as a literary critical term, dates from the early 20th century.

minyan, plural minyanim

Hebrew *minyān* means literally 'number, count', but it is in the very specialized sense of 'minimum number of people who according to Jewish law must be present in order to hold a religious service' that it was introduced into English in the mid-18th century. The relevant number is ten males aged 13 or over.

mir

Russian *mir*, literally 'world' and 'peace', was the term applied to a sort of village commune in pre-revolutionary Russia: all the members of the *mir* community held the land jointly, and it was cultivated by individual families. The term began to appear in English texts in the late 19th century. In the sense of 'peace' it was also the name given to a series of Soviet space stations launched from 1986.

mirabile dictu

Latin *mirabile dictu* means literally 'wonderful to say'. *Mirabile* is the neuter form of *mirabilis* 'wonderful', and *dictu* is the supine of *dīcere* 'say' (the supine is a form of noun derived from a verb). Usually translated as 'wonderful to relate, amazing to relate', it is used as a parenthetical expression of (often ironic) surprise at something unusual or strange: 'The Marshal was anxious to save Otto Abbetz, who, *mirabile dictu*, was considered in certain Vichy circles as a "friend of France"' (L. Marchal, *Vichy*, 1943). Its use in English, which dates from the early 19th century, may have been inspired by this passage from Virgil's *Georgics*: *quin et caudicibus sectis (mirabile dictu) truditur e sicco radix oleagina ligno* 'what's more – and this is a marvel – if you take a saw to the trunk of an olive, a root will come gushing out from the dry wood' (in C. Day Lewis's 1940 translation). A similar Latin construction that is also occasionally used in English is *mirabile visu* 'wonderful to behold'.

mise-en-scène

French *mise-en-scène* means literally 'placement on stage'. It refers both to the staging of a play (its production) and more specifically to a stage setting (the way the props, scenery, etc are arranged on stage). English took it over in the early 19th century, apparently in both these senses, but the 'staging, production' sense seems gradually to have died out. To replace it, however, the word has evolved a vigorous metaphorical application to the 'physical or psychological context in which an event takes place', the 'setting of an action' (as in 'The shadowy back street was an appropriate *mise-en-scène* for their squalid transaction'). This dates from the latter part of the 19th century.

mittelschmerz

Mittelschmerz is a gynaecological term originating in German. Literally 'middle-pain', it denotes pain in the lower abdomen experienced by some women about midway through the menstrual cycle, between periods, which may be associated with the release of eggs by the ovaries. Its use in English dates from the end of the 19th century.

modus operandi

The term *modus operandi* has probably gained its widest modern currency from its use by the police, as portrayed on film and television, where it denotes the characteristic methods used by a particular criminal. Does a certain burglar, for instance, always glue paper over a window pane before breaking it to gain entry? But in fact this is a comparatively recent usage. For a long time following its introduction into English in the 17th century it was used for the way in which a thing, such as a force or cause, operates, and it is only in the past 100 years that it has been applied to human doings. In Latin it means literally 'mode of working' (*operandi* being the genitive form of the gerund of *operari* 'work'). In police usage it is often abbreviated to *m.o.*

modus vivendi

Latin *modus vivendi* means literally 'mode of living' (*vivendi* is the genitive form of the gerund of *vivere* 'live'). Its main use in English, however, is far more specific: it denotes a temporary accommodation reached between two parties in disagreement, which enables them to 'live' together – to get on with each other, work together, etc – until the dispute is finally resolved. This usage seems already to have become fairly common by the middle of the 19th century: '"Modus Vivendi" – This formula is in daily use to express a practical compromise' (*Notes and Queries*, 1879).

monstre sacré

Jean Cocteau's 1940 play *Les monstres sacrés* documents the eccentricities of the theatrical world. By the 1950s the term *monstre sacré* (in French literally 'sacred monster') was appearing in English. It denotes someone – generally a show-business figure – who has a high but somewhat grotesque or eccentric public profile, and who grips the public imagination. A typical example might be Edith Piaf.

mont de piété

French *mont de piété* (literally 'mount of piety') denotes a public pawnshop, set up by the state to enable poor people to obtain money by pledging goods. It was probably a loan-translation from Italian *monte di pietà*, where *monte* 'mount, hill, heap' stands metaphorically for a 'fund' or 'bank'. Such institutions were first set up in Umbria in the 15th century, and the Italian term itself reached English in the early 17th century. It apparently survived into the 19th century, either in original form or translated as *mount of piety*. But it seems eventually to have died out, and *mont de piété* represents a fresh mid-19th-century borrowing from French. It is now disused in French.

morceau, plural morceaux

English originally acquired French *morceau* (or rather its Old French ancestor *morsel*) in the 13th century, and it is now thoroughly naturalized as *morsel*. It goes back ultimately to Latin *morsus*, the past participle of *mordere* 'bite', and so etymologically means 'piece bitten off'. The modern French form was reborrowed in the mid-18th century. It is occasionally used as a general term for a 'piece' or 'fragment', but its main application is to a 'short (and relatively trivial) piece of music' or a 'literary fragment'. In addition it is used in *morceau de salon* 'salon piece', a somewhat dismissive term for a short piece of light classical music.

morgue

French *morgue*, a word of unknown origin, means 'haughtiness, arrogance', and English borrowed it in that sense in the late 16th century. Before the end of the 19th century it had virtually died out, but by then it had been joined by *morgue* 'mortuary'. It is assumed that they are one and the same word, and that the link between the two is an intermediate French sense, now obsolete, 'room in a prison where new prisoners were examined (by disdainful warders, presumably)'. The original mortuary-style *morgue* was an establishment in Paris where unidentified corpses were laid out for visitors in search of missing relatives and friends.

mot

A *mot* is a 'witty saying'. In French, of course, it also means
more broadly 'word', but it is this specialized sense that English
has taken over. An isolated example is recorded from the 17th
century ('That Mot of the Athenians to Pompey the Great,
Thou art so much a God, as thou acknowledgest thy selfe to
be a man, was no ill saying', Richard Brathwait, *The English
Gentlewoman*, 1631), but it does not seem to have come into
general use until the 19th century ('Of the three, for sheer wit
in making *mots* and in comments, *obiter dicta*, always sharp as a
needle and possibly Rabelaisian, Harry Higgins was without
rival', E. F. Benson, *As We Were*, 1930). French *mot* itself goes
back ultimately to Latin *muttīre* 'mutter', which also produced
English *motto* (via Italian) and is distantly related to English
mutter. *Motet* comes from a diminutive form of French *mot*. (See
also **bon mot**.)

mot juste

The *mot juste* is in French literally the 'exact word' – that is, the
most precisely appropriate word or expression to characterize a
particular situation, person, etc. English took the term over
around the turn of the 20th century, and often uses it with its
original French definite article: 'My head is a squeezed rag, so
don't expect le mot juste in this letter' (Ezra Pound, 1915).

moue

French *moue* means 'pout'. English originally acquired it in the
14th century and anglicized it to *mow*, but gradually it dispersed
via dialectal speech into oblivion (in Scotland it came to mean
'joke', and *no mows* was used for 'no joke, no laughing matter').
English reacquired the modern French form in the mid-19th
century, and uses it to suggest a more Frenchly provocative
grimace than a mere English *pout*. It has also come to be
employed as a verb, meaning 'make a *moue*'.

mouton enragé

French *mouton enragé*, literally 'angry sheep', is used metaphorically for someone who is normally calm or passive but
is goaded into rage or violence by extreme provocation. The
expression has been sporadically recorded in English since the
1930s, and may even lie behind Denis Healey's memorable

likening of being criticized by Sir Geoffrey Howe to being savaged by a dead sheep.

mouvementé

French *mouvementé* means 'animated, lively, eventful, full of busy incident' (it is an adjectival use of the past participle of *mouvementer* 'enliven, animate'). Its use in English dates back to the early years of the 20th century.

multum in parvo

Latin *multum in parvo* means literally 'much in little' (*multum* 'much' and *parvo*, the ablative singular form of *parvus* 'small'). Though now little used, the phrase was for many centuries often resorted to by the bookish to denote compendiousness, the packing of much matter into a small space. It was particularly popular with authors in search of a title for their work that would suggest a comprehensiveness not promised by the actual size of the volume: Samuel Maunder, for instance, called a small dictionary of his *The Little Lexicon; or Multum in Parvo of the English Language* (1825). English has also occasionally used the synonymous *magnum in parvo*.

musique concrète

Musique concrète is electronic music made by combining pre-recorded sounds, both natural (eg birdsong or pneumatic drills) and produced by musical instruments. The term was coined by Pierre Schaeffer in Paris in the early 1950s, and first promulgated in his *À la recherche d'une musique concrète* (1952). English has adopted it in its original form, translated as *concrete music*, and in the halfway-house form *musique concrete*.

mutatis mutandis

Mutatis mutandis means 'with the necessary changes made'. It is usually used in the context of making allowances for differences in small, inessential details when comparing cases that are substantially the same: 'What is said of the army here is to be taken also to apply, *mutatis mutandis*, to the air force and the navy' (Samuel Finer, *The Man on Horseback*, 1962). The expression is an ablative absolute construction containing two derivatives of the Latin verb *mūtāre* 'change': *mutatis*, the ablative plural of the past participle, and *mutandis*, the ablative plural of the gerundive, expressing necessity – thus, 'things changed that have to be changed'. Its use in English goes back as far as the late 15th century. It is sometimes abbreviated to *m.m.*

N

natura naturans

Natura naturans is a medieval Latin philosophical term denoting the creative force which produced our world, often equated with God. Its literal meaning is 'nature naturing', but Latin *natura* here still carries the force of its origins as a derivative of the verb *nasci* 'be born, come into being'. *Naturans* is a medieval Latin present participial form derived from *natura*. The term is particularly associated with the philosophy of Spinoza (1632–77). Originally in English it was used in the translated form *nature naturing* (records of this date back to the early 16th century), but the original Latin came into wider use in the 19th century.

nebbich

A *nebbich* is a hapless, useless individual, a nobody, a no-hoper. Still largely restricted to Jewish usage, in America and Britain, it is a Yiddish contribution to English, dating from the end of the 19th century. In Yiddish (where it is generally spelled *nebach* or *nebech*) it is if anything an exclamatory noun, used to express dismay and commiseration over one of God's less fortunate creatures (as English might use *poor thing!*). Early use in English mirrors this, but it has gradually conformed to a more standard noun role, and it is also used adjectivally, in the sense 'hapless, ineffectual'. Yiddish originally acquired it from a Slavic source, and it is related to Polish *nieboze* 'poor thing'.

nécessaire

English originally borrowed French *nécessaire* 'necessary' as an adjective in the 14th century, but it did not catch on (English *necessary* comes direct from Latin *necessarius*), and it was not for another 400 years that it returned. This time, however, it was as a noun, denoting a small receptacle into which a lady puts articles thought likely to come in useful (eg on a journey), such as make-up, needle and thread, a small pair of scissors, even items of jewellery. The word now has an irretrievably dated air, but the *nécessaire* was a vital piece of equipment for

19th-century ladies. The finest examples were richly orna-
mented in gold, enamel, semi-precious stones, etc.

née

Née is prefixed to a married woman's maiden name, when it is
given as an additional piece of information after her married
name – thus, 'Margaret Thatcher, *née* Roberts'. It is the feminine form of the past participle of the French verb *naître* 'be
born', and means literally simply 'born' (indeed, English *born*
is often used in its place). It has been used in English since at
least the mid-18th century, and is now well enough established
occasionally to go without its accent – *nee*. The masculine
form, *né*, is far less common in English, but it is occasionally
encountered before the real name of a man who has adopted a
stage-name, pen-name, etc: 'Then there dawned that most
fateful day when Destiny in the disguise of the admirable Mr
Theodore Watts-Dunton (*né* Watts) came knocking at the door
of Swinburne's rooms' (E. F. Benson, *As We Were*, 1930).

negligee

Negligee appears in the guise of a French word, but in fact it
was an English coinage, of the mid-18th century. Pronounced
to rhyme with *squeegee*, it denoted a long loose outer garment
worn on informal occasions by both men and women. Its basis
is nevertheless firmly French: it was formed from the past participle of the French verb *négliger* 'neglect, treat carelessly', and
so etymologically signifies 'careless dress'. That past participle
itself, in the form *négligé*, began to put in an appearance as a
noun in English in the early 19th century, referring to (in the
words of the *Oxford English Dictionary*) 'unceremonious attire as
worn by women when not in complete toilette'. The original
application of English *negligee* had died out by the end of the
18th century; but it continued in the language, being used for
a sort of necklace made with irregular beads and (in American
English) for a shroud; and in the 1920s the sense we are familiar
with today emerged – 'woman's light flimsy dressing gown
trimmed with frills and lace'. Its 'French' feel is enhanced by a
French-style pronunciation, a tendency to spell it *négligée*, and
the association of France with such frivolously sexy garments.

négociant

Négociant is a French word that has become increasingly familiar in English over the past few decades as a result of the wider dissemination of knowledge about wine. In French it means literally 'merchant, trader' (and indeed it was originally borrowed into English in the 17th century, as *negotiant*, in the broad sense 'negotiator', and later 'merchant'). But it is often used as shorthand for *négociant en vins* 'wine merchant', and it is this application that English has now adopted. A négociant does not only act as a merchant, buying wine from the growers and selling it on to the retailers; most of them hold large stocks of maturing wines, which they bring up and blend in such a way as to give them a distinctive house style.

ne plus ultra

Supposedly this phrase was inscribed in ancient times on the Pillars of Hercules, two mountains (Gibraltar and Abyla) on either side of the Straits of Gibraltar. It literally means in Latin 'not more beyond', its underlying message being a warning to sailors in the Mediterranean not to venture out beyond their home sea into the uncharted waters of the Atlantic. It is only a short step from that to the more general 'command to go no further', which is how the expression was once used in English ('Her fancy of no limit dreams, No ne plus ultra bounds her schemes', Hannah More, *The bas bleu*, 1786). That meaning has now died out, however. It was another metaphorical extension, 'utmost point', and particularly 'point of greatest achievement', that proved to have the staying power. And even this now has the stuffily dated air of Victorian advertising hype ('Bloggs's knife powder, the ne plus ultra of cutlery cleaners'). The synonymous Latin expressions *nec plus ultra* and *non plus ultra* are used in French, and the latter once enjoyed some currency in English ('Seckendorf ... witnesses with unfeigned admiration the non plus ultra of manoeuvring', Thomas Carlyle, *History of Frederick the Great*, 1858).

netsuke

Netsuke (the word can be plural as well as singular) are small Japanese toggles or buttons, whose original use was to fasten a container, such as a purse, tobacco pouch, or medicine box, to the sash of a kimono. They are made usually of wood or ivory, and are carved into elaborate shapes. They were mainly produced during the Edo period, between 1601 and 1867, and it was around the end of this time that English took the word *netsuke* over from Japanese. Netsuke are now widely collected, as miniature sculptures in their own right (cognoscenti are fond of getting one-up on laymen by approximating to a two-syllable Japanese pronunciation of their name, /'netski:/; but the three-syllable form is far more usual in English). They should not, incidentally, be confused with *okimonos*, which are also small Japanese carvings, but are purpose-made decorative objects, without any original practical application.

nihil obstat

For a book to receive the official sanction of the Roman Catholic Church, it must have been subjected to an authoritative review to ensure that it contains nothing doctrinally or morally unsound. When this scrutiny has been satisfied, a declaration of *nihil obstat* is made. This means literally in Latin 'nothing stands in the way, nothing hinders' – that is to say, there is nothing objectionable in the book that need hinder its publication. The next step is for a bishop to grant an *imprimatur* (Latin for 'let it be printed'), giving permission for the book to be printed. *Nihil obstat* is first recorded in an English text towards the end of the 19th century, and it was not long before it was being put to metaphorical use, in the general sense 'permission to proceed, approval'.

nil desperandum

Nil desperandum has been used in English since at least the 17th century as an encouragement to pessimists or to those in an apparently hopeless situation, urging them not to lose heart (Robert Burton, for instance, in his *Anatomy of Melancholy* 1628, says '*Nihil desperandum*, there's hope enough yet'). The expression comes from one of the odes of Horace, the Roman poet and satirist of the Augustan period, and its full context is *Nil desperandum Teucro duce et auspice Teucro; certus enim promisit Apollo ambiguam tellure nova Salamina futuram* 'Nothing (is) to be despaired of with Teucer as your leader and Teucer to protect you; for Apollo assuredly promised that there would be an ambiguous Salamis in a new land'. *Nil* 'nothing' is the subject of the first sentence, with *desperandum* 'to be despaired of' (the neuter gerundive form of *desperare* 'despair') qualifying it, and the verb *est* 'is' understood. The 'Teucer' referred to was a brother of Ajax and son of Telemon, king of Salamis in Greece. When he returned from the Trojan War he went off to found a new city in Cyprus, which he also called Salamis – hence the reference to the 'ambiguous Salamis'.

nisi

Latin *nisi* means 'unless' (it originated as a compound conjunction, formed from the negative particle *ni* and *si* 'if'). It has two uses in English, both of them legal. Adjectivally, it denotes a legal instrument that comes into effect on a stipulated date unless cause is shown why it should not do so. It occurs in collocations like *order nisi* and *rule nisi*, but by far its commonest use is in the term *decree nisi*, denoting a provisional judgment made in divorce proceedings. Its second role is in the term *nisi prius*. This means literally 'unless previously', which had its origin in a provision of the Statute of Westminster 1285 stipulating that all cases were to be brought for trial before the court in Westminster Hall 'unless previously' they had been tried at the assizes in the county in which they originated. It is now a dead letter in English law, but the term is still used in the USA for a civil court in which cases are tried by one judge and a jury.

noblesse oblige

The expression *noblesse oblige* (in French literally 'nobility obliges') is first recorded in English in 1837, in a letter written by the actress Fanny Kemble, but the context ('To be sure, if "noblesse oblige", royalty must do still more') suggests that it was already fairly well known. It carries the rather condescending implication that if one has had the good fortune to be born into the upper reaches of society, one has a duty always to behave honourably and with generosity (as if those not so blessed are somehow absolved of such obligations). It hit the headlines in 1956 with Nancy Mitford's *Noblesse Oblige: an enquiry into the identifiable characteristics of the English aristocracy*, in which she introduced to a wider public Professor A. S. C. Ross's notions of 'U' and 'Non-U' vocabulary.

noli me tangere

In the Vulgate version of St John's gospel, *noli me tangere* are the words spoken by Christ to Mary Magdalene, the first person to see him after his resurrection (the Authorized Version translates them 'touch me not', John 20:17). (Latin *tangere* 'touch' is a relative of English *contact*, *tactile*, and *tangent*). Hence, *noli me tangere* is used as a term in art history to denote a painting of Christ's meeting with Mary. But it also has, or rather had, a lot of other uses in English. In the Middle Ages it denoted a sort of facial ulcer, so named presumably because it hurt to touch it, and it lingered on into the 19th century as a term for lupus, a sort of tuberculosis of the facial skin. It was also used for a type of plant of the balsam family whose seed-pods burst open forcibly when touched, and, more broadly and metaphorically, for a person who will brook no interference, a topic that must not be mentioned, etc.

nolle prosequi

Nolle prosequi is a legal term signifying either that the plaintiff in a civil action wishes to withdraw his case, or that the prosecution in a criminal trial has decided to abandon its case. In Latin it means literally 'do not pursue' (Latin *prōsequī* 'follow, pursue' is the ancestor of English *prosecute*). It languished in the language of the law courts for two and a half centuries, until P. G. Wodehouse took a fancy to it. It crops up quite often in his novels, denoting a 'desisting from undesirable action': 'When an aunt has set her mind on a thing, it's no use trying to put in a nolle prosequi' (*Much Obliged, Jeeves*, 1971). It is commonly abbreviated to *nol pros* or *nolle pros*, and the latter is also used, especially in American English, as a verb, meaning 'abandon a case'.

nolo contendere

If the defendant in a criminal case enters a plea of *nolo contendere*, what he is in effect saying is that he is willing to accept a conviction in this particular case, but without prejudice to his right to plead 'not guilty' to substantially the same charge in a subsequent action. The term means literally 'I do not wish to contend', and it is used mainly in the US legal system.

nom de guerre

One's *nom de guerre* (in French literally 'name of war, war name') is, as it were, the name under which one goes into battle – an assumed name which one adopts for the purpose of engaging in a particular activity, to conceal one's true identity ('When they went upon private adventures, to prevent discovery, each had her *nom de guerre*', Mary Manley, *Secret Memoirs*, 1709).

The term has been used in English since the 17th century, but it has never been as widespread as the similar but semantically narrower **nom de plume**.

nom de plume

Nom de plume 'pseudonym adopted by a writer' is one of those rather rare instances in which a loanword exists side by side with its direct literal equivalent in the language which borrowed it – in this case, English *pen-name*. But to call it a loanword may be going too far. It gives every indication of being a French expression, but in fact it is quite uncommon in French, and it could well be that it was coined in English as a pseudo-Frenchism, perhaps modelled on the long-established *nom de guerre* (it is first recorded in the 1820s, in the works of Thomas de Quincey). The Englished *pen-name* sidled into the language in the mid-19th century, perhaps originally in America: the earliest record of it comes in the 1864 edition of *Webster's Dictionary*, where it is quoted as being used by the American writer Bayard Taylor. Amongst the best-known noms de plume in English literature are Lewis Carroll (real name Charles Lutwidge Dodgson), George Eliot (Mary Ann Evans), and Boz (Charles Dickens).

nomen nudum

Nomen nudum (literally in Latin 'naked name') is a dismissive term used by zoological and botanical taxonomists for a name applied to an animal or plant without reference to the accepted standards of scientific nomenclature, without going through the formal process of ratification, or without being properly published with a full description of the species named. Its use in English dates at least from the early 20th century.

non sequitur

In Latin, *non sequitur* is a sentence. It means 'it does not follow' (*sequitur* is the third person present singular of *sequi* 'follow', which also gave English *sequel* and *sequence*). But English took it over in the 16th century as a noun, with the sense 'conclusion which cannot logically be inferred from what preceded it'. It seems to have emerged from the Latin of the law courts, and for a long time that was its main area of use: 'The Justices need not set forth any Reason of their Judgment, therefore a *Non sequitur* will not vitiate' (Sir Geoffrey Gilbert, *Report of cases in equity*,

1726). But it is also a term in formal logic, and increasingly over
the centuries it has come to be used in a looser, more general
sense 'statement which has no connection with or relevance to
what has previously been said'.

nostalgie de la boue

French *nostalgie de la boue* means literally 'hankering for mud' –
that is to say, an 'overwhelming desire for the lowest aspects of
life, and particularly for sexual degradation'. The phrase
appears to have been coined by Émile Augier in his play *Le
Mariage d'Olympe* 1855, where one character observes that if you
put a duck among swans, it will yearn to return to the mud it
came from. It had begun to appear in English before the end of
the 19th century (Bernard Shaw is the first on record as using
it), and it soon became established in the language. In D. H.
Lawrence's *Lady Chatterley's Lover* (1928), for instance, Clifford
Chatterley describes his wife Constance (referring to her affair
with the gamekeeper Mellors) as 'one of those half-insane, per-
verted women who must run after depravity, the *nostalgie de la
boue*'. Other French expressions based on *nostalgie* to have made
sporadic appearances in English include *nostalgie de la banlieue*
'yearning for the suburbs' and *nostalgie du pavé* or *du trottoir*,
literally 'nostalgia for the pavement', a wish to return to the life
of the city and its streets.

nota bene

Latin *nota bene* is most familiar in English in its abbreviated
form *nb* (or *NB*). Literally 'observe well, note well' (*nota* is the
imperative singular of *notare* 'mark, note, observe'), it is used in
writing to draw the reader's particular attention to an important
comment, request, instruction, etc. *Nota* on its own is first
recorded in English as long ago as the 14th century (it has long
since disappeared), but *nota bene* does not begin to emerge
before the early 18th century. The abbreviation *nb* predates it,
as far as the recorded evidence shows, by about 50 years: Joseph
Addison, in a 1710 edition of the *Tatler*, noted that 'of late Years,
the N.B. has been much in Fashion'.

notes inégales

The term *notes inégales* (in French literally 'unequal notes') is
used in the context of Baroque music, and particularly French
Baroque music of the sort written by Lully and Rameau,

to signify notes that are written as a series of equal notes, such as four quavers, but are played as if they were divided into pairs of notes, the first longer and the second shorter than the notes written, such as dotted quaver-semiquaver, dotted quaver-semiquaver. It came into English in the early part of the 20th century.

nous verrons

French uses *nous verrons* just like its precise English equivalent, *we shall see*, to denote an undecided future possibility. On the face of it, English had no pressing need to borrow the French expression, but nevertheless from the mid-18th century onwards there are sporadic records of its use in English: 'I don't feel much like matinizing at the moment mais *nous verrons*' (Ernest Dowson, letter, 1889).

nouveau riche, plural nouveaux riches

There is nothing new about the nouveaux riches. As a class they were first seen as calling for a special term to define them as long ago as the beginning of the 19th century (Maria Edgeworth noted in a letter of 6 April 1813, 'Larry the footboy and Mrs Rafferty's dinner are nothing to what has been seen at the dinners of les nouveaux riches at Liverpool and Manchester'). *Nouveau riche* was duly borrowed from French (where it literally means 'new rich'), not long after *parvenu* had made the same trip across the Channel – two elegant put-downs for the industrialists and merchants whose newly acquired wealth gained them entry into aristocratic society, but whose vulgarity and ostentation allowed them to be patronized by those with 'old money' who knew how to spend it more discreetly. It remains today one of the most crushingly snooty of insults, often abbreviated to *noov* in Sloane Ranger slang. The similarly inspired *nouveau pauvre* (literally 'new poor'), describing a member of a recently impoverished class, first appeared in English in the mid-1960s.

nouveau roman, plural nouveaux romans

French *nouveau roman*, literally 'new novel', is an alternative term for **anti-roman**, denoting a genre of novel which rejects traditional fictional techniques, and attempts to present events unfiltered by an authorial persona. It was adopted by English at the beginning of the 1960s.

nouvelle cuisine

The term *nouvelle cuisine* – in French literally 'new cooking' – denotes a style of cookery whose main avowed aim is to produce dishes that are light, are not harmful to the health, and emphasize rather than disguise the natural taste of their ingredients. To this end, exponents of the *nouvelle cuisine* use lean cuts of meat rather than fat ones, often preferring fish to either; they use fresh vegetables and fruit (and fruit often features in their meat and fish dishes); they go for cooking methods which are quick (thus preserving the food's natural freshness and flavours) and fat-free, such as steaming or grilling; and they avoid the use of lots of cream and butter in sauces. Also on the hit-list of the original *nouvelle cuisiniers* (whose inspirers in the early 1970s were the French food critics Henri Gault and Christian Millau) was the appearance of food. They wanted to get away from the ornately decorated concoctions of classical haute cuisine, and go for a much simpler approach. But latterly, critics have accused *nouvelle cuisine* of having an ossified visual style, more interested in painting pictures on a plate than in producing tasty food. (See also **haute cuisine**.)

nouvelle vague

Nouvelle vague means literally in French 'new wave'. It was applied in the late 1950s to a school of French film-making which abandoned traditional sequential narrative technique in favour of a more abstract approach based on the reactions of an individual character to events and stimuli. Amongst its leading exponents during the 1960s were Claude Chabrol, Jean-Luc Godard, Alain Resnais, and François Truffaut – indeed, the nouvelle vague did much to make the director, rather than the actor, the star of the film. Examples of the genre include Godard's *A bout de souffle* (1960), Resnais's *Hiroshima mon amour* (1959), and Truffaut's *Jules et Jim* (1961). The expression was first used in English in 1959, and its English translation *new wave* (now the more usual term) followed a year later.

nudnik

A *nudnik* is a 'tiresome or boring person', a 'pest', and also an 'idiot'. This piece of American slang was acquired around the middle of the 20th century from Yiddish. There, it originated as a derivative of Russian *nudny* 'boring', formed with the agent suffix -*nik*.

nuit blanche

A *nuit blanche* is a 'sleepless night'. The phrase means literally 'white night' in French, but here *blanc* is being used in the metaphorical sense 'blank', hence 'without sleep'. The first recorded use of the term in English is in Charlotte Brontë's novel *Villette* (1853), but that is set in Belgium. It was not until the 20th century that it began to gain a more general currency in English.

nulli secundus

Latin *nulli secundus* means 'second to none' (*nulli* is the dative singular of *nullus* 'none'), and English uses it to denote high excellence. Earliest records of it date from the 19th century, which was probably the high point of its popularity. It is the motto of the Coldstream Guards. The neuter form *nulli secundum* is used when referring to things rather than people.

numero uno

Someone who is *numero uno* is the leading person, the top banana, the big cheese, clearly out in front of the rest. English apparently acquired the expression from Italian in the 1960s or 1970s, slotting it into the same colloquial niche as is occupied by the vernacular *number one* (which dates back to the early 19th century).

nunc dimittis

Nunc dimittis, in Latin literally 'now you may send away', originated as the first words of the Canticle of Simeon in the Vulgate, the Latin Bible: *'Nunc dimittis servum tuum, Domine, secundum verbum tuum in pace; quia viderunt oculi mei salutare tuum, quod parasti ante faciem omnium populorum. Lumen ad revelationem gentium, et gloriam plebis tuae Israel'* (Luke 2:29–32). This is translated in the King James Version as 'Lord, now lettest thou thy servant depart in peace, according to thy word: For mine eyes have seen thy salvation, which thou hast prepared before the face of all people; a light to lighten the Gentiles, and the glory of thy people Israel'. The words are those of Simeon, an old and devout man who was promised by the Holy Ghost that before he died, he would see Christ; and when Mary and Joseph brought Jesus to the temple in Jerusalem shortly after his birth, Simeon did indeed see him there, and took him in his arms, offering up this song of thanksgiving which is also a petition for release from the labours of a long life. The canticle has been set to music by numerous composers, both in Latin and in the vernacular, the most familiar modern English version being one by Geoffrey Burgon which served as the title music to the BBC television serialization of John le Carré's *Tinker, Tailor, Soldier, Spy*.

Since its introduction into English in the 16th century, the term has often been used metaphorically, both in the phrase *sing one's nunc dimittis*, meaning 'leave or die willingly' ('I am now contented, and can sing my "nunc dimittis",' Charles Darwin, 1859), and more generally in the sense 'permission to go'.

nyet

Nyet, Russian for 'no', became widely known in English in the 1950s and 1960s as a symbol of Soviet obstructiveness and intransigence. As part of the petty skirmishing of the Cold War, it seemed that whenever the West put forward a proposal at the United Nations, the Soviet Union would veto it with a firm *nyet*, and the word came as a boon to headline writers looking for a shorthand encapsulation of the Russian stance.

O

obiter dictum, plural obiter dicta

An *obiter dictum*, in its original legal sense, is a statement made by a trial judge on a point of law, whether in argument during the course of the trial, in the summing-up, or in giving judgment, which is of only incidental relevance to the case in question, and therefore has no binding authority. The Latin phrase means literally 'statement in passing'. *Dictum* is a noun formed from the past participle of *dicere* 'say', and *obiter* 'incidentally, in passing' is a compound adverb formed from *ob* 'by' and *iter* 'way' – it is collaterally related to English *obituary*, which goes back ultimately to Latin *obīre* 'go down, fall, die'. The phrase is now used in English in the broader, more general sense of 'passing comment, thing said by the way'. A parallel formation that has enjoyed some currency in English is *obiter scriptum* 'thing written hastily or by the way', and *obiter* has even taken on a life of its own as an adjective in legal circles: 'the obiter observations said to have been made by magistrates' clerks' (*The Daily News*, 21 April 1891).

objet d'art

French *objet d'art* was introduced to English in the 1860s, and soon caught on in a big way. At first it was often anglicized to *object of art*, but this has never succeeded in ousting the original version. From the beginning, the French term had a cachet of refinement to it, alluring or faintly ridiculous according to one's point of view: 'the various little tables, loaded with "objets d'art" (as Mrs Gibson delighted to call them) with which the drawing room was crowded' (Elizabeth Gaskell, *Wives and Daughters*, 1866).

First cousin to the *objet d'art* is the *object of virtu*, an 'object of some artistic value, of interest to a connoisseur or collector'. This has occasionally been turned in English into the pseudo-French *objet de vertu*, presumably on the model of *objet d'art*, although in fact French *vertu* does not share the sense of Italian *virtu*, 'artistic taste, knowledge of the fine arts', which originally inspired the expression.

objet trouvé

An *objet trouvé* is literally in French a 'found object' (the 'lost-property office' in French is the *bureau des objets trouvés*). But in English the main use of the term has been as defined by the theorists of Surrealism. It denotes something – a natural object, such as a pebble or branch, or an artefact, such as an old tin can – which is invested with aesthetic significance by virtue of its being found by chance by the 'artist' and put on display as any conventional work of art would be. Amongst the leading British exponents of the *objet trouvé* was Paul Nash.

oeil de perdrix

French *oeil de perdrix* means literally 'partridge's eye', and is used in two metaphorical applications that have been passed on to English. The eye's beady roundness has lent its name to a pattern of dotted circles, originally used on Sèvres porcelain around 1760, and subsequently widely employed on French porcelain and pottery, and also in lace-making. The eye's reddish colour led to the use of the phrase to describe wine: in the 19th and early 20th centuries it was applied to a range of rosé wines, including pink champagne, but nowadays it mainly denotes a type of rosé made from pinot noir grapes in Neuchâtel, Switzerland.

oeuvre

French *oeuvre* means literally 'work' (it comes from Latin *opera* 'works', a derivative of *opus* 'work', which English has also taken up). English adopted it in the second half of the 19th century, and has used it in two distinct senses: for an 'individual work by a painter, writer, composer, etc', and for the 'whole body of a particular artist's work': 'The spreading abroad of [Palestrina's] bulky *oeuvre* gained considerably from the attentions of the romantics' (*The Listener*, 2 October 1958). (See also **chef d'oeuvre** and **hors d'oeuvre**.)

olé

Olé is a Spanish cry of exultation or approval, which might be rendered in English as 'bravo!' It cannot be said to have become fully assimilated into English – it is not an exclamation that springs unbidden to English lips – but since the early 20th century it has become familiar enough to English-speakers for it to be used in appropriate contexts, in descriptions of Spanish festive activities, such as flamenco dancing, and accounts of bull-fighting.

om

Om is a Hindu mantra intoned as a component of prayer and meditation. It is interpreted as typifying the great triad of Hindu gods, Brahma, Vishnu and Siva, who are concerned with integration, maintenance and dissolution. The earliest known reference to it in an English text is in the works of the Sanskrit scholar Sir William Jones (1746–94), but it was the 1960s, with their increased interest in mystic Eastern religions in the West, that first saw English-speakers in large numbers intoning *om*.

ombudsman

Ombudsman is a Swedish contribution to English. Descended from Old Norse *umboðsmaðr*, a compound of *umboð* 'commission' and *maðr* 'man', it denotes a member of a group who is appointed to look after its legal and other interests. In 1809 the office of *justitieombudsman* was established in Sweden. He is a par-liamentary commissioner whose job is to investigate grievances due to governmental maladministration. The idea of such a post spread through the rest of Scandinavia in the 20th century (Finland 1919, Denmark 1954, Norway 1962). New Zealand made a similar appointment in 1962, and in 1967 the concept reached Britain. The post was officially designated *Parliamentary Commissioner for Administration*, but right from the outset the term *ombudsman* was applied to it.

omertà

English found out about *omertà* when the Sicilian Mafia brought its activities to the USA. It denotes the Mafia's code of conduct, and in particular the injunction not to give away the secrets of the Mafia's doings. Those who break silence can expect no mercy. The word is a dialectal variant of Italian *humilità* 'humi-lity', and referred originally to that part of the Mafia code that enjoined humility, or submission, on the part of the members towards the leader. It began to appear in English at the start of the 20th century.

om mani padme hum

Tibetan Buddhists repeatedly intone *om mani padme hum* as an aid to meditation. It means in Sanskrit 'hail, jewel in the lotus', and is known as the 'Shadakshari mantra'. It was first mentioned in an English text as long ago as the 1770s.

on dit

'What is the *on dit*?' means 'What are people saying about this, what is the gossip?' The term *on dit* 'piece of gossip or rumour' comes from French, where it originated as a nominalization of the clause *on dit*, literally 'one says', thus 'people say, they say'. The first record of its use in an English text goes back as far as 1826 and Benjamin Disraeli's *Vivian Grey*, and it was soon turning up in Australia: 'Our various Australian journals furnish intelligence and *on-dits*' (Peter Cunningham, *Two Years in New South Wales*, 1828).

opus

Latin *opus* was a general term for 'work', denoting especially the repetitive application of effort expected of slaves, animals, machines, etc (as opposed to the derivative *opera*, source of English *oeuvre*, which suggested effort willingly exerted). But it was also used for something produced by work, including a work of art or literature. And it was in this sense that English adopted the word in the late 18th century. At first it was a fairly general term (a usage which survives in **magnum opus**), but before the end of the 19th century we find it being used specifically in the numerical designation of pieces of music, listing a particular composer's works in (roughly) chronological order (thus Elgar's *Sevillana* Opus 7 dates from early in his career, but his Cello Concerto Opus 85 is a late composition). In this context the word is often abbreviated to *op*. Recent decades have seen a revival of the more general application of *opus*, but generally with an ironic twist, suggesting that the work referred to does not live up to its pretensions – as in 'Jeffrey Archer's latest opus'.

origami

Origami is the Japanese art of paper-folding, in which sheets of paper are bent and twisted into shapes suggesting flowers, birds, boats, etc. Masters of the art can make models that move – birds that flap their wings, for instance. It is also used for the decorative wrapping of presents. It began to be popularized as a hobby in the West in the 1950s, which was when the term *origami* first appeared in English – it was originally a compound formed from Japanese *ori* 'fold' and *kami* 'paper'. Origami should not be confused with kirigami, which is also concerned with producing decorative paper designs, but uses cutting as well as folding (from Japanese *kiri* 'cut').

Ostpolitik

In its broadest sense, the term *Ostpolitik* now denotes any country's policy with regard to the (formerly Communist) countries of Eastern Europe, but as its German origin (literally 'east-policy') suggests, it at first referred much more specifically to Germany's attitude towards its eastern neighbours. It was applied to Germany's dealings with Russia towards the end of World War 1, leading to the treaties of Brest-Litovsk, under the terms of which Russia lost control of the Ukraine and its Polish and Baltic possessions. And indeed, Hitler used it when referring to his plans for extending German lebensraum eastwards: 'The goal of *Ostpolitik* is to open up an area of settlement for one hundred million Germans' (quoted by Terence Prittie in *Germany Divided*, 1961). Its common use in English, though, really began in the later 1960s, when it was applied to the Federal Republic of Germany's policy of fostering good relations with the Soviet Union and other Communist-bloc countries. During the 1950s and early 1960s the Christian Democrats, under Konrad Adenauer and later Ludwig Erhart, had taken a fairly distant if not frosty line with Moscow, but after the Social Democrats were elected to power in 1969, the new Chancellor, Willi Brandt, began to open up a friendly dialogue, negotiating treaties with the USSR, Poland and East Germany – some might say setting in train the series of events that led, through many vicissitudes, to the abandonment of the Cold War at the end of the 1980s.

o tempora! o mores!

In his *In Catalinam* ('Against Catalina'), his prosecution speech against Lucius Sergius Catalina for plotting to overthrow the Roman state, Cicero inveighs against the moral decline of the modern world, saying in effect 'what have things come to when people can behave like this?' He punctuates his comment with the lament *o tempora! o mores!*, which has been taken up in English as a condemnation of the perennial degeneracy of

221

present times, as contrasted with an always golden past: '[Queen Victoria] had established the annual calendar, whereby the royal Christmas was spent at Windsor Castle. O tempora, o mores! These days, the only people who take any notice of this calendar are the royals themselves' (*The Sunday Times*, 2 December 1990).

outré

Something that is *outré* is extreme or excessive, especially in going beyond the bounds of conventional taste or propriety, or simply in being eccentrically odd. *Outré* is an adjectival use of the past participle of the verb *outrer* 'go to excess', which comes ultimately from Latin *ultra* 'beyond'. English borrowed it from French in the early 18th century.

P

pace

Pace is the ablative case of Latin *pax*. This originally meant 'peace', but it spread semantically to 'grace, favour' and, in ablative constructions, to 'permission'. Thus, *pace tua* meant 'by your leave, with your permission'. When Ovid in his *Amores* wrote *pace loquar Veneris: tu dea major eris*, it meant 'With Venus's permission I will speak: you will be a greater goddess'. Over the centuries this 'by your leave' became a polite or ironic way of showing disagreement with someone. A particular use of it was in the expression *pace tanti viri* 'with the permission of such a great man', a sycophantically polite demurral which crops up in Tobias Smollett's *Humphrey Clinker* (1771): 'Dr Shaw ... says, he has seen flakes of sulphur floating in the well. – *Pace tanti viri*, I, for my part, have never observed any thing sulphur, either in or about the well'. It was not until as recently as the second half of the 19th century, though, that *pace* came to be used on its own in English to express disagreement or contradiction, as in 'The rain in Spain falls mainly, pace Professor Higgins, on the hills'.

padre

Padre has come at English from many sides. Descended ultimately from Latin *pater* 'father', it is the word for 'father' in Italian, Spanish and Portuguese, and consequently is used in those languages as a term for 'priest'. Its first major impact on English probably came in India, from the 17th century onwards, where British people encountered it amongst Portuguese colonists. Here it remained a relatively unassimilated term (Mary Sherwood, for instance, felt obliged to include '*Padre*, a Christian minister' in the glossary to her *The Lady and her Ayah*, 1813), but it became familiar enough to British soldiers serving in India, and also to British sailors in parts of the world where Italian, Spanish and Portuguese were spoken, that by the end of the 19th century it was the established term for a military or naval chaplain. This has led in the 20th century to its use in general British English as a jocular term for any clergyman.

palais de danse

French *palais de danse*, literally 'dance palace', denotes a public dance hall. It came into English after World War 1, and in the 1920s, '30s, and '40s enjoyed a considerable vogue in Britain as the luxurious-sounding term for the dance halls of the time which young people attended in large numbers to dance to big-band music. It was frequently shortened to *palais*. In the late 1930s a communal dance known as the *palais glide* was briefly popular: the dancers linked arms and progressed with a mixture of high kicks and gliding steps.

palio

The *Palio* is a horse race run every July and August through the streets of the Italian city of Siena. First held in 1482, it is now a considerable tourist attraction. The term *palio* is also applied to similar races in other Italian cities, and indeed the earliest recorded use of it in an English text, as long ago as the 1670s, is a reference to a *palio* in Florence. Italian *palio* is descended from Latin *pallium* 'cover' (source of English *pall* and possibly *tarpaulin*), and refers to the painted silk banner presented to the winner.

panem et circenses

When the Roman satirist Juvenal wrote of the typical Roman citizen *Duas tantum res anxius optat, panem et circenses* 'Only two things does he worry about or long for – bread and circuses' (*Satires* x, 80), he was starting up a metaphor that was to endure for nearly 2000 years. 'Bread and circuses' – or translated into modern terms, 'food and the big match' – represents the ruling classes' idea of what the average Joe needs to keep him happy and out of mischief. As long as he is well fed and has sufficient entertainment to divert him from the more unpleasant realities of life, he will not start a revolution. The phrase *panem et circenses* has been used in English since at least the late 18th century, although nowadays the translated version *bread and circuses* is commoner.

papabile, plural papabili

Someone who is *papabile* is worthy of being or likely to be elected pope. The Italian word, a derivative of *papa* 'pope', first came into English in the late 16th century via French as *papable*, but this had essentially died out within 100 years, and *papabile*

224

represents a 20th-century reborrowing. In the 1980s it began to be used metaphorically with reference to someone suitable or likely to be chosen for any high office. It can function as both an adjective and a noun.

paparazzo, plural paparazzi

Paparazzi are part of the price fate exacts for fame. If editors decree that your photograph will help to sell their newspapers, you will be pursued by paparazzi – freelance photographers – who will stop at nothing, flinch from no deviousness or importunity, in order to get it. English acquired the word *paparazzo* in the 1960s from Italian, where it originally denoted a reporter rather than a photographer. And Italian in turn may have got it from French *paperassier* 'scribbler', a derivative of *paperasse* 'scrap paper', which itself was formed from *papier* 'paper'.

papier mâché

Papier mâché is a substance made from paper pulp that is mixed with paste or glue, moulded into the required shape, and then allowed to set. *Papier* 'paper' and *mâché* 'chewed' are of course French words, but the term *papier mâché* appears to have been concocted in English in the mid-18th century: the usual French expression for what we call papier mâché is *carton-pâte*. The word is often partially anglicized to *paper mâché*.

Genuine French *papier* compounds that have made an appearance in English include *papier collé*, literally 'glued paper', a sort of collage made from paper and other materials; *papier déchiré* 'torn-up paper', a collage technique developed by Picasso using torn paper; *papier découpé* 'cut-up paper', a collage technique using cut paper; and *papier poudré* 'powdered paper', paper impregnated with talcum powder.

parador

Spanish *parador* originally denoted an 'inn' or 'tavern'. It now has as archaic an air as those two words have in English, but it was revived as a term for the state-owned, state-run hotels that have been called into being in Spain since World War 2 in reconstructed castles, monasteries, stately homes, etc. In this application its use in English dates, as far as the records show, from the beginning of the 1960s. There are also paradors in Portugal and Puerto Rico.

par avion

France played a big role in the early history of aviation, as the French influence on English aeronautical terminology bears witness (*aeroplane, aileron, fuselage*, etc). This was the case in air transportation too, and a living reminder of this is *par avion*, literally 'by aircraft', which, although it has never really entered the active vocabulary of English, has nevertheless become an internationally recognized term through its use on airmail letters and packets, alongside English *by airmail*. Formerly the element *avion* appears to have had some limited independent currency in English: James Joyce, for instance, in a letter of 1935, wrote of 'an avion letter from Bailly'.

parens patriae

Parens patriae is a legal term denoting an authoritative person or body – a sovereign, an attorney general, etc – regarded as being in the relation of a guardian to the citizens of a state, or to those of them (eg children or lunatics) unable to take legal action in their own name. The *parens patriae* is empowered to afford legal protection to such people, to sue on their behalf, etc. The term in Latin means 'parent of the country', and has been in use in English since the 18th century.

par excellence

Par excellence has been around in English for so long now – since the 17th century, in fact – that its second element is often pronounced as if it were the English word *excellence*. But in fact the expression is a borrowing from French, where it means literally 'by way of excellence, by way of pre-eminence', hence 'pre-eminently, above all others' – as in 'Vintage port is the dessert wine *par excellence*'.

pari passu

Pari passu is Latin. It means literally 'with equal step' (its constituent parts are the ablative forms of *par* 'equal' and *passus* 'step', ancestor of English *pace*). In English it is used, and has been since the 16th century, to mean 'at an equal rate of progress', both literally and figuratively ('proceed with warlike measures and conciliatory measures *pari passu*', John Adams, 1775), and also, in legal contexts, 'equitably, without unfair preference'.

parti pris

English adopted French *parti pris* in the middle to late 19th century. It means literally 'decision taken', and is used in two distinct ways: it denotes 'set purpose' (the phrase *de parti pris* is frequently used for 'of set purpose, with deliberation'), but it is also used more metaphorically for 'prejudice, bias'. It is this latter application which English has taken over: 'that fatal spirit of *parti-pris* which has led to the rooting of so much injustice, disorder, immobility and darkness in English intelligence' (John Morley, 1871). French *parti* also means 'marriageable person', and for a while in the 19th century English used it in this sense as well.

parvenu

French *parvenir* means 'arrive at a place, reach a place', and hence figuratively 'attain a particular rank or position, succeed'. Its past participle, *parvenu*, is used as a noun meaning 'person who has risen above the station in which he or she was born, but does not have the education or social graces to fit in to the class to which he or she now aspires' – in other words, an 'upstart'. English adopted the term around the start of the 19th century. (Compare **arriviste**.)

pas de deux

For long the butt of English music-hall jokes that would translate it facetiously as 'father of twins', French *pas de deux* literally means 'step for two, dance for two people', and is applied to a ballet figure for two people, typically a man and a woman. English has adopted a number of other ballet terms from French incorporating *pas*, including *pas de chat* a cat-like, springing step, *pas de cheval* (literally 'horse-step'), in which the dancer paws the ground with one foot, *pas de ciseaux* a scissors step, *pas de trois* a dance for three people, and *pas seul* a solo dance. Many of these had become established before the end of the 18th century, and indeed in Richard Sheridan's *The Rivals* (1775) we find Acres complaining, when reluctantly practising his dancing, 'These outlandish heathen allemandes and cotillons are quite beyond me! – I shall never prosper at 'em, that's sure – mine are true-born English legs – they don't understand their cursed French lingo! – their *pas* this, and *pas* that, and *pas* t'other! – damn me, my feet don't like to be called paws!' A *pas de deux* danced by the prima ballerina and the leading male dancer is termed a *pas de deux grand*.

pas devant les enfants

French *pas devant les enfants* 'not in front of the children' has become a catch-phrase in English, warning of the inadvisability of referring to delicate or scandalous topics, using strong language, etc within the hearing of impressionable young ears. It is often shortened for convenience to *pas devant*, and applied more widely to any person or group condescendingly regarded as unfit to be privy to one's proceedings (as in the vernacular 'not in front of the servants').

passé

Passé is the past participle of the French verb *passer* 'pass', used adjectivally to mean 'past, gone by', and by extension 'past its best, faded'. English acquired it in the late 18th century, and for a long time used it chiefly with reference to women who had passed the apogee of their youthful beauty: 'Even a Frenchman would not have called her *passée* – that is for a widow. For a spinster, it would have been different' (Edward Bulwer-Lytton, *My Novel*, 1853). In the 20th century, however, it has predominantly been used in the sense of 'out of date, old-fashioned' – a meaning not actually present in French. English has also borrowed *passé* as a noun, denoting a movement in ballet in which the leg is transferred from one position to another.

passéisme

When the Italian poet and novelist Filippo Marinetti proclaimed the doctrine of Futurism in his Paris manifesto of 1909, his targets were the traditional artistic aims and methods of the past, the stifling weight of academicism. He had no time for such outdated literary conventions as metre and syntax. He saw the future of art in power, speed, technology, mechanization. Regard for traditional values was scornfully dismissed with the French term *passéisme*, a derivative of *passé* 'dated'. This and the adjective and noun *passéiste* were adopted into English by British disciples of Futurism, notably Percy Wyndham Lewis, and they have remained in the language ever since, used mainly in the field of the arts.

passim

In classical Latin, *passim* meant simply 'scattered about randomly, here and there or everywhere' (it was a derivative of the verb *pandere* 'spread out, scatter', ancestor of English *expand*). In Virgil's *Aeneid*, for instance, we read that *Tyrii comites passim ... diversa per agros tecta metu petiere* 'The Tyrian retinue scattered in alarm all over the fields in search of shelter'. English, however, which has used it since the beginning of the 19th century, has taken it on in a much more restricted sense. It is employed in the annotations and other textual apparatus of learned volumes, and denotes that a particular word or phrase occurs 'throughout' a particular book – in other words, in too many places to cite each one individually.

paterfamilias

In Roman law, a *paterfamilias* was the male head of a household, the person who had authority over all those living in a house, including the servants as well as his family. The term was a compound formed from Latin *pater* 'father' and *familias*, the archaic genitive form of *familia*, here in the sense 'household'. (Collateral terms included *materfamilias* 'mistress of a household' and *filiusfamilias* or *filiafamilias*, denoting a son or daughter still under the father's legal guardianship.) By the time English acquired the term, in the 15th century, it had lost its legal implications, and had become a general term for the 'male head of the family', perhaps with connotations of wise but stern paternal control – indeed, a short-lived adjective *paterfamiliar* was coined from it in the 17th century that reflected these.

paternoster

Pater noster are the first words of the Lord's Prayer in the Vulgate: *Pater noster, qui es in coelis ...*, 'Our father, which art in heaven ...' Since Anglo-Saxon times, *paternoster* has been used in English to refer to the Lord's Prayer, particularly the Latin version of it, and over the centuries a number of secondary meanings of the word have evolved. When Catholics say their prayers, counting the beads of the rosary, at every eleventh bead they say the Lord's Prayer, and so this bead, which is of a different appearance to the rest, became known as the *paternoster*. By extension the term was applied to the rosary itself, and this led to a variety of metaphorical uses: to a sort of fishing line, for instance, with alternately arranged weights and hooks, and to a chain with a number of buckets on it for raising water (later re-applied to a sort of continuous lift which one can step on to or off without its stopping). Paternoster Row, a street in the City of London traditionally associated with publishers and booksellers, got its name because makers of rosaries once worked there. And although the expression has now died out, for a long time to do something 'in a paternoster while' was to do it in the time it takes to say a paternoster – that is, in quite a short time: 'He pissede a potel in a pater-noster while' (*Piers Plowman*, 1362).

patois

In French, *patois* means strictly a 'local form of speech used in an area alongside a national variety' (as opposed to a *dialecte*, which is a 'local variety that is the sole form used in a particular area'). However, it is also used more broadly for the jargon of a particular group, and both these meanings have been taken over by English since the 17th century. In addition, the word is used as a term for the creole languages of Caribbean islands, both English-based (especially in Jamaica) and French-based (as in St Lucia). It is not known for certain where French *patois* came from, although its original Old French meaning, 'rough speech', suggests that it may be derived from the Old French verb *patoier* 'handle roughly', itself based on *patte* 'paw'.

patron

English has acquired *patron* twice. It first crossed the Channel from French in the 14th century, meaning 'protector' or 'supporter', and is still very much with us. Its pronunciation has become anglicized to /'peɪtrən/. In this century, however, it has been reborrowed as a term for the proprietor of a restaurant or other hostelry, particularly one in France or elsewhere on the continent; and in this incarnation it retains an approximation to its original French pronunciation, with the nasalized vowel in the second syllable, /pa'trɔ̃n/. In this sense, too, English has taken over the feminine form *patronne*, denoting a female patron, or the wife of a patron. Another heavily disguised relative is the English word *pattern*, which also comes from Old French *patron*; the circuitous semantic link is that 'patrons' of tradesmen (such as shoemakers) would give them a model or 'pattern' of what they wanted, for them to copy.

pension

Pension 'money paid regularly' and *pension* 'boarding house' are ultimately the same word, and their common denominator is 'payment.' Both were borrowed from French, the former long enough ago (in the 14th century) to have become thoroughly anglicized, and their common French source originally meant literally 'payment' or 'rent'. One of its particular applications was to money paid for board and lodging, and from this it was extended to the lodgings themselves. English has been using the word in this sense since the 17th century, but at first in its anglicized form, and it does not seem to have been until the end of the 18th century that it began to be regarded as a foreignism, pronounced *à la française*, and restricted in its application to continental boarding houses. At around the same time French *en pension* was substituted for the native *in pension* (as in *live in pension* 'be a lodger'). (See also **demi-pension**).

pentimento, plural pentimenti

Italian *pentimento* means literally 'repentance'. When an artist 'repents' of his first effort, or makes a mistake, he may change it or correct it by painting over it. Over the decades and centuries the top layer of paint may fade, allowing the painter's original version to emerge from beneath its covering. This re-emergence, or the image thus revealed, is called *pentimento*. The term began to be used in English around the beginning of the 20th century.

per annum

Latin *per annum* means literally 'by the year, for each year', thus 'annually' (this use of Latin *per* for 'for each one' is a medieval development; it was not present in classical Latin). English took the phrase up in the 17th century, and for much of the time since has used it mainly in the context of annual salaries and similar payments ('The professor in divinity, hath per annum 1125 florens', Robert Johnson, *The Worlde, or an historicall description of the most famous kingdomes and commonweales therein*, 1601), but these days it is more widely employed in giving various sorts of statistics. Related terms are *per diem* 'per day' and *per mensam* 'per month'.

per capita

Latin *per capita* means literally 'by heads'. Its original use in English was as a legal term, denoting the inheritance of property when divided up equally between a number of individuals (it contrasted with *per stirpes*, literally 'by [family] stocks', in which the inheritance is divided up equally between different branches of a family). However, in the early 20th century it found a new use for itself, denoting 'per head of the population' in statistical contexts. This usage was resoundingly censured by Henry Fowler in his *Dictionary of Modern English Usage* (1926) ('This use is a modern blunder, encouraged in some recent dictionaries') on the grounds that it is plural, and logically the singular form *per caput* should be used (as indeed it has been in English in the 20th century). However, *per capita* remains the main form, and is now often encountered as an adjective (as in 'per capita income').

perestroika

When Mikhail Gorbachev came to power as General Secretary of the Soviet Communist Party in 1985, he found a Soviet Union ossified in the ways of the past, the machinery of its industry and commerce unchanged, both literally and figuratively, since the days of Stalin. He realized that if the whole system was not revitalized, the country would gradually grind to a halt. So he set in train a programme of economic 'rebuilding, reconstruction' – in Russian, *perestroika*. The word quickly became familiar in the West, particularly after the publication of his book *Perestroika: Our Hopes for Our Country and the World* (1987), and established itself in English alongside **glasnost** as one of the key terms to emerge from the political and economic sea change in Eastern Europe. It became fashionable to use it for any restructuring of an organization, and it even spawned its own English adjectival derivative, *perestroikan*.

perpetuum mobile

The term *perpetual motion*, denoting the motion of a hypothetical mechanism that will go on for ever without an external power source, dates from the late 16th century. The English philosopher Ralph Cudworth, one of the so-called Cambridge Platonists, in his *Treatise concerning morality* (1688) introduced a Latin equivalent, *perpetuum mobile*, apparently modelled on *primum mobile*. This seems not to have caught on, for there is no further record of it for over 200 years, but it reappeared at the beginning of the 20th century (in the works of Bertrand Russell), and it has been in use ever since. It has also been employed, since the late 19th century, as a musical term, synonymous with *moto perpetuo*, denoting a piece of music that unfolds at a rapid pace in an apparently never-ending stream of equal-value notes.

per pro

Per pro is short for Latin *per procurationem* 'by procuration' – that is, by getting someone else to do something on one's behalf. It is found in commercial usage, generally indicating that someone else has signed a letter on behalf of the named sender. The full form first appeared in English in the early 19th century, and from the start its length guaranteed a reduction to *per pro*, *per proc*, or (nowadays the commonest form) *pp*.

per se

Latin *per se* means literally 'by itself' (*se* is the accusative form of the Latin third-person reflexive pronoun), and English adopted it in the 16th century in the sense 'as such, intrinsically, without reference to any outside considerations' (as in 'It is not dangerous per se, but wrongly used it could cause harm'). It is also used more narrowly as a technical term in logic, denoting 'by virtue of an intrinsic cause' (in this sense it contrasts explicitly with *per accidens*, literally 'by accident', which signifies 'by virtue of an external factor').

persona non grata

The term *persona non grata* originated in the terminology of international diplomacy. It denotes a diplomat who is not acceptable to a foreign government (in Latin it means literally 'unacceptable person') and either is not permitted to take up a post in its country or is required to leave. It has been used in English since at least the late 19th century, as has its positive version, *persona grata* (although this usually appears in negative contexts – 'The envoy is no longer *persona grata*'). It is sometimes abbreviated to *p.n.g.* It is also widely used in the more general sense 'person who is or would be unwelcome': 'Your recent book has ... caused a lot of annoyance here, and you would not be *persona grata* at Eton on the Fourth of June' (*The Daily Telegraph*, 2 June 1972).

petit bourgeois, plural petits bourgeois

Petit bourgeois has a dual role in English. In French, where it means literally 'little citizen', it denotes someone from the humbler end of the urban middle class, and it was taken up in Marxian theory to signify a member of the social class consisting of small businessmen, clerical workers, and skilled manual workers (the *petite bourgeoisie*). English adopted it in the 19th century (sometimes partially anglicizing it to *petty bourgeois*), and in the 20th century has turned it into a term of abuse, encompassing narrow conventionality, conservative attitudes, and smug self-righteousness. In present-day English, it is commoner as an adjective than as a noun: '[Harold Wilson's] natural modesty has remained unchanged. So have his modest tastes, his simple liking of high tea, his completely unaffected petit bourgeois habits' (Richard Crossman, *Diaries*, 1974).

petit maître

In French a *petit maître* is a 'foppish fellow', an 'effeminate dandy'. English borrowed the term as long ago as the early 18th century. But consciousness of its literal French meaning, 'little master', has, especially in recent times, been influencing English-speakers increasingly to use it to signify a 'minor master', a painter, composer, etc capable of accomplished work but not of reaching great artistic heights: 'Liadoff, a real petit-maître, produced at rare intervals a few miniatures of extraordinary felicity' (Constant Lambert, *Music Ho!*, 1934).

petit mal

The term *petit mal* (in French literally 'small illness') denotes the less severe of the two forms of epilepsy, in which the sufferer often loses consciousness for brief periods, but seldom collapses or has full-scale seizures. English took it over in the 1830s or 1840s. (Compare **grand mal**.)

petit point

In French literally 'small point', *petit point* denotes both a type of embroidery done on canvas with relatively small stitches, and a type of fine lace. Phonetically, English has the term in two forms: an approximation to the original French, and an anglicized form in which *point* is pronounced as English *point*. The contrasting term is *gros point*, literally 'large point', which signifies a type of large embroidery cross-stitch worked across a double thread of canvas.

piano nobile

Italian *piano nobile* means literally 'great floor, noble storey' (*piano* is a noun use of the adjective meaning 'flat, level', and is related to English *plane*). The term was applied originally to the main floor in Italian *palazzi* and other grand houses, on which the chief reception rooms and salons were situated (generally the first floor), but its application soon spread to non-Italian contexts. It was acquired by English around the beginning of the 20th century.

pièce de résistance

French *pièce de résistance* denotes first and foremost the 'main or most splendid dish in a meal'; and if this seems a curious jump from its literal meaning, 'piece of resistance', the explanation is that *résistance* is being used here in the sense 'substantialness, weighty or enduring quality', so the *pièce de résistance* was originally the most substantial dish, typically the meat course. English took it over early in the 19th century, and its metaphorical sense, 'most outstanding item amongst many', soon followed. (There is a record from the late 18th century, in the writings of Edmund Burke, of a move to anglicize the expression – 'Our appetite demands a *piece of resistance*' – but this seems never to have caught on.)

pied à terre

A *pied à terre* is somewhere where one can, metaphorically speaking, put one's 'foot to the ground'. It is a flat, small house, etc which one can use for temporary accommodation – typically a flat in a town which is owned by someone who lives in the country or is constantly travelling about, and who uses it as a home base when working for a short while in that town. British English took the term over from French in the early 19th century, but it has never really caught on to any extent in American English.

pince-nez

The term *pince-nez* (in French literally 'pinch-nose') denotes spectacles that do not have side-arms, but are kept in place by a spring-loaded clip that holds them firmly on to the nose.

English acquired it in the mid-19th century, and at first used it as an ordinary countable noun – one said 'a pince-nez': 'Our young Charles ... was slightly short-sighted and used only occasionally a pince-nez' (George Eliot, letter, 1876). By the middle of the 20th century we see clear evidence of its being drawn into the pattern of *glasses* and *spectacles*, and treated virtually as a plural noun: 'There was a frail creature in pince-nez at the other end of the table' (*Punch*, 13 August 1941).

pinxit

Pinxit is the third-person singular perfect tense of Latin *pingere* 'paint' (source of English *paint*). Literally 'he or she painted (it)', it was formerly used by artists in signing their paintings, and placed after their name. It was often abbreviated to *pinx*. (Compare **sculpsit**.)

pis aller

A *pis aller* is something one does or accepts because there is no better alternative, even though in itself it is not what one would have wanted. In its original French its literal meaning is 'go worst', or, with the verb *aller* turned into a noun, 'worst course'. There is an isolated record of its use in English in the 17th century, in George Etherege's *Man of Mode* (1676), but it was not until the 19th century that it became firmly established in the language.

pissoir

Differences in urinal design and a preference for euphemistic circumlocution have prevented French *pissoir* (a derivative of the verb *pisser* 'piss') from becoming a general term in English for a public lavatory, but it has been fairly widely used in English since at least the early 20th century in the more restricted sense of a public urinal on the pavement in a Continental European country. In 1919, H. L. Mencken noted in his *The American Language* 'The French *pissoir* ... is still regarded as indecent in America, and is seldom used in England, but it has gone into most of the Continental languages'.

pistolero

A *pistolero* is literally 'someone who wields a pistol'. The word is Spanish in origin, and has been used in English since the 1930s to denote a rough-housing Spanish gunman – or more generally, any gun-toting gangster. It was preceded into English by its French equivalent *pistolier*, which enjoyed a brief vogue in the late 16th and early 17th centuries; and in the 19th century the native formation *pistoleer* was used for a 'soldier armed with a pistol'. Other Spanish words with the suffix *-ero* acquired by English over the years include *bandolero* 'bandit', *caballero* 'Spanish gentleman', *ranchero* 'rancher', *sombrero* and *torero*.

plongeur

A *plongeur* is someone who does the washing-up and other menial jobs in the kitchens of a hotel or restaurant – lowest of the low in the pecking order of catering. The word is of French origin – a derivative of *plonger* 'plunge', referring to the plunging of the dirty pots and pans into the water – and its *locus classicus* in English is George Orwell's account of his career as a washer-up at the Hôtel X in his *Down and Out in Paris and London* (1933): 'Except for about an hour, I was at work from seven in the morning till a quarter past nine at night; first at washing crockery, then at scrubbing the tables and floors of the employees' dining-room, then at polishing glasses and knives, then at fetching meals, then at washing crockery again, then at fetching more meals and washing more crockery'. As Orwell learned, 'a *plongeur* is a slave's slave', with 'a chance of rising to lavatory attendant if trade was good'. Most of the recorded uses of *plongeur* in print in English since Orwell introduced it have been in direct or indirect reference to his.

plus ça change

The French aphorism *Plus ça change, plus c'est la même chose* 'The more things change, the more they stay the same' has been traced back to a passage by A. Karr in 1849: *On change quelquefois le prix, quelquefois le bouchon, mais c'est toujours la même piquette qu'on nous fait boire. Plus ça change – plus c'est la même chose* 'Sometimes the price is changed, sometimes the cork, but it's always the same plonk that we have to drink. The more things change – the more they stay the same'. English began to find a use for its cynical view of the basically unchanging nature of the world, confounding attempts at 'improvement' or 'progress', at the beginning of the 20th century (it is first recorded in Bernard Shaw's *Man and Superman*, 1903), and by the middle of the century its abbreviated form *plus ça change* was in common use.

pocho

Pocho is a derogatory American English word for a US citizen of Mexican ancestry. It was acquired from Mexican Spanish in the mid-20th century, and it goes back ultimately to the Spanish adjective *pocho*. This means literally 'discoloured, pale' and also, in Latin America, 'squat, stubby'.

poilu

Poilu is the slang term used by the French for their soldiers. It is a noun use of the adjective *poilu*, whose original meaning is 'hairy' (it is a derivative of the noun *poil* 'hair, fur', which goes back ultimately to the same Latin source as English *pile* of a carpet). From 'hairy', its connotations spread to 'virile, pugnacious, brave', so in effect the French *poilus* are their 'brave' lads. It was in the trenches in France that English-speakers had their first significant encounter with it, and since then it has been used in English particularly for a 'French soldier of World War 1'.

point d'appui

French *point d'appui* means literally 'point of support' (*appui* is a 'prop' or 'support', and the word goes back ultimately to a Vulgar Latin formation based on Latin *podium* 'support', which also produced English *appoggiatura* 'grace note in music'). It has two principal applications in French, both of which have found their way into English at various times since the early 19th century. First, the literal 'point at which something is supported or gets purchase', often with specific reference to the 'fulcrum' of a lever ('the boatman, with his spoon-shaped paddle fixed against a jutting rock, for a *point d'appui*', Sydney Morgan, *Florence Macarthy*, 1819); this has latterly most often been used figuratively ('Raymond used to arm himself with the newspapers as the safest *point d'appui*', Charlotte Yonge, *The Three Brides*, 1876). Its other use is as a military term, denoting a 'secured position, acting as a base of operations'.

politburo

The *politburo* is the chief policy-making committee of a Communist country, most notably the Soviet Union. The word is Russian, a portmanteau term formed from *politicheskoye byuro* 'political bureau', and it was already a well-established term in English by the mid-1920s. From time to time the semi-anglicized version *politbureau* puts in an appearance, but it has never succeeded in ousting the original Russian form. At the end of the 1980s, politburos were going out of business in Eastern Europe at a rate of knots, and it may not be long before the term is of purely historical significance.

pons asinorum

In former times, the fifth proposition in Euclid's geometry (that the base angles of an isosceles triangle are equal) was thought to be a particular stumbling block for beginners, its difficulty sure to show up those who had no aptitude for the subject. And so it was termed the *pons asinorum*, in Latin literally 'asses' bridge', signifying that those without sufficient brain-power could not cross over it: 'Peregrine ... began to read Euclid ... but he had scarce advanced beyond the *Pons Asinorum*, when his ardor abated' (Tobias Smollett, *Peregrine Pickle*, 1751). Since at least the 19th century the expression has been used in English in the much more general sense 'difficulty which exposes the inexperienced or inept'.

port de bras, plural ports de bras

Port de bras is a ballet term. Literally in French 'carrying of the arms', it denotes the way in which dancers move their arms and the position in which they are placed. A critic may praise a ballerina for an 'exemplary *port de bras*'. The first recorded use of the expression in English is in the August 1912 issue of the *Dancing Times*.

posada

Spanish *posada* means 'inn'. It is a derivative of the verb *posar* 'put down, settle, lodge' – a relative of English *pose* and *pause* – and so is etymologically a 'place for stopping at or lodging at'. It first appeared in English as long ago as the 1760s, and has eked out an existence ever since as a term for a 'Spanish inn'. More recently English has also adopted the Mexican application of the word to any of a series of visits paid to one's friends in the twelve days leading up to Christmas, in remembrance of the days spent by Mary and Joseph trying to find lodging in Bethlehem. And the derivative *posadero* 'inn-keeper' has made occasional guest-appearances in English.

pose plastique

Until the relaxed 1960s ushered in no-holds-barred striptease, gentlemen in search of the unencumbered female form on stage often had recourse to the *pose plastique*. This was a theatrical presentation in which naked or minimally clothed women posed motionless on stage in a scene often suggesting some mildly salacious episode in the life of a beauty of former times (such as 'Cleopatra emerging from her bath'). The golden age of the *pose plastique* was the Victorian era, but it lived on in the statuesque nudes of the Windmill Theatre in the 1930s and 1940s. The French term means literally 'flexible pose', and it came into English in the 1840s. Although it has come to be associated with naked women, it has also been used more generally for any posed scene – in which sense it is more or less synonymous with **tableau vivant**.

post coitum

Post coitum (in Latin literally 'after sexual intercourse') is most commonly used in English, either directly or allusively, with reference to the Latin proverb *post coitum omne animal triste est* 'after sexual intercourse every animal is sad'. There is no actual evidence that such a proverb existed, in so many words, in classical times, but the *Oxford English Dictionary* quotes two sources that express the same sentiments. In *Problems* (once attributed to Aristotle, but no longer accepted as his) we find: *Dia ti hoi neoi hotan prōton aphrodisiasdein arkhōntai, hais an homilēsōsi meta tēn praksin misousin* 'Why do young men, on first having sexual intercourse, afterwards hate those with whom they have just been associated?' Also, Pliny writes in his *Natural History*: *Homini tantum primi coitus paenitentia* 'Man alone experiences regret after first having intercourse'.

post factum

Latin *post factum* – literally 'after the thing done, after the event' – has been used in English since at least the 17th century to denote retrospectiveness, particularly with the advantage of hindsight: 'But textbooks are post-factum rearrangements of long and devious processes of inquiry' (Arthur Koestler, *Insight and Outlook*, 1949). It is by no means uncommon to find it replaced by *post facto* (presumably under the influence of the phrase *ex post facto*, which is also used in English), even though in Latin terms this is a grammatical solecism. (The Latin preposition *post* 'after' took the accusative case, which in the case of *factum* is *factum*. The ablative form *facto* in *ex post facto* – where *post* is an adverb – depends on the preposition *ex* 'from'.) The synonymous Latin *post eventum* has also had some currency in English.

post hoc

Latin *post hoc* – literally 'after this' – is widely used in English as shorthand for the expression *post hoc, ergo propter hoc* 'after this, therefore because of this'. This encapsulates the logical fallacy that because one thing happened after another, it must necessarily have been caused by it – particularly if some causal connection has been demonstrated in an apparently similar case before. For example, if someone falls ill after eating a meal, it does not necessarily follow that the food caused the illness.

post meridiem

Latin *meridies* meant 'noon' (its ultimate origin was the phrase *mediei die*, literally 'at the middle of the day'); and since classical times, *post meridiem* has been used for 'after midday, after noon'. The first record of its occurrence in English dates back to the 1640s, but as far as English is concerned, the full form has never been anything like as common as the abbreviation *pm*. In World War 1 this was expanded in the British Army's signalling code to *pip emma*, and the expression enjoyed some currency in the general language for a while. A close relative in English is *postmeridian* 'of the afternoon', descended from the Latin adjectival derivative *postmeridianus*.

post mortem

Post mortem has gone through four distinct stages of development in English. At first it was a simple prepositional phrase, as in Latin (literally 'after death'), with adverbial function: 'evidence by offices *post mortem*, charters, pedigrees' (Roger North, *The Life of Francis North*, 1734). Then, in the 19th century, it began to be used as an attributive adjective; and by the middle of the century, its frequent occurrence in the phrase *post-mortem examination*, an examination of a body in order to determine the cause of death, had led to its use as a noun, denoting such an examination. Its subsequent metaphoricization to 'retrospective discussion of the course of events, particularly an inquiry into the reasons for the failure of something' appears to date from the early years of the 20th century.

post partum

Latin *post partum* means literally 'after childbirth'. The noun *partus* 'birth' was formed from the past participial stem of the verb *parere* 'bring forth', which is also the source of English *parent* and *parturition*. The use of the phrase in English, often in attributive contexts ('a post-partum examination'), is largely restricted to medical language; its equivalent in general English is *post-natal*.

pot de chambre

The English term *chamber pot* dates back to the 16th century, but (apart from an isolated example in the 18th century) it was not until the late 19th century that it was joined by its French counterpart *pot de chambre*, clothing its earthy function in the decent obscurity of a foreign language. This was often shortened, for convenience, to *pot*, whose French-style pronunciation has been signalled since the 1880s by the spelling *po*.

poule de luxe

French *poule*, literally 'hen', is used for a sexually attractive (and accommodating) young woman (and indeed it occasionally appears in English in the same sense). A *poule de luxe* is a more glamorous version of the same, particularly one who has turned professional – a prostitute. English began to use the expression in the 1930s, and it continues to crop up sporadically: 'The girls, they come around the whole time: they practically picket the place. When I tell these pictures and visions, little duchesses, dazzlers and *poules de luxe* that Mark Asprey isn't around – they're devastated' (Martin Amis, *London Fields*, 1989).

pour encourager les autres

When Voltaire wrote in *Candide* (1759) *Dans ce pays-ci il est bon de tuer de temps en temps un amiral pour encourager les autres* 'In this country [England] it is thought well to kill an admiral from time to time to encourage the others', he was referring to the execution of the English admiral John Byng in 1757. Byng commanded a fleet sent in 1756 to relieve Minorca, at that time under attack by the French. He failed ignominiously in this enterprise, retreating to Gibraltar, and in order to dissuade others from such inept and cowardly behaviour he was court-martialled and shot. The expression *pour encourager les autres* began to creep into English as shorthand for 'putting people on their mettle by the exemplary punishment of a colleague' in the early 19th century.

pourparler

French *pourparler* 'preliminary discussion' is a noun use of an obsolete verb *pourparler* 'discuss in advance, plot', which was formed from *pour-* 'before' and *parler* 'speak'. English took it over towards the end of the 18th century, and uses it (usually in the plural form *pourparlers*) for 'informal discussions preliminary to official negotiations'.

pour-soi

It was the French existential philosopher Jean-Paul Sartre (1905–80) who coined the term *pour-soi*, literally 'for itself'. He used it to designate the individual consciousness, which has freedom of action, as contrasted with what he called the *en-soi* 'in itself', which is simple identity. He introduced both expressions in his *L'Être et le Néant/Being and Nothingness* (1943), and they came into English soon afterwards.

pousse-café

A *pousse-café* is a small glass of spirits, typically brandy or a liqueur, taken with or after coffee, often at the end of a meal. In its most elaborate and highly evolved form it consists of several liqueurs poured into the same glass in layers, without mixing, producing a striped effect. The term *pousse-café*, which has been in fairly common use in English since the 1880s, means in French literally 'push-coffee', the notion being that the spirits help the coffee on its way down to the stomach. The synonymous *chasse-café*, also occasionally used in English, brings us nearer to the closest native-English conceptual equivalent, the *chaser*, a glass of spirits drunk after a glass of beer, or vice versa.

First cousin to the *pousse-café* is the *trou normand*, literally 'Norman hole', a glass of calvados (an apple-brandy produced in Normandy) drunk between courses to make room for the next course.

précis

Like its English cousin *precise*, the French adjective *précis* means 'exact'. But its etymological roots lie in the notion of 'cutting short' (it goes back to the past participle of Latin *praecīdere* 'cut short, abridge', a compound verb based on *caedere* 'cut'). It is this idea of abridgement (preserved in the related *concise*) which survives in the noun use of the adjective for a 'condensed version' or 'summary', which English adopted in the mid-18th century. And in the mid-19th century, English went a step further than French, turning the noun into a verb, meaning 'summarize' – although the mismatch between sound and spelling in its inflected forms (*précising, précised, she précises*) has probably given writers pause ever since.

premier cru

French *premier cru* means literally 'first growth', and it denotes wine of the highest quality in a system of classification. This may sound perfectly straightforward – and in the case of claret from the Médoc, it is. There, the classification introduced in 1855, on the occasion of the Great International Exhibition in Paris, decreed that there were four *premier cru* clarets: Chateaux Haut Brion, Lafitte, Latour, and Margaux (Mouton Rothschild was added in 1973, after a long and vigorous campaign by its proprietor). But elsewhere it is not so simple. The search for ever more hyperbolic superlatives has introduced *grand cru* 'great growth' as a grade above *premier cru*. In Burgundy, for instance, it is the wines of second-ranking vineyards that are termed *premiers crus*; only the absolute *crème de la crème* (Le Montrachet, La Romanée-Conti, Le Musigny, Le Chambertin, etc) are entitled to the designation *grand cru*. And in St-Emilion and Pomerol, the situation is even more anarchic: the latter has the grades *premier grand cru*, *premier cru*, and even *deuxième premier cru* 'second first growth'.

pré salé

French *pré salé* means literally 'salted meadow' (*pré* is descended from Latin *prātum* 'meadow', which also lies behind English *prairie*). The term denotes meadows near the sea, whose grass becomes impregnated with salt and iodine. This grass makes excellent pasture for sheep, whose flesh is thereby made especially tasty and tender, and so over the years *pré salé* has become an adjective designating such sheep. References in

English to '*pré salé* mutton' (now more usually '*pré salé* lamb') go back to the 1830s.

prêt-à-porter

Prêt-à-porter was contributed to English by the French fashion industry. Literally 'ready to wear', it denotes clothes, particularly women's clothes, that are made in standard sizes and can be bought off the peg (as opposed to made-to-measure clothes which are fitted to each individual customer). It seems first to have crossed the Channel in the mid-1950s. In American English in the 1980s it began to be abbreviated to *pret*: 'Christian Lacroix's pret and luxe collections' (*San Francisco Sunday Examiner and Chronicle*, 12 June 1988).

prie dieu

A *prie dieu* was originally a sort of low desk with a sloping shelf for a prayer book or bible and beneath it a footpiece for kneeling on while saying one's prayers. Latterly the term has been extended to a sort of chair with a tall sloping back, originally used for praying. In French it means literally 'pray God'. English has been using it since the mid-18th century.

prima ballerina

A *prima ballerina* is the leading female dancer in a ballet company. The term was borrowed into English from Italian, where it means literally 'first ballerina', in the late 19th century. *Ballerina* 'female ballet dancer' is itself an 18th-century acquisition from Italian, where it is a derivative of the verb *ballare* 'dance'. A *prima ballerina* of particular excellence or eminence is awarded the accolade *prima ballerina assoluta*, literally 'absolute first ballerina'. The equivalent English term for a leading male ballet dancer comes not from Italian but from French: *premier danseur*, literally 'first dancer' (English also uses the feminine form *première danseuse*).

prima donna

Prima donna, in Italian literally 'first lady', came into English in the late 18th century as a term for the 'leading female singer in an opera'. The term dates from the late 17th century, when it very specifically referred to the principal female vocalist in a particular opera cast (the leading male – a castrato – was termed the *primo uomo* 'first man'), but over the centuries its signification has broadened out to 'operatic soprano of great eminence (and fees)'. Greater prestige still is conferred by the honorific *prima donna assoluta* 'absolute first lady'.

Operatic first ladies evidently being felt to be typically 'difficult' and always wanting things their own awkward way, the metaphorical use of *prima donna* for a 'demandingly temperamental and self-centred person, female or male, in any field of activity' grew up. The earliest records of this usage date from the 1930s, and the corresponding adjective *prima donna-ish* appears in the early 1960s.

prima facie

Latin *prima facie* meant 'at first sight' (it depended on a metaphorical extension of *facies* 'face' to 'sight'). Its use in English dates back at least to the early 15th century. At first it was a fairly general term, but by the 18th century there are clear signs of its moving into the legal lexicon, which is its most familiar role today. It can be used as an adverbial phrase (as in 'His action was *prima facie* illegal'), but probably its commonest function now is an adjective, in contexts like *prima facie case* and *prima facie evidence* (that is, evidence that is assumed to be true unless disproved by other evidence). The literal anglicization *at prime face* or *of prime face* has in the past been used in English (perhaps inspired by French *de prime face*), but it has never succeeded in ousting *prima facie*.

There is a single isolated example from the 18th century of the use in English of the synonymous Latin *prima fronte*, literally 'at first forehead'.

primum mobile

In medieval cosmological theory the whole universe, consisting of eight (later nine) concentric spheres, with the Earth at the middle, was put in revolving motion by an additional outside sphere, which went round the Earth from east to west once every 24 hours. Arabic astronomers termed this final sphere *al-muharrik al-awwal* 'the first moving thing', which was variously translated into Latin around the 11th or 12th century AD as *primus motus*, *primus motor*, and *primum mobile* – respectively, 'first moved', 'first mover' and 'first movable'. It was the last which established itself, and it has been used in English texts since at least the mid-15th century. Its metaphorical application to any 'instigator of action' dates from the early 17th century, although nowadays it is more familiar in its anglicized version *prime mover*.

primus inter pares

Latin *primus inter pares* means literally 'first among equals'. In its use in English, which dates from the early years of the 19th century, it generally occurs in the context of a group of equal-ranking persons, one of whom is chosen to be leader. The feminine form *prima inter pares* is occasionally used for a female leader so selected.

princesse lointaine

La Princesse lointaine was the title of a play written in 1895 by the French dramatist Edmond Rostand (1868–1918) (better known for his *Cyrano de Bergerac*). It was based on a theme from the poems of the 12th-century troubadour Jaufré Rudel. Rudel's *princesse lointaine* (literally 'distant princess') was a woman whose love was unobtainable, and the expression has come to be used in English in the 20th century for the ideal of female grace and beauty who remains out of reach.

prix fixe

French *prix fixe* 'fixed price' is used to denote a meal in a restaurant that is offered at an all-inclusive price for a restricted choice of courses. It began to infiltrate English towards the end of the 19th century, but it is only within recent years that it has begun to challenge **table d'hôte** as the major foreignism used in English for such meals.

pro bono publico

Latin *pro bono publico*, literally 'for the public good', has been used in English since the early 18th century, designating in broad terms anything that is done for the benefit of the community at large rather than for the sake of private gain. Never more than a marginal item in British English (although it enjoyed a vogue in the early 20th century as a pseudonymous signature appended to letters written to newspapers), in American English it has established itself firmly enough to be widely used in the abbreviated form *pro bono*, denoting something done or given without charge – a lawyer doing *pro bono* work, for instance, would be giving his services free of charge for the benefit of those unable to afford it.

procès-verbal, plural procès-verbaux

French *procès-verbal* denotes a written record of some proceeding – minutes of a meeting, for instance, or an official report
submitted by the police following some incident. There are signs
of its influence on English as early as the 17th century, but at
first it seems always to have been anglicized, either partially to
process verbal or wholly to *verbal process*. The authentic French
form did not begin to make headway in the language until the
early 19th century.

pro forma

Latin *pro forma* has had a long and curious history in English.
It means literally 'for form' – that is, 'for the sake of form, as a
matter of form' – and it has been used in that sense in English
since the 16th century. Denoting something that is done purely
as a formality, it has commonly been employed adjectivally in
the combination *pro-forma invoice*, signifying usually an invoice
that is sent either before an order is placed or before the goods
are delivered, in order to describe the goods, give advance
notification of cost, etc. Probably since at least the beginning of
the 20th century, *pro forma* has been used on its own as a noun
meaning 'pro-forma invoice', and before the century was very
old it had been extended to any 'form to be filled in' – presumably on the model of *form*.

pronto

The adverb *pronto* has a range of connotations in Spanish,
including 'soon' and 'early', but it is in the very specific and
urgent sense 'at once, immediately' that it has come into English.
It made its first appearance as long ago as the mid-19th century,
introduced into American English by Spanish-speakers in the
southwest USA, and it has never become fully naturalized in
British English. Spanish *pronto* itself is descended from Latin
promptus 'ready', which also produced English *prompt*.

pro rata

Pro rata means 'according to a rate or proportion' – that is,
'proportionately'. But although the element *rata* looks like a
noun (and indeed was the source of the English noun *rate*), it
was not originally so. In medieval Latin, *pro rata* was in fact
short for *pro rata parte* or *pro rata portione* 'according to a fixed
part'. *Rata* was the feminine ablative singular form of the adjec-

tive *ratus* 'fixed, established', from which English *ratify* comes. *Pro rata* first appears in English texts in the 16th century, but its offspring *rate* was already established as an English word 100 years earlier.

prosit

Latin *prodesse* meant 'be beneficial', and its third person singular present subjunctive *prosit*, literally 'may it be beneficial', has found its way into several modern European languages as a toast preparatory to drinking wine, beer, spirits, etc (the 'it' refers to the drink). It was through German that the term first came into English in force, in the early years of the 20th century, and the contracted German form *prost* has also enjoyed some currency, but neither has become fully naturalized – for the most part they are used in contexts which call for a flavour of Continental conviviality.

pro tempore

Pro tempore 'for the time being, temporarily' is one of those Latin expressions that is more familiar in English in its abbreviated form (*pro tem*) than in its full form. But it was not always so. Records of the use of *pro tempore* in English texts go back to the 15th century, but *pro tem* does not appear, at any rate in print, until the early 19th century. In classical Latin, incidentally, *pro tempore* did not mean 'for the time being, temporarily'; *ad tempus* was the Latin term for 'temporarily', and *pro tempore* stood for 'according to circumstances, according to the situation'.

proxime accessit

If someone is declared *proxime accessit*, it means that he or she is the runner-up in some academic contest – has finished second in a competitive examination, for instance, or just failed to win a scholarship or prize. It counts as an 'honourable mention'. The Latin expression means literally 'he or she came next' (*accēdere* 'go to a place, approach' is the source of English *accede* and *access*), and it has been around in English since the mid-19th century. It is sometimes abbreviated to simply *proxime*, and *accessit* can be used on its own with the same meaning.

puna

Punas are cold, arid, inhospitable plateaux in the high Andes, at or above 10 500 feet. The name is ultimately from Quechuan, the language of the Andean Indians, but it reached English in the 17th century via Spanish. Samuel Purchas in his *Pilgrimage* (1613) reported that 'there are other Deserts in Peru, called Punas, where the Ayre cutteth off mans life without feeling'. The term is also used as a synonym for 'mountain sickness', the difficulty in breathing experienced at high altitudes.

punto banco

Punto banco is a casino gambling game similar to baccarat, in which the players bet on whether the banker (*banco*) or the punter (*punto*), both representing the house, will win a particular trick. The two components of its name are Italian (*punto* 'point' and *banco* 'bank'), but the term itself does not appear to have been of Italian origin, and it may be that it was concocted in English.

Q

quaere

Quaere is the imperative form of Latin *quaerere* 'seek, ask' (which is the ancestor of English *acquire*, *inquire*, *require*, *quest*, etc). It has been put to two uses in English, both dating back to the 16th century. First, it appears as a sort of introductory device signalling a question. This was a legacy of the rhetoric of medieval Latin scholarship ('*Quaere*, how many angels can stand on the head of a pin?'), and today it puts in an appearance only as a self-conscious revival, bringing a whiff of candle-wax and dusty volumes. Second, it appears as a noun, meaning 'question'; but since the 17th century this has been gradually anglicized, under the influence of *inquiry*, so that *query* is now its only extant form.

quai hai

When in former years a cry of *Quai hai!* penetrated to the kitchen of a bungalow in Camberley or a villa in Eastbourne, it was a sure sign that the person calling for his servant was an old India hand. The exclamation is an adaptation of Urdu *koī hai?* 'is anyone there?', and was used by the British in India for summoning servants. Records of it in English, variously spelled *qui hy*, *quai hi*, and even *koi hai* as well as *quai hai*, go back to the early 19th century, and it continued in use well into the 20th: 'That he [Major Flint] had seen service in India was, indeed, probable by his referring to lunch as tiffin, and calling to his parlourmaid with the ejaculation of "Qui-hi". As her name was Sarah, this was clearly a reminiscence of days in bungalows' (E. F. Benson, *Miss Mapp*, 1922). It was also used as a noun to denote a British person living in India, and particularly in Bengal.

quantum meruit

Quantum meruit is a legal term meaning in Latin literally 'as much as he or she has deserved'. It is used in circumstances where someone sues for payment for work done when no price has been fixed (and often no formal contract entered into), on the basis of what would be a reasonable price for such work. Its use in English law goes back at least to the mid-17th century.

quattrocentro

The Italian system of designating centuries often causes confusion to English-speakers who try to use it, and *quattrocento* is a case in point. To begin with, it means literally 'four hundred,' but Italian uses it for 'fourteen hundred'; and as if this were not bad enough, it goes directly against standard English usage, which uses an ordinal system rather than a cardinal system for naming centuries, so that *quattrocento*, which denotes the 'fifteenth century', is always in danger of being misinterpreted as the 'fourteenth century'. Nevertheless, English persists in employing it, and its relatives (see also **cinquecento**, **secento**, and **trecento**), when referring to Italian fine arts and literature. In the case of *quattrocento*, this means essentially the early work of the giants of the Renaissance, including Leonardo, Michelangelo, Raphael, Giorgione and Ariosto.

que será será

The fatalistic Spanish expression *que será será* made its greatest impact on English in a song of that title, written by Ray Evans and Jay Livingston and made famous by Doris Day. She sang it at full volume in Alfred Hitchcock's film *The Man who Knew Too Much* as part of a ruse to rescue her young son from the clutches of would-be assassins – and it won an Oscar for Best Film Song in 1956. The lyrics gave its literal English translation: 'whatever will be, will be'. The Italian equivalent *che sarà sarà* has also enjoyed some currency in English.

Quicunque vult

Quicunque vult is an alternative name for the Athanasian Creed, a 5th-century statement of the Christian faith which expounded and defined the doctrine of the Trinity. It comes from the first words of the Creed in Latin, *Quicunque vult salvus esse* 'Whosoever wishes to be saved'. Its use in English dates back at least to the 15th century, and it is sometimes abbreviated to *Quicunque*.

quid pro quo

Latin *quid pro quo* means literally 'something for something'. English originally used it, in the mid-16th century, in the straightforward sense of 'something in place of something else', and two particular usages arose out of this that have now died out. Apothecaries employed it to denote a medical substance that was substituted for another, sometimes on purpose and for valid reasons, but also fraudulently or by mistake. And the notion of mistaken substitution led to the use of *quid pro quo* for a 'blunder caused by replacing one thing by another or mistaking one thing for another'. Guy Miege's *Great French Dictionary* (1687) equated *quid pro quo* and *mistake* when glossing French *quiproquo* – and indeed French *quiproquo* still means 'mistake caused by taking one thing for another, misunderstanding'. The English term's main modern connotation of 'one favour or advantage given in exchange for another' had already emerged by the end of the 16th century.

quien sabe

Spanish *quien sabe?*, typically uttered with a shrug of the shoulders, means 'who knows?' English began to use it in the early 19th century, generally in contexts referring to Spain or Spanish-speaking coutries, and generally also with an underlying suggestion of indifference, of a reluctance to bestir oneself in order to find out the answer to the question, of a fatalistic acceptance that some things will always remain unknown.

quis custodiet ipsos custodes

The Roman satirist Juvenal had cynical views on the possibility of keeping one's wife's attentions from wandering to other men. 'Lock her up!' said one man. *Sed quis custodiet ipsos custodes? Cauta est et ab illis incipit uxor* 'But who will guard the guards themselves? Your wife is as cunning as you, and begins with them'. The expression *quis custodiet ipsos custodes?* has passed into English to denote the inadvisability of reposing total trust in those put in charge of a situation that offers temptations to wrongdoing. It is often abbreviated to *quis custodiet?* by those who cannot remember the rest of it.

qui vive

French *qui vive?* (literally 'who lives?') is used as a sentry's challenge, roughly equivalent to English 'Who goes there?' *Vivre* 'live' is being employed here in the sense 'long live', as in *vive la France*, the force of the question being to require the unknown person to state which side he supports. The verbal phrase was turned into a noun *qui-vive*, meaning 'sentry's challenge', and this is frequently used in the expression *être sur le qui-vive* 'be on the alert, as sentries are supposed to be'. English took this over in the early 18th century, translating most of it, as *be on the qui vive* (Jonathan Swift is the first writer on record as using it).

quod erat demonstrandum

Demonstrandum is the gerundive of the Latin verb *demonstrare* 'show' – that is to say, the form which expresses the desirability of showing something. *Quod* is 'as much as, what' and *erat* means 'was', so the complete Latin clause signifies 'that which was to be demonstrated'. The technical usage which brought it into English appears to have been as an appendage to the proof of a theorem in Euclidian geometry, affirming that what the theorem set out to show had indeed been proved. But it has also – and particularly in its abbreviated form *qed* – long been widely used in a much more general context, asserting that the truth of something uncertain or doubtful had been convincingly demonstrated.

Other Latin expressions of the same pattern to have been used in English include *quod erat faciendum* 'that which was to be done' and *quod erat inveniendum* 'that which was to be found'.

quod vide

Quod vide is part of the learned Latin superstructure of textual organization that has been inherited by English. It means literally 'which see' (*vide* is the imperative form of Latin *videre* 'see'), and is used to indicate that a particular word or other item is treated more fully elsewhere in the book in question, particularly as an entry in its own right in a dictionary, glossary or encyclopedia. It is usually encountered in its abbreviated form *qv*, the first record of which in English is in Edward Phillips's dictionary *The New World of English Words* (1678).

quo warranto

Medieval Latin *quo warranto?* meant 'by what warrant?' It was used in legal terminology for a writ issued by the Court of King's Bench, requiring a person to show by what authority he or she claimed a particular office or privilege. Such writs have long since gone out of use, but the term survives as the name of a legal proceeding designed to elicit the same information. In the 17th century it was used as a verb, meaning 'serve with a writ of *quo warranto*'.

R

raison d'être

The *raison d'être* of something is the rational justification for its
existence. The phrase was imported into English, apparently in
the mid-19th century, from French, where it means literally
'reason to be'.

raison d'état

Raisons d'état (the plural is commoner than the singular) are
invoked by a government when it has to defend some unpopular
action, withhold some piece of information, etc without revealing the real reason for doing so. This Machiavellian concept,
with its subtext of concealment of shady dealing, has been
familar to students of statecraft since at least the 16th century,
and at first it was generally expressed in English by the native
term *reason of state* (a translation either of French *raison d'état*
or of Italian *ragione di stato* – a term which appeared in John
Florio's *Queen Anna's New World of Words*, 1611). The French
version did not make its English debut until the mid-19th
century, but it is probably now commoner than its vernacular
alternative.

rapporteur

A *rapporteur* is someone who attends a committee meeting, con-
ference, etc and is delegated to give a report on its proceedings
to another body. The French word is a derivative of the verb
rapporter 'give a report on', and there is an isolated example of
its use in English around 1500 in the sense of 'reporter'. In its
modern, more specialized sense it is on record as being used by
Lord Palmerston in a diary entry for 13 July 1791, but its
full-scale incorporation into English, originally as part of the
terminology of international diplomacy, did not begin until the
20th century.

rapprochement

If you bring about a *rapprochement* between two antagonists, you restore harmonious relations between them. The word is an early 19th-century borrowing from French, where it originally meant literally a 'bringing closer together' (it is a derivative of the verb *rapprocher* 'bring together'). It is most commonly used in the field of international relations, to denote a re-establishment of friendship between countries which had been hostile to each other.

rara avis, plural rarae aves

When the Roman satirist Juvenal wrote of the *rara avis in terris nigroque simillima cygno* 'a rare bird on this earth, like nothing so much as a black swan', he was creating a metaphor which has survived nearly two millennia into modern English. On the whole the vernacular version, *rare bird* (first recorded in the 1890s), is now the commoner, but *rara avis* goes back in English to the early 17th century, and is still used by those with a leaning towards classical tags. The term denotes 'something or someone remarkable and unusual', although awareness of its literal meaning leaves it open to an application to birds, real or artificial. The character Gutman, for instance, played by Sidney Greenstreet in the film of *The Maltese Falcon*, referred to the priceless statuette of the bird as a *rara avis*.

ras

In the Amharic language of Ethiopia, *rās* means 'head, chief'. It has been used in English since the 17th century to denote an Ethiopian king or chieftain, but it is most familiar now as part of the name by which the Emperor Haile Selassie of Ethiopia was known between 1916 and 1930, when he came to the throne: *Ras Tafari*. This was adopted by a Jamaican sect that regards Haile Selassie as God, the Rastafarians. Italian designs on Ethiopia from the late 19th century established a link between the two countries, and in the 1920s English began to use *ras* for a local boss in fascist Italy.

ratskeller

German *ratskeller* denotes literally the 'cellar of a town hall' (*rat* is short for *rathaus* 'town hall' and *keller* is related to English *cellar*). Such cellars are standardly the venue for establishments dispensing beer and other refreshments, and it is this particular aspect that has brought the word into English. In American English it is used for a restaurant or bar that echoes the style or ambience of a German *ratskeller*.

re

Re is the ablative case of Latin *res* 'thing'. The *Oxford English Dictionary* records one isolated quasi-prepositional use of *re* in 18th-century English meaning 'relating to': 'amused by Charlett's trick *re* Tacitus' (Thomas Hearne, *Remarks and Collections*, 1707). But it was not until the late 19th century that the usage we are familiar with today – 'about, concerning, with reference to' – began to emerge. It appears to have started in commercial usage (as in '*Re* your order of the 12th inst') but soon spread into the general language, and it has frequently been the butt of commentators who regard it as pretentious. (See also **in re**.)

realpolitik

German *realpolitik* means literally the 'politics of realism' – that is, the pursuit of policy based not on idealism or morality, but on a clear-sighted, not to say cynically ruthless view of what is advantageous or practicable. The term is particularly associated with the career of Bismarck (1815–98), the 'Iron Chancellor', who by force of ambition and political acumen raised Prussia and latterly Germany to the status of a world power, and who coined the saying 'Politics is the art of the possible' (*Die Politik ist die Lehre von Möglichen*). The use of *realpolitik* in English dates from the period of World War 1 (it is first recorded in the writings of George Bernard Shaw).

réchauffé

French *réchauffé*, a noun use of the past participle of *réchauffer* 'heat up again', denotes literally 'heated-up dish, dish made from reheated left-overs', but it is widely used metaphorically for a 'rehash', a 'reworking of previously used material'. It was in this derogatory sense that English took the word over at the beginning of the 19th century. Since then it has been joined by the adjectival usage 'rehashed' (together with the anglicized *rechauffeed*) and by the derivative *réchauffage*, also used for a 'rehash'.

recherché

Etymologically, something that is *recherché* has to be carefully 'sought' out, and hence is particularly choice or rare. The word is an adjectival use of the past participle of French *rechercher* 'search for' (whose Old French ancestor gave English *research*). English adopted it early in the 18th century, and by the 19th century it had become fashionable to use it to refer to refined or dainty dishes, exquisite clothes, etc (*exquisite*, incidentally, also means etymologically 'sought out'). In present-day usage the balance of its meaning has shifted to 'out-of-the- way, exotic, rare'.

recherche du temps perdu

Marcel Proust's seven-part novel *À la recherche du temps perdu* (1913–27) views in a vast span the life of the narrator Marcel as it led up to the point at which he began writing the book. A major theme is the recreation of an apparently irrecoverable past, both through the promptings of sensory recall (as in the episode of the madeleine dunked in lime-blossom tea, whose taste conjures up a range of forgotten impressions) and through the work of art itself. In the second half of the 20th century, several instances are on record of the use of French *recherche du temps perdu* (literally 'search for the lost time') in English to denote an attempt to recapture the past, either in reality or imaginatively.

réclame

French *réclame* means 'publicity, advertising' (it is a derivative of the verb *réclamer* 'lay claim to'). English borrowed it in the latter part of the 19th century, using it particularly with the connotation of 'self-publicity', of the sort which leads to notoriety ('Byron was an adept in the art of *réclame*', Mary Braddon, *The Golden Calf*, 1883), and in the 20th century it has come to mean mainly 'public acclaim, fame, glory'.

reculer pour mieux sauter

The French expression *reculer pour mieux sauter*, literally 'move backwards in order to jump better', encapsulates the potential advantage of a strategic withdrawal: if you give a little ground now, you will retain enough strength to return to the attack later. The sentiment is first recorded in English in a translation of Jean d'Arras's *Mélusine* of around 1500 ('Alwayes wyse men goo abacke for to lepe the ferther'), but the French formulation does not seem to have passed into English until the early 19th century.

redivivus

Latin *redivivus* means 'that lives again, brought back to life' (it was formed in the post-classical period from *red-*, a variant of the prefix *re-* 'again', and *vivus* 'alive'). It was adopted into English in the early 17th century, but although it was occasionally used in its original form in the titles of books, it was more usually anglicized, to *redivive*. This was also turned into a verb *redivive*, meaning 'bring back to life', and formed the basis of another adjective, *redivivous*, meaning 'liable to revive'. These had all largely disappeared from general scholarly usage by the end of the 17th century, and the modern English use of *redivivus* is a 19th-century revival. It is used for 'revived, brought back into existence, repeated in a new form'. It usually follows the noun (so for example 'Munich *redivivus*' might refer to a perceived repeat of Neville Chamberlain's 1938 agreement with Hitler).

reductio ad absurdum

Latin *reductio ad absurdum*, literally 'reduction to the absurd', has a very specific, and also a wider, more general meaning in English. It is used in logic for a method of refuting an argument or proposition by pursuing it to a logical conclusion that is manifestly ridiculous, or for a method of proving a proposition by assuming that its negative is true and showing that this leads to a logical absurdity. In non-technical parlance it denotes the following through of an idea or principle until it reaches an absurd conclusion. Its introduction into English dates from the mid-18th century. Also occasionally used, when the depths of absurdity are to be plumbed, is *reductio ad absurdissimum*, using the Latin superlative form. And based on the same model is the *reductio ad impossibile*, denoting the destruction of an argument by demonstrating the impossibility of its conclusion.

régisseur

French *régisseur* can mean generally 'manager', but it was specifically as a theatrical term that English began to use it in the early 19th century. It covers a range of roles, from the relatively humble stage-manager to someone who has artistic control over the staging of a work, or of a company's whole output. In recent years it has also begun to come into use for the manager of a French wine estate: 'The Smith team, *oenologue* [technical expert in wine-making] Dominique de Beauregard and *regisseur* [sic] Claude Gérin ... are wary of leaving the white wine too long on its lees' (*The Vine*, January 1991).

remuage

Remuage is a technique used in the making of champagne and other sparkling wines. As the wine ferments in bottle, dead yeast cells and other debris are deposited. These must be removed or the wine will be cloudy. The normal processes of racking and fining are not available once the champagne is in bottle, because they would also remove the fizz. So instead, the sediment is brought to the top of the bottle, where it can be frozen and swiftly removed without letting out too many bubbles. The method of bringing the deposit to the top is termed *remuage*: the bottles are placed horizontally in special racks (known in French as *pupitres* 'desks'), and every day are given a slight shake and turn, to disturb the sediment, and upended a fraction, to move it towards the cork. By the end of the process the bottles are upside-down, with the sediment in their necks. Traditionally this is done by hand, by a *remueur* (many of whom get arthritic wrists after long years in damp cold cellars), but for the most part machines have now taken over. English acquired *remuage* and *remueur* in the 1920s. Both are derivatives of French *remuer*, used here in a specialized sense, but also being a general verb meaning 'move around'.

rentier

A *rentier* is someone whose income is largely or wholly unearned, deriving not from wages or salary but from dividends on stocks and shares, rents from property, etc – what used to be known euphemistically as a 'private income'. The term was borrowed into English from French (where it is a derivative of *rente* 'revenue, income') in the mid-19th century, and now, although it is still used by economists and sociologists, it has rather the air of a past age: 'This book ... catches and holds with deadly accuracy the extinct world of pre-war rentier society; the majors, padres and lady water-colourists – with their private incomes and servant problems; their bridge teas and games of golf' (cover blurb for E. F. Benson's *Mapp and Lucia*, 1970).

repêchage

In a sporting competition, the *repêchage* is an additional round in which contestants who finished as runners-up in the semi-finals get another chance to win a place in the final. It was originally a rowing term, and first appeared in English in the 1920s; it has since become more widely applied to other sports. It was borrowed from French, where it originated as a derivative of the verb *repêcher*. This means literally 'fish out again' (*pêcher* is 'to fish'), and has been extended metaphorically via 'rescue a drowning person' to 'give someone who has failed an examination another chance to succeed at a later exam'.

répétiteur

A *répétiteur* is a musician employed by an opera house to play the piano at rehearsals and also to coach the principals in their parts. The term is also applied to someone who supervises ballet rehearsals. English adopted it in the first half of the 20th century from French, where it also denotes more generally a 'private tutor' or 'coach', and a 'teacher in charge of pupils' preparation time'. It is a derivative of the verb *répéter* 'repeat', hence 're-hearse'. Also occasionally used in English are the feminine form *répétiteuse*, the corresponding Italian term *repetitore*, and also German *repetitor*, which denotes a 'private tutor at a German university'.

répondez, s'il vous plaît

This request for an answer (in French literally 'reply, please') is familiar in English mainly in its abbreviated form, *RSVP*, which appears on invitations. Its force is to get the invitee to say whether he or she accepts the invitation. Its use in English goes back at least to the 1830s, and over the years it has blossomed from a mere abbreviation to a noun ('Is there an RSVP on the card?') and even, somewhat anomalously, to a verb, meaning 'reply to an invitation, as requested': 'The printed invitations to 27 journalists were delivered.... We all RSVP'd' (*The Observer*, 19 February 1978).

requiescat in pace

Latin *requiescat in pace* means 'may he/she rest in peace'. *Requiescat* is the third person singular present subjunctive form of *requiescere* 'rest, repose'. The phrase, or its plural form *requiescant in pace* 'may they rest in peace', is found carved on gravestones, invoking a peaceful afterlife for the person interred underneath. It is in its abbreviated form, *RIP*, that it has truly become part of the English language, though. First recorded in the early 19th century, it has become a shorthand term for signalling metaphorical as well as physical demise. It is often interpreted as short for English *rest in peace*, which happily fits the abbreviation as neatly as the Latin original, and it has even been facetiously interpreted, when the departed was the victim of a bomb, as 'rest in pieces'.

réseau, plural réseaux

French *réseau* means literally 'net' or 'network'. It is descended from Old French *resel* 'little net', a diminutive form of *rais* 'net', which in turn went back to Latin *rēte* 'net', source of English *reticulated*. English has adopted the word in four distinct specialized applications: first, and by far the earliest (from the 16th century) as a 'piece of netting used as a foundation in lacemaking'; and then, in the 20th century, as a 'network of fine lines laid over a photograph of stars for the purpose of measurement'; as a 'screen with a pattern of tiny coloured dots or lines, formerly used in colour photography'; and as an 'intelligence network, especially within the French resistance in World War 2'.

res gestae

Latin *res gestae* means literally 'things done'. *Gestus* was the past participle of the verb *gerere* 'carry, carry on', which has also given English *gerund*, *gestation*, *gesticulation*, *gesture*, and *register*, amongst many others. As an English term, there are two main strands to its history. The first evidence of its adoption comes in the early 17th century, when it was used in the general sense of 'things accomplished, achievements'. But from at least the mid-18th century it has also been used as a legal term, denoting 'facts or remarks that are incidental to a case but are nevertheless admissible in court as throwing light on the matter at issue'.

res ipsa loquitur

Res ipsa loquitur enshrines a legal principle. In Latin literally 'the thing speaks for itself' (Latin *loquī* 'speak' lies behind English *locution* and *loquatious*), the term denotes that if an accident has been established as happening, that in itself is sufficient to prove negligence on the part of the defendant unless he or she can show that the injury to the plaintiff was due to another cause. It has a long history in English legal terminology, stretching back at least to the mid-17th century.

resurgam

Latin *resurgam* means 'I shall rise again'. It is the first person singular future of *resurgere* 'rise again, reappear', which has given English *resurgence*. Its first known appearance in English dates back to the mid-17th century, and it has been used both in a specifically Christian context, to express faith in the resurrection of the soul and one's own participation in it (it is often carved on tombstones), and more generally as an assertion of a determination to surmount present difficulties.

retroussé

A *retroussé* nose is one that turns up slightly at the end (generally speaking the term is one of approval for a charming feature of a woman's nose, not of condemnation for an unsightly malformation). *Retroussé* is an adjectival use of the past participle of French *retrousser* 'turn up, roll up, tuck up' (a relative of English *truss*). It began to be used in English around the beginning of the 19th century. A related word acquired by English is the noun derivative *retroussage*, a term applied to the process of wiping some of the printing ink out of the etched lines of a plate into a thin film over the unetched surface, so as to give the resultant print some background colour other than white.

revenons à nos moutons

The French expression *revenons à nos moutons*, literally 'let us return to our sheep', means 'let us get back to the main point'. It is a signal to abandon a digression. It comes ultimately from an episode in the late 15th-century French comedy *La farce de Maistre Pierre Pathelin*, in which a cloth-merchant accuses a shepherd of ill-treating his sheep. While making his charges in court he continually wanders off the point, and the judge has to say to him several times '*Mais, mon ami, revenons à nos moutons*'. The expression was frequently quoted by the French author Rabelais (c.1494–1553), and the first recorded allusion to it in English dates from 1617; but it was not until the 19th century that it came to be widely used in English. It is sometimes facetiously anglicized to 'let us return to our muttons'.

rien ne va plus

Film scenes featuring the rich and glamorous losing money in the casino at Monte Carlo have made the expression *rien ne va plus* familiar to generations of English-speakers who have never been near a roulette wheel. In French literally 'nothing further goes', it is the signal by the croupier in a game of roulette that he is about to spin the wheel, and that therefore no more bets will be accepted. French being the international language of roulette, *rien ne va plus* has established itself firmly in English (although the vernacular *no more bets* is also heard). French *rien* 'nothing', incidentally, is descended from Latin *rem*, the accusative form of *rēs* 'thing'.

rijsttafel

Rijsttafel is in origin and inspiration a dish of the East Indies, but the extensive history of Dutch colonization in that region has made it a cornerstone of Dutch cuisine. In fact, it is more of a meal than a dish: its centrepiece is a large bowl of rice (hence its name, a Dutch compound formed from *rijst* 'rice' and *tafel* 'table'), but surrounding it like satellites are lots of smaller dishes containing various Indonesian specialities, such as satay, curry, spicy soup, dried shrimps, and scrambled eggs. The use of the term *rijsttafel* in English dates back at least to the late 19th century.

Risorgimento

The Risorgimento was the 19th-century Italian nationalist movement that led to the unification of all the independent Italian states into a single Italy. Activists had started uprisings as early as the 1820s, but things really got under way in 1859, when Piedmont under Cavour freed Lombardy from Austrian control. The following year Garibaldi led his celebrated Expedition of the Thousand to liberate most of southern Italy, which was subsequently joined to northern states, such as Tuscany and Romagna, under the umbrella of Piedmont; and in 1861 the independent kingdom of Italy was proclaimed. Italian *risorgimento* is the etymological equivalent of English *resurgence*, and means literally 'renewal, renaissance'. English was using the term by the 1880s, and in recent decades there has been some evidence of its metaphorical application to any 'renewal' or 'revival'.

risqué

French *risqué* means broadly 'risky, hazardous' (it is an adjectival use of the past participle of the verb *risquer* 'risk'), but it also has the narrower sense of 'on the verge of impropriety, especially in being sexually suggestive'. It is this sense of the word, which has the advantage of combining euphemism with a hint of French naughtiness, that English has taken over. Records of its use in English go back to the 1860s, and over the past 130 years it has established itself very firmly in the language – firmly enough to fight off sporadic attempts in the 19th century and later to anglicize it to *risky*.

rite de passage

The anthropological term *rite de passage* was coined by Arnold van Gennep, and used by him as the title of a book published in 1909. It denotes a ritual or ceremony that marks a person's transition from one status to another – for example, childhood to adulthood, or the unmarried to the married state. It first appeared in English in 1911, but over the years the anglicized version *rite of passage* has become commoner than the original French form.

roche moutonnée

Geographers use the term *roche moutonnée* to denote a large mass of rock that has been shaped by glacial action: its front has been rubbed smooth and round by the passage of the glacier, but its rear is rough and craggy. However, this was not its original meaning. It was coined in the late 18th century by Horace-Bénédict de Saussure, and he used it to refer to any of a terrain of small rounded hillocks, usually covered with scrub or trees, which supposedly resembles a fleece (French *moutonné* means 'fleecy', and is a derivative of *mouton* 'sheep') or a wig of a sort then called *moutonné*. The term in its present-day application came into English in the middle of the 19th century.

roi fainéant

French *roi fainéant* means 'lazy king' (the adjective *fainéant* was formed from *faire* 'do' and *néant* 'nothing'). It was originally applied as an insulting epithet to any of the later Merovingian kings of Gaul, from the death of Dagobert to the overthrow of Childeric III in 751. They ruled virtually in name only, real power being exercised for much of this period by Charles Martel.

The term was introduced into English in the latter part of the 19th century, and is often used metaphorically to refer to any inactive or nominal ruler. *The Economist*, for instance, in 1966 called US President Eisenhower a '*roi fainéant*'.

roi soleil

Roi soleil, in French literally 'sun king', is an epithet applied to the French king Louis XIV (1638–1715). It comes from the figure of a sun surrounded with rays which was used by him as a heraldic device, but it is now generally interpreted as referring to the splendour of his reign, as symbolized by the sumptuous palace of Versailles. It first appeared in English towards the end of the 19th century, and is sometimes used metaphorically to denote anyone who exercises ostentatiously pre-eminent power. In 1966, for instance, *The Guardian* referred to the British newspaper publisher Cecil King as 'the *roi soleil* of Long Acre'.

roman à clef

A *roman à clef*, in French literally a 'novel with a key', is a novel in which real people or events are depicted under a more-or-less thin veneer of fiction. The 'key' is what reveals who the characters were based on. It may be a literal list of correspondences – for example, Mrs Manley in her novel *The New Atlantis* (1709) attacked several notable figures of the day, and provided a glossary identifying the real people beneath the pseudonyms – or it may be a more subtle clue hidden within the body of a text. The earliest recorded use of the term *roman à clef* in English dates from the 1890s.

roman-fleuve

The French term *roman-fleuve*, literally 'stream novel', denotes a novel, or series of novels, that in a broad sweep of narrative tells the story of a character or set of characters (such as the members of a family) over an extended period of time. As a genre the *roman-fleuve* reached its apogee in France in the first four decades of the 20th century: an example is Roger Martin du Gard's *Les Thibault*, a ten-volume sequence following the careers of two brothers. It never caught on to the same extent in Britain, although notable *roman-fleuves* have been produced by the likes of Anthony Trollope, whose 'Palliser' novels have a cast of recurring characters, and John Galsworthy, whose sequence *The Forsyte Saga* tells the story of three generations of the Forsyte family. The term *roman-fleuve* is first recorded in English in the 1930s.

roman policier

A *roman policier* is a detective novel. The French adjective *policier* 'of the police' is a derivative of *police*, but it is only used in certain restricted combinations. The term was borrowed into English in the 1920s (it is actually first recorded in the works of Agatha Christie), but does not appear to have become at all common until the 1960s. English of course already has a perfectly adequate term for a detective novel – *detective novel* – and the particular niche into which *roman policier* has fitted is as a literary-critical term, considering detective fiction as a literary genre.

routier

French *routier*, a derivative of *route* 'road', means 'long-distance lorry-driver', but its use in English in the latter part of the 20th century has been inspired mainly by the *Guide des Relais Routiers*, whose nearest English equivalent would be a 'Guide to Transport Cafés'. This is a guidebook giving advice on good-value hotels and restaurants to be found by the roadside in France, intended originally for lorry-drivers but increasingly used by travellers and tourists. So now in English one refers to '*routier* guides', '*routier* restaurants', etc.

ruat caelum

Latin *ruat caelum* means literally 'though heaven fall'. *Ruat* is the third person singular present subjunctive of Latin *ruere* 'fall', which also lies behind English *ruin* and *congruent*. The phrase is used in the sense 'come what may, though the worst happen'. Probably the best-known context in which it appears (in the plural) is the maxim *Fiat justitia et ruant caeli* 'Let justice be done though the heavens fall', an assertion of the primacy of justice over all other considerations. The first known example of its use in an English text is in William Watson's *A Decacordon of Ten Quodlibeticall Questions Concerning Religion and State* (1602). Similar sentiments are expressed in *Fiat justitia et pereat mundus* 'Let justice be done though the world perish', attributed to the Holy Roman Emperor Ferdinand I (1503–64).

rus in urbe

It was the Roman epigrammatist Martial who coined the phrase *rus in urbe*, which means literally 'the country in the town'. It has been used in English since at least the mid-18th century to convey the notion of creating the illusion of a rustic idyll in the centre of a city – for example with an approximation to a cottage garden tucked in behind an urban terrace. The poet Thomas Gray (1716–71) even created the nonce-adjective *rus-in-urbe-ish* from it.

S

sabra

Modern Hebrew *sābrāh* literally means 'prickly pear'. This sharply bristled cactus, with edible fruit, grows quite commonly in the Negev desert, in the southern part of Israel; and this, together perhaps with the plant's toughness and endurance, led to a new metaphorical application of the term *sābrāh*. It came to be used first for a Jew born in Palestine and then, after the creation of the state of Israel in 1948, for a native-born Israeli. It came into English, in the slightly anglicized spelling *sabra*, around 1945. In about 1970 a new liqueur made in Israel was put on the market. It was called *sabra*, although it had no trace of prickly pear among its ingredients: it was made from orange and chocolate.

sachem

Sachem is a North American Indian contribution to the English language. Specifically, it comes from the Narraganset language of the Rhode Island area, in which *sâchim* means 'chief'. English adopted it as early as the 1620s as the term for the chieftain of certain tribes or confederations of Native Americans, and already by the 18th century it was being turned to metaphorical use in American English. It now has two such applications: generally to the 'top man', the 'big cheese', such as a party boss or political leader; and more specifically to a top official of the Tammany Society, a 19th-century New York political association affiliated to the Democratic Party which was notorious for its corruption. The Narraganset word is descended from a prehistoric Algonquian **saakimaawa*, which also produced *sagimau* in the Abnaki language of Maine and Southern Quebec. English took this over and anglicized it as *sagamore* 'Indian chief'.

sacré bleu

Sacré bleu has become for English-speakers an archetypal French expression of explosive exasperation, indignation, surprise, etc. Now in French usually *sacrebleu*, it means literally 'sacred blue', but its literal meaning is of no consequence. It is a euphemistic alteration of *sacré Dieu*, one of a range of mild French oaths based on *sacré*, roughly equivalent to English *blessed*. Others include *sacré nom* 'sacred name' and *sacré tonnerre* 'sacred thunder'. *Sacré bleu* is first recorded in an English text in the 1860s. Part of the same family is the exclamation *sapristi*, often used in English when a Gallic flavour is required; it is an alteration of *sacristi*, literally 'sacred Christ'.

saeva indignatio

The Irish-born satirist Jonathan Swift composed his own epitaph: *ubi saeva indignatio ulterius cor lacerare nequit* 'where fierce indignation can no longer lacerate his heart' (it was carved on his tomb in St Patrick's Cathedral, Dublin, where he lies beside his beloved Stella). It expressed the bitter fury which Swift felt in the face of humankind's multifarious inhumanities, and which he poured into his scathing satires. Since the mid-19th century the phrase *saeva indignatio* has come to be used in English, in reminiscence of Swift, to denote the burning, passionate anger that fires the committed artist, reformer, etc.

Salon des Refusés

The *Salon* was an exhibition, latterly held every year, of paintings and sculptures produced by members of the French Royal Academy (somewhat akin to the British Royal Academy summer exhibition). Its name came from its being held in the Salon d'Apollon in the Louvre. It was the only public art exhibition in Paris, which meant that artists who did not belong to the Academy could not get their work seen. This became an increasingly sore point, and finally, in 1863, Napoleon III ordered the setting up of a so-called *Salon des Refusés* (literally 'exhibition of refused works') at which those who had been rejected by the Academy's jury could exhibit. Amongst its contributors were Manet (whose *Déjeuner sur l'herbe*, featuring a naked woman having a picnic with two clothed men, caused a scandal which closed the exhibition), Pissarro and Whistler. Use of the term *Salon des Refusés* in English dates from at least the 1890s, and since then it has often been employed metaphorically for any 'exhibition of works of art not officially sanctioned'.

salus populi suprema est lex

In his *De Legibus* the Roman orator and statesman Cicero wrote *salus populi suprema est lex* 'the good of the people is the chief law'. The maxim has been adopted by English jurists (sometimes in the abbreviated form *salus populi*). It implies that, for instance, an injury to an individual may not be remediable at law if to do so would be against the 'public interest'.

samizdat

The term *samizdat* denotes the system of illegal underground publishing carried on in the USSR and other Eastern European countries during the years of Communist sway, when only material that was ideologically pure was allowed to be put out. Those with a message critical of the official party line had to tap it out secretly on ancient typewriters, turn it into pamphlets and books on clapped-out duplicating machines, and risk arrest and prison to distribute it. Russian *samizdat* is short for *samo-izdátel'stvo* 'self-publisher', a compound formed from *sam* 'self' and *izdátel'stvo* 'publisher' (which itself is derived from *izdát'* 'publish', a compound verb made up of *iz* 'out' and *dat'* 'give'). It began to be widely used in English in the mid-1960s. Also sporadically employed in English is the derivative *samizdatchik* 'someone who writes or publishes samizdat material'.

san

San is a Japanese honorific title equivalent to English *Mr, Mrs, Ms*, etc. With the increasing importance of Japan in the world community, English-speaking businessmen, academics, and so on have had to get used to handling the term, and particularly its placement after the name (so *Mr Moto* becomes *Moto-san*). It is a contracted form of Japanese *sama*, which is a title of respect for particularly exalted personages. An additional subtlety in the use of *san* is that when it is placed after a female name, the prefix *O-* is often put before the name.

sanbenito

The *sanbenito*, or *sambenito*, is a garment associated with the Spanish Inquisition, which those accused of heresy were forced to wear. It was a sort of tunic, and it came in two styles: those who admitted their heresy and professed penitence were given a yellow sanbenito with a red T-shaped St Anthony's cross on the front and back; but impenitents were forced to wear an altogether more grisly garment, black with flames and devils painted on it, to remind them of the consequences of their impiety, both in this world – they would be burned at the stake – and the next (this sort of sanbenito was also called a *samarra*). The name of the garment, borrowed from Spanish and first recorded in English in the mid-16th century, is an ironic allusion to its resemblance to the outer garment worn by Benedictine monks (*San Benito* is Spanish for 'St Benedict').

sancta simplicitas

Legend has it that when Jan Hus (c.1369–1415), the Bohemian religious reformer, was tied to the stake waiting for the executioner to light his fire, an old peasant came up and threw an extra bundle of twigs on to the pile. Hus is supposed then to have said *O sancta simplicitas!* 'Oh holy simplicity!' – the implication being that the man did not really realize what he was doing. The expression has come to be used in English as an exclamation of wonderment or exasperation at someone's naivety (the earliest record of its use is in a letter from the actress Fanny Kemble written in December 1847).

sanctum sanctorum

Latin *sanctum sanctorum* means literally 'holy of holies'. It is a word-for-word translation, via Greek *to hagion tōn hagiōn*, of Hebrew *qōdesh ha-qqodashīm* 'holy of holies'. This was the name given to the innermost chamber of the Temple, where the Ark of the Covenant was kept, and as such crops up several times in the Bible. English began to use it towards the end of the 14th century, but it has always had competition from the translated English version *holy of holies*. From the 18th century, in addition, it has been employed metaphorically, and often jocularly, for a private room or other secluded place where one can do one's own thing without interference or interruption.

sang froid

French *sang froid*, literally 'cold blood', denotes 'composure under stress or danger, imperturbability' – what would be meta-phoricized in English as *coolness* (*cold-blooded* being a negative term, evoking the ruthless aspect of impassivity). English has used it since about the middle of the 18th century. It is interesting to note, incidentally, that in 17th-century written French, *sang froid* often became *sens froid*, literally 'cold sense', *sens* in this context being phonetically close to *sang*.

sans

French *sans* 'without' (a descendant ultimately of Latin *sine* 'without') made its debut in English in the 13th century. It never succeeded in ousting the native *without*, and by the end of the 17th century had died out of general use. However, the fame of the passage in the 'Seven Ages of Man' speech in Shakespeare's *As You Like It*, in which old age is characterized as 'sans teeth, sans eyes, sans taste, sans everything', led to its retention in the language in direct (and often facetious) allusions to this (as in Lytton Strachey's 'I am sans teeth, sans eyes, sans prick . . .'). It is pronounced more or less as it was in the English of Shakespeare's day, to rhyme with *bans*, not with the modern French nasalized vowel.

sans-culotte

In late 18th-century France the upper-crust gentry wore knee-breeches (in French *culottes*, a derivative of *cul* 'arse'), but the ordinary working-class man in the street had a garment more akin to modern long trousers; accordingly, the former were wont to label the latter with the nickname *sans-culottes*, literally those 'without knee-breeches'. The epithet took on a more specific role in the Revolution, when it came to denote an 'extreme working-class republican'. It was quick to cross the Channel (it first appeared in English in 1790), and before long its meaning had spread to the more general 'extreme radical or revolutionary'. It was quite a high-profile term in this wider sense in the 19th century, and spawned a number of derivatives (*sansculotterie*, *sansculottic*, *sansculottish*, *sansculottism*, etc), but nowadays it has largely returned to its historical roots.

sasquatch

Down the Pacific coast of North America, in British Columbia and down into the northwestern USA, they have a legend of a large hairy manlike monster that lives up in the mountains and leaves its footprints in the snow. As with the yeti, no confirmed sightings have been made and no concrete evidence has been found, but the myth lives on, and is inordinately popular. Its name originated in the Salish languages, spoken by the native

Americans of that region, and first appeared in English in the 1920s; it means literally 'hairy men'.

satyagraha

Satyagraha is the Sanskrit term applied to the policy of passive resistance advocated by Gandhi as a means of bringing about political reform in India and ultimately independence. He began it soon after his return to India from South Africa in 1914, and in 1920 he published a book on it called *Non-Co-operation*. He would not allow his followers and supporters to commit any violent act in pursuit of their political aims. Amongst the highlights of his campaign were several fasts and the walk from Ahmedabad to the sea in 1930 to protest against the government's salt monopoly. Sanskrit *satyāgraha* means literally 'insistence on truth'; it is a compound noun formed from *satya* 'truth' and *āgraha* 'act of holding on, insistence'. It is first recorded in English in 1920.

sauve qui peut

French *sauve qui peut* means literally 'save who can' – that is, 'let anyone who is able, save himself'. But from being a verb phrase it was turned into a noun, denoting the sort of often panic-stricken stampede that results when a crowd of people are trying to save themselves from a dangerous situation and it is 'every man for himself'. This is the sense in which English acquired the term, in the early 19th century, and since then it has even occasionally been converted back into a verb phrase, *à la française*: 'All the baboons do in such a case is *sauve qui peut* with an alarm call that makes the mountains echo' (E. N. Marais, *My Friends the Baboons*, 1939).

savoir faire

Someone who has *savoir faire* knows what to do in any situation, has in particular the social tact that enables him or her always to do or say the right thing. In French the expression means literally 'knowing what to do', and it was adopted into English in the early 19th century (apparently, as far as the record shows, as one of Sir Walter Scott's many introductions). Of greater antiquity in English is the similarly formed *savoir vivre* (French 'knowing how to live'), which denotes a 'sophisticated knowledge of life and the usages of the world'; it dates back at least to the mid-18th century.

sayonara

Sayonara is Japanese for 'goodbye'. It has been turning up in English texts since the latter part of the 19th century. It is nearly always used in Japanese contexts, but it has become well enough known to be recognizable out of its Japanese environment. Rudyard Kipling is even on record as using it as a verb, meaning 'say *sayonara* to'.

schadenfreude

For long a gap existed in the English lexicon for a term that would encapsulate the notion of gaining pleasure out of the misfortune of others. Possible candidates included Greek *epikhairekakia* (literally 'rejoicing at bad things') and German *schadenfreude*. It was the latter which caught on, in the second half of the 19th century. It is a compound noun made up of *schade* 'harm' (a relative of English *unscathed*) and *freude* 'joy'. In a 'Words' column on foreignisms in *The Observer* (24 February 1991), John Silverlight noted the same sentiment expressed in La Rochefoucauld's maxim 'In the suffering of our dearest friends there is something that is not displeasing', and in the possible Confucianism 'There is no spectacle more agreeable than to observe an old friend fall from a rooftop'.

schola cantorum

Medieval Latin *schola cantorum* means literally 'school of singers'. It was a term originally applied to the papal choir in Rome, founded in the 4th century AD and greatly developed and expanded by Pope Gregory I (after whom 'Gregorian chant' is named) in the 6th century. The tradition of having a choral school attached to a cathedral or monastery, which trained the choir for that institution, evolved through the Middle Ages, and continues in various forms to this day. In that context the term *schola cantorum* now has a rather antiquarian air, but it is still used in the name of singing groups that specialize particularly in church music of earlier centuries (eg the *Schola Cantorum Basiliensis*).

schuss

Schuss is a skiing term. Literally in German 'shot', it denotes a straight steep downhill course or section of a course. It is also used for the act of skiing down such a run. It appears to have been introduced into English by Otto Lang in his book *Downhill*

Skiing (1937). It has since been put to work as a verb too, both transitive and intransitive, meaning 'ski down a steep slope'.

schwärmerei

German *schwärmerei* is a derivative of the verb *schwärmen*. This means literally 'swarm', but it is also used metaphorically for 'enthuse', and so *schwärmerei* denotes 'enthusiasm' – particularly 'excessive or gushing enthusiasm'. English took it over in the middle of the 19th century, often applying it specifically to 'religious enthusiasm' or 'fundamentalist zeal', but its more recent usage has centred on 'sexual infatuation', and especially the 'adolescent crush' of one schoolgirl for another or for her teacher. English has also acquired the related noun *schwarm* 'enthusiasm, craze, crush' and the adjective *schwärmerisch* 'infatuated', and it has even adopted the verb *schwärmen* as *schwärm*: 'It's true we weren't allowed to schwärm' says Amanda of her school in Joyce Cary's *The Moonlight* (1946).

schweinehund

Schweinehund is one of those expressively aggressive-sounding German words seized on enthusiastically by writers of pulp World War 1 and 2 fiction to give a touch of supposed authenticity to the lurid utterances of German soldiers ('Die, English schweinehund!' and so on). In German literally 'pig-dog', its force as a term of abuse is roughly similar to that of English *bastard*. It was imported into English in the World War 2 period, and it is quite common to find it altered to the not-quite-authentic form *schweinhund*.

scilicet

Scilicet is far more familiar in its abbreviated form, *sc*, than in full; indeed, there must be many who use the abbreviation without knowing what its expansion really means. Latin *scilicet* is a contracted form of the verbal phrase *scīre licet* 'it is permitted to know'. *Scīre* means 'know', and lies behind English *science*; and *licet* is the third person present singular of *licēre* 'be allowed', source of English *licence* and *licit*. From being 'permitted to know', it moved on in sense to 'being obvious', and *scilicet* came to be used as an explanatory interpolation in texts, denoting 'what this means of course is ...'. Its role is to introduce an elucidation of an obscure word or passage, or to supply a missing piece of text. Formerly often abbreviated to *scil*, it is now most commonly encountered as *sc*.

scire facias

Latin *scīre facias* means 'you should make [him] know'. The verb *scīre* 'know' is the ancestor of English *science*, and *facias* is the second person singular present subjunctive of *facere* 'make, do'. The phrase was a characteristic feature of the wording of a type of writ formerly issued to instruct someone to appear in court and show cause why a judicial record entered against his or her name should not be acted upon (eg enforced or annulled). It came to be used as a term for the writ itself, and also for the proceedings instituted under the terms of such a writ. Such writs are now virtually legal museum pieces, although they are still used for the revocation of royal charters.

sculpsit

Sculpsit is the third person perfect singular of Latin *sculpere* 'scratch, carve'. It is often inscribed on a piece of sculpture, an engraving, etc, together with the name of the artist, denoting 'he/she carved this'. (Compare **pinxit**, used similarly on paintings.)

seicento

The *seicento* is the 17th century in Italian art, literature, etc (on the Italian system of nomenclature for centuries see **quattrocento**). This was the period of the baroque, whose leading figures included the architect and sculptor Bernini, the painters Caravaggio and Caracci, the architect Borromini, the painter and poet Salvator Rosa, and the poets Giovanni Battista Marini and Gabriello Chiabrera. Use of *seicento* as an art-historical term in English dates from the 19th century, as does that of the Italian derivative *seicentismo*, a synonym of *seicento* which is also used for the 'character or style of Italian works of art produced in this period'.

senex, plural senes

The Latin adjective *senex* means 'old' (it lies behind English *senile* and *senate*, and its comparative form has given English *senior* and *sir*). It was used as a noun to denote 'old man', and this has come to be employed in English as a technical term in literary criticism, referring to the stock character of the 'old man', particularly as he appears in the classical comedies of Terence and Plautus and later works which continue their tradition. It is sometimes qualified with an adjective: for example, the *senex amans* is the 'old man in love', the 'infatuated old fool'.

sensu stricto

Latin *sensu stricto* (or *stricto sensu*, as it is sometimes formulated) means 'in the strict sense, in the narrow sense' (it is in the ablative case). English has used it since at least the middle of the 20th century to denote that a term is being used in its narrowest or most accurate sense, rather than broadly or loosely. In particular, biologists and other natural scientists employ it to stress that a name is being used in its scientific sense rather than in a general sense. It is sometimes explicitly contrasted with *sensu lato* 'in the broad sense', and also with **grosso modo**. Other similar Latin phrases sometimes encountered in English include *sensu bono* 'in a good sense', *sensu malo* 'in a bad sense', and *sensu proprio* 'in its proper sense'.

seppuku

English-speakers are used to referring to the Japanese form of ritual suicide involving disembowelment as *hara-kiri* (first recorded in the 1850s). But in fact *hara-kiri* is a relatively colloquial word: the more dignified Japanese term for the practice is *seppuku*. This is a conflation of *setsu fuku*, which comes ultimately from Chinese and means literally 'cut open the stomach'. The first evidence of it in English texts comes from the latter part of the 19th century.

se tenant

Se tenant, in French literally 'holding together', is a philatelic term. It denotes two stamps that are printed together as a pair, or are not separated for some reason: for instance, it might be a pair of similar design but different denominations, or a pair of stamps identical except for an imperfection or printing error in one of them. Its use in English dates from the early part of the 20th century.

Sezession

German *Sezession* means literally 'seceding', and was used in the late 19th century for various groups of artists who, impatient of the hidebound traditionalism of the official academies, 'seceded' from them to form their own associations. The first such grouping came into being in Munich in 1892, but the best-known is the Vienna Sezession. This was founded in 1897 by Gustav Klimt, and it took the lead in promoting the German version of *art nouveau*, which is known as the *Jugendstil*. At first, in the 1890s, English tended to translate the German term as *Secession*, but *Sezession* is first recorded in English in 1905, and since then has gradually taken over as the main form. An artist of the *Sezession* is known as a *Sezessionist*.

shiksa

Shiksa is a Jewish word for a gentile woman or girl. It was adapted into English in the late 19th century from Yiddish *shikse*. This is the feminine form of *sheygets* 'gentile boy', which in turn goes back to Hebrew *sheques* 'defect, blemish, abomination'. Yiddish *shikse* also lies behind English *shickster*, an English slang term dating back to at least the 1830s. Like its model, this originally denoted a 'gentile woman', with no hint of non-respectability, but gradually it came down in the world until it was being used for a 'prostitute'. (Compare *goyah* at **goy**.)

shlemiel

In American slang, a *shlemiel*, or *schlemiel*, is a person who is inept, unlucky, or always being put upon by others – a 'loser', in other words. The term was adopted, in the late 19th century, from Yiddish *shlumiel*, but it is not entirely clear where this came from. The likeliest explanation is perhaps that it represents the name of a character in the Bible (Shelumiel the son of Zurishaddai, leader of the tribe of Simeon, as named in Numbers 1:6), who apparently always came off worst when he led his people into battle. An additional possibility is that this could have been reinforced by the name of Peter Schlemihl, hero of the novel *Peter Schlemihls wundersame Geschichte* ('The strange story of Peter Schlemihl') (1814) by the German writer Adelbert von Chamisso (1781–1838). This tells the story of a poor young man, Schlemihl, who gives away his shadow to the devil in return for money, but finds that his wealth cannot save him from becoming an outcast in society because of his lack of a shadow.

shlep

If you *shlep* something, or *schlep* it, you don't just carry it, you complain about it afterwards. The verb denotes the lugging of something wearisomely heavy, usually over a long distance, at the cost of much trouble and exertion. It was introduced into English, in the early part of the 20th century, from Yiddish *shlepn*. This in turn came from German *schleppen* 'drag'. It is also used intransitively, in the sense 'go or travel effortfully or at great inconvenience to oneself, traipse'. From it was derived the noun *shlepper*, which is a general derogatory term for a 'foolish, clumsy, or untidy person', and has also been used for a 'scrounger' or 'beggar'. The abbreviated *shlep* is also used in these senses, and the noun *shlep* 'tedious period or piece of work' is presumed to be the same word.

shlimazel

A *shlimazel*, or *schlimazel*, is someone whose bread always falls butter-side down, an unlucky jerk, a born loser. The word was introduced into American English in the early part of the 20th century from Yiddish. The Yiddish language developed from a basis of medieval German, with an admixture of Hebrew (plus some Romance and Slavic elements), and in *shlimazel* its two major sources are combined. Middle High German *slim* meant 'crooked' (it is the ancestor of modern German *schlimm* 'bad' and is related to English *slim*), and Hebrew *mazzāl* is 'luck' (as in *mazel tov* 'good luck'). Put them together and you get 'bad luck'. It seems likely in fact that the word's first brush with English came not in the USA, but in Britain. It occurs, in forms such as *shlemozzle*, in late 19th-century East End slang, but meaning not 'unlucky person' but 'row, rumpus'. Apparently over the decades the *l* dropped out to give the modern British colloquialism *shemozzle*.

shlock

Something that is *shlock*, or *schlock*, is of low quality, cheap and shoddy. The word can be used either as an adjective or as a noun – 'shoddy material or goods, junk'. It came into American English in the early 20th century from Yiddish, where it originally meant 'broken or damaged merchandise'. It is generally assumed that this was derived from the verb *shlogn* 'hit', which in turn came from German *schlagen* 'hit', a relative of English *slay*. A *shlockmeister* or *shlockmaster* in American English is someone who deals in cheap trashy goods.

shmaltz

Shmaltz, or *schmaltz*, in Yiddish means literally 'melted fat, dripping'. It comes from German *schmalz*, which is related to the German verb *schmelzen* 'melt' and also to English *enamel* and *smelt*. English took it over in the 1930s as applied specifically to the melted chicken fat used in Jewish cookery, and also in the metaphorical sense (in which it has since become widely known) 'unctuous sentimentality, particularly in writing, music, art, etc'. In this sense it has spawned the derogatory adjective *shmaltzy* (first recorded in 1935) and also a verb, *shmaltz something up*, meaning to make it shmaltzy, and especially to play music in an oversentimental way. In Jewish cuisine a *shmaltz herring* is a sort of pickled herring.

shmatte

The original meaning of *shmatte*, or *schmatte*, is 'rag'. It is a Yiddish word, introduced into American English in the 20th century, but Yiddish got it from Polish *szmata* 'rag'. It has a range of applications in English. From 'small cloth, rag' it has spread out metaphorically to 'something cheap or shoddy', which is presumably the basis for the further extension of its meaning in American English to 'contemptible person'. This is the American version of the word. But it has also made its way into British English, in slightly altered form, as *shmutter*. This is used for 'garments, clothing' ('a nice bit of shmutter' would be a complimentary reference to a new suit or dress) and also by extension for 'rubbish' ('a load of old shmutter').

shmuck

Shmuck, or *schmuck*, is one of a long line of words for 'penis' that have been pressed into service for '(male) idiot, fool' (others include *prick* and *plonker*). This particular one is a Yiddish contribution to English, first recorded at the end of the 19th century. And Yiddish in turn got it from German *schmuck*, which means 'ornament, decoration'. Also current in American slang is *shmo*, which is an abbreviated version of *shmock*, a variant of *shmuck*.

shnozzle

The most famous of all shnozzles belonged to Jimmy Durante
(1893–1980), the American comedian. His nose was so promi-
nent that it became his trademark, and the word *shnozzle* 'nose'
(sometimes fancifully altered to *shnozzola*) became his nickname.
The word is Yiddish in origin, and is probably an adaptation
of Yiddish *shnoitsl*, with some contribution no doubt being made
by English *nozzle*. *Shnoitsl* is a diminutive form of *shnoits* 'snout',
which in turn came from German *schnautze* (a relative of English
snout). An alternative form of the word in English is *shnozz*,
which is either an abbreviated form of *shnozzle* or a direct
borrowing from Yiddish *shnoits*. In American slang, *on the shnozz*
means 'exactly, precisely'.

shogun

The shoguns were for many centuries the real rulers of Japan.
Their period of control began in the 12th century, and lasted
nearly 700 years, during which time their dynasty wielded actual
power while the emperor, or *mikado*, was a mere figurehead.
Their rule came to an end in 1867, when the feudal system was
abolished. The original shoguns had been supreme military
commanders in Japan, from the 8th century AD onwards. Their
name was a Japanese adaptation of Chinese *jiāng jūn* 'general',
a compound noun formed from *jiāng* 'lead, command' and *jūn*
'army'. When the military leaders took political power in 1192,
the title *sei-i-tai shōgun* 'barbarian-subduing great general' was
conferred on them, usually shortened to *shōgun*. The first record
of the term in English dates from the early 17th century (mis-
spelled *shongo*).

shtetl, plural shtetlach

A *shtetl* was a Jewish village or other small community as found
in Eastern Europe and Russia before World War 2. Virtually
isolated ghettoes, the last of them were destroyed and depopu-
lated as Hitler made his way East. The word means literally
'little town'. It is a Yiddish diminutive form based on German
stadt 'town' (a relative of English *stead*). The first records of it
in English date from the late 1940s.

shtik

An entertainer's *shtik* is his or her 'turn' or 'set': for example, a
comedian's routine of gags would be his *shtik*. The word (which
comes in a variety of alternative spellings, such as *shtick* and
schtick) came into American English from Yiddish in the mid-
20th century; and Yiddish in turn got it from German *stück*
'piece, play'. It is used in a range of extended senses, denoting
a person's particular talent, a gimmick, or the sort of thing
someone does for preference, someone's 'bag'.

shul

English *shul* and *school* are doublets: that is to say, they share a
common source, but have developed along very different lines.
That source is medieval Latin *scōla*, which was borrowed into
Old English as *scōl* and has subsequently become *school*. Old
High German acquired the Latin word as *scuol*, which has
become modern German *schule* 'school'; and Yiddish adopted
this as *shul*, but uses it not for 'school', but for 'synagogue' (as
being the place where the Jewish religion is taught). It passed
into English in the late 19th century, where, like *school*, it can
be used for the institution and the activities that go on there as
well as for the building: *after shul*, for instance, denotes 'after the
synagogue service'.

sic

Latin *sīc* had a variety of uses, amongst them (albeit rarely) as
an affirmative equivalent to English *yes* (from which Italian,
Spanish and French get *si*). But the common semantic denominator of most of them is 'in this way, thus'. That is the general
sense in which English adopted it in the late 19th century, but
it uses it only in very restricted contexts – as a parenthetical
insertion into a piece of text, after an erroneous or apparently
erroneous form in a quotation, indicating that it accurately
represents an error in a source being quoted and absolving the
writer of any possible charge of misquotation (eg 'He was said
to have "flaunted" [sic] all the rules').

sic transit gloria mundi

Latin *sic transit gloria mundi* means literally 'thus passes the glory
of the world', and it has been used as an aphorism in English
since at least the 16th century, conveying the notion that all
earthly fame is transitory, certain to be consigned in the end to

the dustbin of history. So familiar has it become that it is often used in the abbreviated form *sic transit*, with the same meaning. It is thought that the source of the expression may be in the *Imitation of Christ* by Thomas à Kempis, a 15th-century German Augustinian monk, where we find *O quam cito transit gloria mundi* 'Oh how quickly passes the glory of the world'. Its form has made it the natural butt of punning transformations based on the name Gloria (eg *Sic transit Gloria Swanson*).

siècle

French *siècle* means 'century', or more broadly 'age'. Its ultimate source is Latin *saeculum* 'generation, age', which also produced English *secular*. English has adopted it in two distinct and long-separated stages. First, its Old French ancestor *siecle* was taken over into Middle English, and anglicized in various forms such as *sekil* and *seicle*. It was used for 'the secular world' as well as for 'age' and 'century', but it seems to have died out by the end of the 16th century. However, in more recent times English has turned its attention to the modern French form, using it particularly in certain fixed expressions, such as **fin de siècle**, **grand siècle**, and *siècle d'or*, literally 'golden age', which is often used specifically to refer to the period of Louis XIV's reign in France.

sieg heil

German *sieg heil* means 'Hail victory'. *Sieg* 'victory' is a component part of many German forenames, including *Siegfried* 'Victory-peace' and *Siegmund* 'Victory-protection'. The phrase was adopted by the Nazis as their salute and war-cry, to be shouted almost as an incantation by the crowds who attended their mass rallies. English adopted it during World War 2, and has since quite often used it allusively for any mindlessly aggressive chant that asserts superiority. It has even occasionally been turned into a verb.

siffleur

The *siffleur*, nowadays a virtually extinct species, was once a hardy perennial of music-hall bills. He was, put simply, someone who whistled. But this was no ordinary whistling: popular tunes of the day were dispatched powerfully to every corner of the house via a vigorous embouchure, embellished with tongue-twirling trills and often bird calls. The last of the famous *siffleurs* in Britain was probably Ronnie Ronalde. The term *siffleur* was borrowed in the early 19th century from French, where it is a derivative of the verb *siffler* 'whistle'; the feminine form *siffleuse* is occasionally encountered in English too. *Siffleur* is also used in Canadian English for various animals that make a whistling sound, notably the hoary marmot.

simpatico

It was French *sympathique* that in the 1850s introduced the notion of 'congenialness' into the English group of *sympath-* words, but it was quickly followed by *simpatico*, borrowed from Italian, with a little help from Spanish *simpático*, and around 1911 German *sympathisch* joined them. Since the beginning of the 20th century English *sympathetic* has increasingly moved in to take the place of these, but *simpatico* has retained a place as expressing an intuitive rapport and understanding, perhaps considered as a characteristic of outgoing southern European temperaments. The whole family of words goes back ultimately to Greek *sumpátheia*, a compound formed from the prefix *sun-* 'together' and *páthos* 'emotions, feelings'.

sine die

Latin *sine die* means literally 'without a day' (*sine* with the addition of the adverbial suffix *-s* produced French *sans* 'without'). It has been used in English since the early 17th century with reference to the adjournment of a session of a court, parliament, or other meeting, to denote that no day has been fixed for its resumption or reassembly – and hence often, by implication, that no plans exist to do so. Right from the start, too, it has been employed from time to time in the more general sense 'indefinitely'. It is sometimes abbreviated to *sd*.

sine prole

Latin *sine prole* means 'without offspring'. Latin *proles* 'offspring' produced *proletarius*, source of English *proletarian*, which originally denoted a Roman citizen of the lowest class who had no money or property with which to serve the state, and therefore served it by producing children. The phrase is used mainly in legal contexts, and particularly in the expression *demisit sine prole* 'died without issue, died having no children'. Other variants occasionally used in English include *sine legitima prole* 'without legitimate offspring' and *sine mascula prole* 'without male offspring'. It can be abbreviated to *sp*.

sine qua non

A *sine qua non* is an indispensable factor, something without which matters cannot proceed. The Latin term means literally 'without which not' (*qua* is the feminine ablative singular form of the pronoun *qui* 'which', whose unexpressed antecedent is *causa* 'thing' – thus, 'thing without which not'). The phrase was widely used in medieval Latin religious and philosophical writings, and appears to have its origins in the works of Aristotle (its Greek antecedent is *hōn ouk aneu* 'which things not without'). Its earliest appearance in English, in the late 16th century, was as an adverbial phrase, but since the beginning of the 17th century it has been employed as a noun, and that is by far its commonest use today. In the 19th century its plural, *sine qua nons*, was included briefly in the panoply of euphemisms adopted by the Victorians for 'nether garments' (apparently modelled on the contemporary vernacular *indispensables*), and the extent of its naturalization can be gauged by the 19th-century nonce derivatives *sine-qua-nonical* and *sine-qua-nonniness*. In Scottish legal terminology, the alternative version *sine quo non*, with the masculine form *quo*, is used.

singspiel

Singspiel was a type of opera, developed probably from English ballad opera, that enjoyed a vogue in Germany and Austria in the second half of the 18th century. Its name (in German literally 'sing-play') suggests its main characteristic: it had passages of spoken dialogue interspersed with songs. Examples include Mozart's *Die Entführung aus dem Serail* and *Die Zauberflöte*, but perhaps the most prolific composer of such operas was one J. A. Hiller (1728–1804). Use of the term in English dates from the latter part of the 19th century.

skoal

It is thought that *skoal* may first have impinged on English in 1589, when James VI of Scotland visited Denmark. There, he would have encountered the Danish toast *skaal*, a descendent of Old Norse *skál* 'bowl' (which also produced English *scale* 'pan of a balance', hence in the plural 'weighing machine'). Certainly it was as a Scottish term that it was first in common use, in the

17th century. Its later relaunch, in the mid-19th century, was probably helped out by the related Swedish *skål*. In present-day English the spelling *skol* has probably taken over from *skoal* as the main form. Scottish English also originated the use of the word as a verb, meaning 'drink toasts', and this too was revived in the rest of Britain, in the 20th century.

slainte

Slainte, relatively unfamiliar in print, becomes more easily recognizable when it is heard (it is pronounced roughly 'slahncher'). It means literally 'health' in Gaelic, and is used in Ireland and Scotland as a salutation when drinking a toast. It has been appearing in English in the appropriate contexts since the early 19th century. It is commonly found in the expression *slainte mhath* (in Scots Gaelic) or *slainte mhaith* (in Irish Gaelic) (pronounced /'slaːntʃə vaː/), which means 'good health'.

sobriquet

To say that someone has a particular *sobriquet* is a posh way of referring to their nickname, or to some descriptive epithet applied to them: thus the boxer Jack Dempsey rejoiced in the sobriquet 'the Manassa Mauler', because he was born in Manassa, Colorado. English adopted the term, in the 17th century, from French, where it appears to be the same word as *soubriquet* 'tap under the chin'. This in turn may have been an alteration of an earlier **souzbequet*, formed from *souz* 'under' and *bec* 'beak'. Defying chronology, English actually borrowed the word's original form, *soubriquet* (now superseded in French), in the 19th century, and this is now if anything commoner than *sobriquet*.

société anonyme

A *société anonyme* is the French equivalent of a limited company. The term means literally 'anonymous society' (the underlying connotation being that the company is not (necessarily) registered in the name of the principal interested party or parties). It is most familiar in English in its abbreviated form *S.A.*, which also stands for Spanish *sociedad anónima* and Italian *società anonima*.

soi-disant

French *soi-disant* denotes that which one is 'saying about one-self' – one's own estimation or claim for one's qualities, not necessarily endorsed by others, and quite possibly exaggerated or fraudulent: 'As I get older ... I become increasingly disturbed by the suffering inflicted by the *soi-disant* human race on lesser creatures, which ... should be our responsibility' (*The Sunday Times Magazine*, 2 December 1990). The French term means literally 'oneself- saying', and was adopted into English in the early 18th century. The extended sense 'so-called', applied to things or abstract qualities rather than people, emerged in English in the 19th century.

soigné

French *soigné* is the past participle of the verb *soigner* 'look after, care for', itself a derivative of the noun *soin* 'care'. English took it over in the early 19th century, and has always used it to convey an aura of sophisticatedly precise elegance, particularly in regard to a person's grooming – it implies not a hair out of place, not a speck of dust on the collar. The niceties of French gender are particularly carefully preserved, so that when an immaculately turned-out woman is referred to, the feminine form *soignée* is generally used. In colloquial French *soigné* has another meaning, 'first-rate, excellent', but this has never crossed the Channel. In the Middle Ages the related French *soigneux* 'careful' was borrowed into English, as *soignous*, but it has not survived.

soirée

French *soirée* is a derivative of *soir* 'evening'. It shares its meaning, but it also goes one step further, and denotes an 'entertainment held in the evening', typically a small private party at someone's home or other premises. It is in this latter sense that English acquired the word in the late 18th century. It was very much the fashionable term in the 19th century, so much bandied about that a semi-humorous anglicized spelling *swarry* enjoyed some currency, and it was even turned into a verb (meaning 'entertain at a soirée'); but nowadays it has a air of antiquated pretentiousness. English has also occasionally used the French term *soirée dansante* for an evening party with dancing.

soixante-neuf

French *soixante-neuf*, literally 'sixty-nine', is used metaphorically for a form of sexual stimulation involving mutual simultaneous fellatio and cunnilingus – the metaphor depends on the supposed resemblance between the figure 69 and the relative positions of the participants involved in the activity. It appears to have been in use in English in the late 19th century – there is an isolated recorded example in P. Perret's *Tableaux Vivants* (1888), an English book – but it is not until the influence of sixties' permissiveness begins to make itself felt that we find evidence of its frequent usage, either anglicized to *sixty-nine* or in its original French.

solvitur ambulando

The 4th-century BC Greek philosopher Diogenes, who was renowned for his sometimes quirky and iconoclastic behaviour, is said to have proved the theoretical possibility of motion by the simple expedient of walking. This procedure was later encapsulated in Latin in the phrase *solvitur ambulando*, literally 'it is solved by walking', which has been used in English since the mid-19th century to express the notion of solving a problem by taking practical action, by trial and error, rather than by thinking about it.

sommelier

French *sommelier* originally meant 'butler'. It came from an Old Provençal word meaning 'one who drives a pack animal' (modern French *somme* still denotes 'pack-saddle'). English originally borrowed it, in that sense, in the 16th century, anglicizing it to *somler*. That soon died out, however, and modern English *sommelier* represents a much more recent, late 19th-century borrowing, reflecting the word's semantic evolution in French to 'wine waiter'. It is much commoner in American English than in British, which prefers the native compound *wine waiter*.

son et lumière

The technique of *son et lumière* was invented by Paul Robert-Houdin, and first used in 1952 at the Château de Chambord, in the Loire valley, France, of which he was curator. It consists of illuminating a place of historical interest, such as a castle, with theatrical lighting effects at night while playing a synchronized soundtrack that includes music and a narrative – hence the name, which in French means literally 'sound and light'. The term is first recorded in English in 1957, and since then the increasing popularity of the technique at tourist venues has established its place in the language. There is even evidence of its metaphorical use, which tends to convey the notion of a superficially brilliant, razzmatazz approach to the presentation of history.

sortes

Latin *sortes* is the plural of *sors* 'lot, fate, chance' (source of English *sortilege* 'divination by drawing lots'). It has been used in English since the 16th century in the expressions *sortes Biblicae*, *sortes Homericae* and *sortes Virgilianae* to refer to the practice of looking up at random a passage in, repectively, the Bible and the works of Homer and Virgil and using it to foretell the future. The underlying principle is the same as that of reading the tea-leaves: a person's apparently chance selection of a passage, like the apparently chance disposition of his or her tea-leaves, is in fact guided by some unknown force to reveal what is yet to come.

sotto voce

Italian *sotto voce* means literally 'under the voice', hence 'in a low voice, in an undertone' (*sotto* comes from Latin *subtus* 'below, underneath'). English borrowed it in the mid-18th century, in two distinct modes: first as a general term, with the connotation of speaking quietly in order to avoid being overheard; and second (as with many acquisitions from Italian) as a musical term, signifying 'to be sung or played very softly, so as to be barely audible'.

soupçon

French *soupçon* means literally 'suspicion' (it is a lineal descendant of Vulgar Latin *suspectio* 'suspicion'), but it is also used figuratively for a 'slight trace of something', a 'mere hint that gives grounds for suspecting the presence of something'. This was the sense in which English acquired the word in the middle of the 18th century. Around 1800 it began frequently to be anglicized to *suspicion* (as in 'A suspicion of a smile played around her lips'), and nowadays *soupçon* tends to be used in English mainly for a 'faint trace of a particular ingredient in a particular dish' or, perhaps even more commonly, for a 'minute quantity to be eaten or drunk' ('More sherry?' 'Just a soupçon, thanks').

spécialité

Someone's *spécialité* is something he or she specializes in – does particularly well or for preference, or is well known for doing. One might, for instance, say that someone has made a bit of a *spécialité* of Sèvres porcelain, if he or she has built up a large collection of it or become an expert on it. Similarly, the *spécialité* of a place is something – a product, for instance – which it is especially well known for. English started using French *spécialité* in the early 19th century, and it was not until the middle of the century that the vernacular *speciality* began to fall in semantically with it. Its best-known application is in the expression *spécialité de la maison* 'speciality of the house', denoting a dish in which a particular restaurant specializes.

sportif

English began to use the French adjective *sportif* in the 1930s. It is roughly parallel in meaning to the native formation *sporty* (itself no older than the late 19th century): it means either 'interested in or actively engaged in sport' or (particularly of clothes) 'suitable for sports, especially in being casual or jaunty'.

sprechgesang

German *sprechgesang*, literally 'speaking-song', is a musical term denoting a type of vocal delivery halfway between singing and speaking, in which each word or syllable is begun at a particular notated pitch but then falls away. It was pioneered by the Austrian composer Arnold Schoenberg, who used it first in his *Pierrot Lunaire* (1912), a set of recitations of poems by Giraud accompanied by five instruments. The term began to appear in English in the 1920s. The word used by Schoenberg to denote the sort of voice that characterizes *sprechgesang* was *sprechstimme* 'speaking-voice', and this too has been adopted by English.

sprachgefühl

The German term *sprachgefühl* (literally 'speech feeling') denotes that indefinable quality which makes people at home in a language, their own or a foreign tongue, and enables them intuitively to select the most appropriate or idiomatic expression for the circumstances, and to avoid solecisms. English began to feel the need for a word to express this rather nebulous concept at the beginning of the 20th century. The first record of *sprachgefühl* in an English text is in J. B. Greenough and G. L. Kittredge's *Words and their Ways in English Speech* (1901).

spritzig

German *spritzig* denotes wines that are slightly sparkling – not wholeheartedly bubbly like champagne, but with small intermittent bubbles. It is equivalent to French *pétillant*. It began to come into English in the first half of the 20th century, as did its related noun *spritz* 'slight sparkle' (as in 'a wine with a certain *spritz*'). From the same word-family comes *spritzer* 'drink that is a mixture of white wine and soda water', which came into American English in the 1950s and has since crossed the Atlantic.

sputnik

When the Soviet Union launched its, and the world's, first artificial satellite on 4 October 1957, it gave it the name *Sputnik*. This means literally in Russian 'travelling companion', and was short for *sputnik zemlyi* 'travelling companion of the earth' – that is, something that travels round the earth. *Sputnik* itself is a compound word formed from *s* 'with', *put'* 'path, way', and the agent noun suffix -*nik*. It was applied to the whole series of unmanned satellites launched by the USSR between 1957 and 1961, and it was immediately welcomed into English as a term for such Russian satellites, and even for unmanned earth-orbiting satellites in general.

In bridge, the term *Sputnik double* is used for a take-out double of a suit overcall of one's partner's opening bid.

stalag

In World War 2 Germany, a *stalag* was a 'prisoner-of-war camp'. The German term is short for *stammlager*, literally 'base camp, main camp', which is a compound noun formed from *stamm* 'base, stem' and *lager* 'camp'. The first record of its use in English dates from 1940. It was, and is, widely employed as a general term for any such prisoner-of-war camp, but strictly speaking it denoted a camp for non-commissioned officers and other ranks; camps for officers were known as *oflags* (short for *offizierslager*). Such a camp for airforce personnel was called a *stalag luft*, literally 'air camp'. Other types of camp were the *dulags* (short for *durchgangslager*), for prisoners in transit, and the *ilags* (short for *internierungslager*), for civilian internees.

status quo

Classical Latin had expressions such as *in statu quo ante* and *in statu quo nunc*, literally 'in the condition in which before' and 'in the condition in which now' – that is, the way things were before and the way things are now (*quo* here is the ablative case of the pronoun *qui* 'which'). These were the basis of the quasi-Latin noun *status quo* 'present state of things', which first appeared in English in the 1830s. A variation on the theme is *status quo ante* 'previously existing state of affairs', first recorded in English in the 1870s.

stet

Stet originally was the third-person present subjunctive of Latin *stāre* 'stand', and meant 'let it stand'. It came to be used as an annotation in correcting proofs, instructing the printer not to make an alteration indicated by an earlier proofreader – to 'let it stand' unchanged, in other words. It is typically written in the margin, and is reinforced by a row of dots under the letter, word, etc it refers to. English has taken it over not just as an injunction, but also as a fully-fledged verb, meaning 'mark a deletion or correction with the word *stet*, indicating that the original version should be retained'.

sturm und drang

The term *sturm und drang* originated as the title of a play by the German dramatist F. M. von Klinger (1752–1831): written in 1775, this was an overwrought romantic drama set in the American War of Independence. The phrase means literally 'storm and stress', and was taken up in the early 19th century by historians and theoreticians of literature, including Goethe, as the name for a German literary movement of the last quarter of the 18th century. Its characteristic features were its rejection of hidebound literary conventions of the past and its glorification of the impulsive hero, the man of genius, as opposed to the rational man of the 18th century (all very much of a piece with the emerging Romantic movement in Britain and the rest of Europe). Leading *sturm und drang* figures included Goethe, Schiller and Herder. The term is first recorded in English in the mid-19th century, and it is frequently anglicized to *storm and stress*.

subbotnik, plural subbotniki

In the Soviet Union, a *subbotnik* is a Saturday on which people work voluntarily, without payment, for the good of their collective or of the national economy as a whole. The word is a derivative of Russian *subbóta* 'Saturday' (a relative of English *sabbath*). The pattern for the *subbotniki* was set by workers on the Moscow-Kazan railway on 10 May 1919. By 1920 the word had arrived in English. At first it was sometimes anglicized as *Saturdaying*, but the Russian form has now become established.

sub judice

Latin *sub judice* means literally 'under a judge'. *Judice* is the ablative case of Latin *judex* 'judge', from which English gets *judge* and *judicial*. The phrase has been used in English since the early 17th century to denote that a particular matter is still under consideration by a judge or a court of law. All the evidence of its use in former centuries suggests that the implication behind it was that the matter in question was therefore still undecided, but nowadays by far its commonest use is to convey the warning that an affair which is the subject of legal proceedings should not be commented on publicly, particularly by the press and other media.

subpoena

A subpoena is a writ issued by a court of law requiring a particular person to appear before that court. It gets its name from the first two words of its text, Latin *sub poena* 'under penalty', which spell out the consequences of refusing to obey the writ (Latin *poena* is the source of English *pain, penal*, and *punish*). The term *subpoena* has been used in English for a very long time, since the early 15th century in fact, and its use as a verb, meaning 'serve with a subpoena', is also well established, going back to the mid-17th century. There are technically two types of subpoena: one is a *subpoena ad testificandum*, literally a 'subpoena in order to testify', which requires a person to come to court to give evidence; and the other is a *subpoena duces tecum*, a 'subpoena you shall bring with you', ordering a person to bring a piece of evidence to court (this is often abbreviated to *duces tecum*).

sub rosa

Latin *sub rosa* means literally 'under the rose', but it is used in English for 'in secret, in strict confidence' – usually with reference to the proceedings of meetings, courts, etc. What is the connection between these two widely separated concepts? There was a legend that Harpocrates, Greek god of silence and secrecy (modelled ultimately on the Egyptian god Horus, and usually represented as a naked boy with his finger to his lips), was presented with a rose by Cupid as an inducement not to reveal the secrets of Venus's amorous dalliances. This led to the use of the rose as a symbol of silence and confidentiality, and the practice grew up (perhaps originally in Germany) of actually carving a rose into the ceiling of banqueting halls, to warn guests not to let secrets unloosed by wine go any further. A symbolic rose was also placed over confessionals. The phrase *sub rosa* has been used in English since the 16th century, often anglicized to *under the rose* (German has the parallel *unter der rose*).

sub specie aeternitatis

Latin *sub specie aeternitatis* means literally 'under the aspect of eternity'. The phrase was coined by the Dutch philosopher Spinoza (1632–77), in his *Ethics* 5.29. He used it in the very specific sense 'considered in relation to God's perfection'. But in English (where it is first recorded in 1896) it is generally used as an invitation to draw back from a too narrow focus on a problem and see it in a wider perspective. The converse is expressed by the phrase *sub specie temporis* 'under the aspect of time'.

sub voce

Sub voce is part of the bibliographical terminology bequeathed to English by Latin. It means literally 'under the word' (Latin *vox* originally denoted 'voice' – it is the ancestor of English *voice* – but it evolved metaphorically via 'that which is spoken' to 'word, sentence, maxim'), and it is used to direct a reader's attention to another word or entry in a reference book under which further relevant information can be found. An alternative term which serves the same function is *sub verba*, also literally 'under the word'. Both are usually abbreviated to *sv.*

succès de scandale

A book, painting, film, etc that achieves a *succès de scandale* gains notoriety because its content shocks public sensibilities, or because some scandal surrounds it or its author, rather than through any intrinsic merit of its own. English acquired the term, around the end of the 19th century, from French, where it means literally 'success of scandal'. Other similar English adoptions involving French *succès* include *succès d'estime* (literally 'success of esteem'), an artistic work that gains critical acclaim but is not a popular success; *succès fou* ('mad success'), a work which is received with wild enthusiasm; and *succès de mouchoir* ('handkerchief success'), a work which achieves its success by a strong emotional appeal.

sui generis

Something that is *sui generis* is in a class by itself; there is nothing else like it. The expression in Latin means literally 'of its own kind' (*generis* is the genitive case of *genus* 'kind, class'). English took it over in the late 18th century, and uses it to mean 'unique'.

summa cum laude

Summa cum laude is part of the terminology of the American educational system. If a college student graduates *summa cum laude*, he or she gains the highest level of academic distinction. The phrase means literally in Latin 'with the highest praise', and its use in English dates back to the turn of the 20th century. It is sometimes abbreviated in American English to *summa* (as in 'an AB summa in philosophy'), and an alternative term which is sometimes substituted for it is *maxima cum laude*. Further down the hierarchy of success are *magna cum laude* 'with great praise' and simply *cum laude* 'with praise'.

summum bonum, plural summa bona

It was the Roman author Cicero, in his *De Officiis* ('On Duties'), who apparently coined the term *summum bonum*, which in Latin means literally 'highest good'. English took it over in the 16th century, and has used it in a dual role: as a technical term in ethics, where it denotes the underpinning principle of goodness from which all moral virtues flow, and as a more general word, signifying 'the best thing you can get, the most desirable goal'. Philosophers have differed over the centuries in their identification of the *summum bonum*: for the Stoics it was the attainment of virtue, for Aristotle it was happiness, and for Jeremy Bentham the greatest happiness of the greatest number of people.

Other English phrases on the same Latin model are *summum jus* (literally 'highest law'), which denotes the most strict and severe application of the law, and *summum pulchrum* ('highest beauty').

suppressio veri

Latin *suppressio veri* means 'suppression of the truth, concealment of the facts'. It has been used in English since the mid-18th century to denote a way of misleading people in which one omits to mention certain material facts in order to give a false impression. It is often paired with *suggestio falsi* 'suggestion of that which is untrue', which denotes a roundabout form of lying by implying (but not directly stating) what one knows to be false.

T

tableau vivant, plural tableaux vivants

In the 19th century and the early 20th century, *tableaux vivants* were very popular forms of public and private entertainment in Britain. People dress themselves up in appropriate costumes, arrange themselves on a stage set in positions illustrative of a well-known incident from history, legend, or literature, such as the death of Nelson, and then ... just stand there. At one time, house-parties and village fetes were not complete without a *tableau vivant* – Britannia was a common centrepiece – but films and television have killed off this static form of entertainment. French *tableau vivant* means literally 'living picture', and is first recorded in English in 1817.

table d'hôte

If one dines at one's 'host's table' (which is what French *table d'hôte* literally means), one naturally eats the dishes he has had prepared for the meal. Translated into the terms of early inns and other hostelries, this meant that if you wanted a meal, you had little or no choice; the inn-keeper would have produced a single set of courses, to which all the guests would have sat down at the same time and at the same table. In modern restaurants, the choice will often have expanded somewhat, but essentially the concept of the *table d'hôte* remains the same: a set list of dishes from which to choose, with a single fixed price to pay whichever one chooses. It contrasts with **à la carte**, which denotes a far longer list of items, each individually priced. Use of the term in English dates back to the early 17th century, but nowadays it is on the wane; it is commoner to speak of a *set menu* or of a **prix fixe**.

tabula rasa

Latin *tabula rasa* means 'scraped table' (*rasa* is the feminine form of the past participle of *radere* 'scrape, shave', from which English gets *abrade* and *erase*), and it literally denotes a writing surface from which previously written words have been removed, so that it is blank and can be written on again. But in English it has, like its vernacular near equivalent *clean slate*, largely been used metaphorically, and its main modern application is as a psychological term, signifying the new-born child's mind thought of as a blank, before it receives any sensory or experiential impressions. This concept was originated by the 17th-century English philosopher John Locke.

taedium vitae

Latin *taedium vitae* means literally 'weariness of life' (*taedium* is the source of English *tedium* and *tedious*). Its use in English dates essentially from the mid-18th century, and it denotes a state of generalized boredom or ennui, a feeling that life has nothing stimulating or pleasing to offer – often with the implication of clinical depression. As a concept it appealed both to the world-weariness of the *fin de siècle* (Oscar Wilde wrote of 'that ennui, that terrible *taedium vitae*, that comes on those to whom life denies nothing') and to the gloomier exponents of mid-20th-century existentialism.

tai chi

Tai chi is a Chinese system of 108 physical exercises, performed slowly and deliberately, the aim of which is not just to improve muscular coordination and physical condition generally, but also to promote spiritual well-being and the meditative faculty. Each exercise has a name (eg 'Embrace Tiger and Return to Mountain' and 'The White Crane Spreads its Wings'). It is believed to have been developed by a Taoist priest in the Sung dynasty (960–1279). Its name is short for Chinese *taì jí qúan*, which means literally 'great ultimate fist, great ultimate boxing' (it is regarded as one of the Chinese martial arts). It is a newcomer to the West, and so records of *tai chi* in English, in this sense at least, are comparatively recent. But *Tai Chi* 'Great Ultimate, Great Absolute' is also the term used in Taoism for the soul of the universe, which is represented pictorially by a circle divided by a wavy line into two tadpole-shaped halves; and this goes back in English to at least the early 18th century.

tant mieux

French *tant mieux* means 'so much the better'; it expresses pleasure at a satisfactory turn of events, especially one which improves on an already adequate situation. The first recorded use of it in English is in one of the letters of Lord Chesterfield to his son, dated 8 March 1754, and it crops up intermittently in print from then onwards. Perhaps rather commoner in English is its opposite, *tant pis*, literally in French 'so much the worse'. It is roughly the equivalent of 'what a pity!', 'too bad!', said often with a real or imaginary shrug of the shoulders over something unfortunate that cannot be helped. It too dates back in English to the 18th century.

tastevin

A *tastevin* is a very shallow cup, typically of silver or silvery-coloured metal, which is used for tasting and assessing wine. The surface area of liquid it contains is large in relation to its depth, allowing easy access to the bouquet of the wine, and its bottom is usually fluted or embossed, allegedly to highlight the colour of the wine in the dimly candle-lit cellars where it is often used. The word is a French borrowing, first recorded in English in the mid-20th century, but in its own language it has a distinctly archaic air. The modern French form of the word is *tâte-vin* (literally 'wine-taster'), but *tastevin* began to be revived in the early 20th century by various newly-formed French organizations for the promotion of wine (notably the *Confrérie des Chevaliers du Tastevin* 'Brotherhood of the Knights of the Tastevin', founded in 1933) whose members have a fondness for dressing up in medieval-style robes and evoking France's Rabelaisian past. In English-speaking countries, and particularly the USA, the tastevin is perhaps most likely to be encountered as a badge of office suspended round a wine waiter's neck.

te igitur

The first prayer of the canon of the Roman Catholic Latin Mass begins *Te igitur clementissime pater* 'Thee therefore most merciful father'. Hence the prayer itself came to be known as the *te igitur*; and the name is also applied to the service book in which it is printed. Use of the term in English dates from the early 19th century.

tempora mutantur

Latin *tempora mutantur* means 'times change'. It encapsulates the fleeting nature of human institutions, the fickleness of fashion, and also often suggests that 'things aren't what they used to be'. Use of the expression in English dates back to the 15th century.

A lengthier variation on the theme is *tempora mutantur et nos mutamur in illis* 'times change and we change with them', which is first recorded in English in William Harrison's *Description of Britain* (1577). Its origins are not known, but a comparison has been drawn with the expression *Omnia mutantur et nos mutamur in illis* 'all things change and we change with them', attributed to the Holy Roman Emperor Lothair I (795–855).

tempus fugit

Tempus fugit is the perennial cry of the impatient: 'Time flies!', so no delay can be tolerated. It is not a direct quote from a Roman author, but was presumably inspired by these words from Virgil's *Georgics*: *Sed fugit interea, fugit irreparabile tempus, singula dum capti circumvectamur amore* 'But meanwhile it is flying, irretrievable time is flying, while beguiled by love [for the topic under discussion] we linger around each detail' (the poet is rhetorically telling himself to get on with it). Latin *tempus* 'time' lies behind English *tempo, temporal, temporary*, etc and also the noun *tense*, while *fugere* 'flee, fly' has given us *fugitive*.

terminus

Latin *terminus* 'end, limit, boundary' is most familiar in English as a term for a main station or stopping place at either end of a railway line, bus route, etc – a use first recorded in the 1830s and in which it has now become thoroughly anglicized. But it is also used in a small set of demarcatory Latin phrases. *Terminus ad quem* (literally 'end towards which') denotes a finishing point, a goal towards which one is aiming. *Terminus ante quem* ('end before which') is used in establishing the date of something, such as an ancient text; it signifies the most recent possible date. *Terminus a quo* ('end from which') has a dual role, as the converse of both the above; it means 'starting point', and also 'earliest possible date'. This last is also expressed by *terminus post quem* ('end after which'). These expressions originated in the Latin of the medieval schoolmen, writers such as Albertus Magnus, Roger Bacon and Duns Scotus.

terra firma

Nowadays in English *terra firma* simply means 'dry land', usually used jocularly by ship or airborne passengers (or even someone up a tall ladder) to express a desire for a swift return to the security of the earth's solid surface. But when English first borrowed it from Latin, in the mid-17th century, it had a wider range of applications than that. Ancient geographers had used it for a 'continent', as distinct from an 'island', and its first English borrowers took this sense over. It was also used more specifically for the area of the Italian mainland under Venetian control, and for the northern coastal area of South America, as distinguished from the islands of the Caribbean. But all these early usages had effectively died out by the beginning of the 19th century. Latin *terra firma* means literally 'firm land'.

terra incognita

Latin *terra incognita* means literally 'unknown land'. It was originally adopted into English in the early 17th century, in the midst of the great age of exploration, and was used to designate areas as yet unpenetrated by Europeans. It can be found on maps of the period. But right from the start it was also used metaphorically, and that is its main role today: it denotes an area of study or activity about which little or nothing is known.

tertium quid

A *tertium quid* (in Latin literally a 'third something') is something intermediate between two other things, particularly something unknown or indefinable that stands between two categories thought of as being exhaustive (eg 'There is good and evil but no *tertium quid*'). The origins of the expression lie in Greek rather than Latin. *Tríton ti* 'some third thing' is found in Plato, and this was subsequently adapted into Latin as *tertium quid*. Amongst its earliest uses was as an alchemical term, denoting a substance created by combining two other substances, and different from the sum of its parts. This accounts for its earliest application in English, in the 17th and 18th centuries. It did not begin to be used in its familiar modern, philosophical sense until the 19th century.

tête-à-tête

French *tête-à-tête* means literally 'head-to-head', and at first, in the 16th century, it was used much as *head-to-head* is in modern English, to denote single combat, one-on-one. By the 17th century it had come to mean an 'intimate or private conversation between two people', metaphorically with their 'heads' together, and that is how English borrowed it at the end of the 17th century. Its adverbial use (as in 'dine *tête-à-tête*') came with it, and it was not long before it was being employed as an adjective ('a *tête-à-tête* supper'). The word is also used in English for a sort of sofa, typically S-shaped, on which two people can sit facing each other.

tête-bêche

Tête-bêche is a philatelic term. It denotes a pair of stamps, one of which is printed upside-down. It dates from the 1870s, and in its original French was adapted metaphorically from an expression that was used literally of people sleeping head to foot. *Tête* is 'head', and *bêche* is a reduced form of *béchevet* 'double-headed'. This was originally used with reference to bed-heads, and was a compound formed from *bes* 'twice, double' and *chevet* 'head (of a bed)'. *Tête-bêche* pairs are much sought after by stamp collectors.

theatrum mundi

The concept of the *theatrum mundi* (in Latin literally 'theatre of the world') originated in Renaissance times. It views the theatre as a stage on which every aspect of human life can be played out. Side by side with this went the idea of the world, God's creation, as a theatre (as in Shakespeare's 'All the world's a stage, and all the men and women merely players', *As You Like It*).

thé dansant

The *thé dansant* was a particularly popular form of entertainment in the 1920s and 1930s. It was a dance held in the afternoon, in a hotel, large private house, etc, to the sober accompaniment of tea (the French expression literally means 'dancing tea'). John Betjeman encapsulated the genteel atmosphere in his *Margate, 1940*: 'How restful to putt, when the strains of a band announced a *thé dansant* was on at the Grand, while over the privet, comminglingly clear, I heard lesser "Co-Optimists" down by the pier'. Records of the term in English actually go back as far as the early 19th century, and the parallel *soirée dansante* for an evening party with dancing is also 19th century. Similarly inspired was the *thé musical*, an afternoon tea party at which music was performed.

touché

Touché originated as a fencing term. In French literally 'touched' (it is the past participle of the verb *toucher* 'touch'), it is used by fencers to acknowledge that their opponent has scored a hit – something that in the days before swords were wired up to indicate contact was not always easy for the referee to tell. The word is not recorded in English before the early 20th century, and almost immediately we begin to see evidence of its metaphorical use, which is today much the commoner: as a light-hearted admission that the person to whom one is speaking has made a telling point against one, usually as a riposte to a point of one's own.

tour de force, plural tours de force

A *tour de force* is a remarkable feat of skill, that fills everyone with admiration. French *tour* means literally a 'turning movement' or a 'journey round something', but it is also used metaphorically for a 'trick' or 'feat' – a *tour d'adresse*, for instance, is a piece of sleight of hand. So a *tour de force* was originally a physical 'feat of strength', but already when English began to adopt it at the beginning of the 19th century the emphasis was shifting to artistic virtuosity or the mastery of some other sort of skill. The plural *tours de force* is used in musical terminology for 'bravura passages'.

tour d'horizon

The French term *tour d'horizon* denotes literally a 'tour of the horizon' – that is, an extensive but not exhaustive tour, taking in places of importance. English adopted it after World War 2, and uses it mainly in the metaphorical sense 'broad survey which touches the main points in a general way but does not go into details'.

tout

The French adjective *tout* 'all' is used before the name of a city to denote the fashionable society of that city: thus *le tout Paris* is equivalent to 'everybody who is anybody in Paris'. The usage began to infiltrate English towards the end of the 19th century. To begin with it was restricted to 'Paris', but it was not long before it spread to non-French cities ('Le tout Bagdad', Gertrude Bell, 1921). Sometimes it is preceded by the French definite article *le* ('*le tout* London'), sometimes not ('*tout* London').

tout court

French *tout court* (literally 'quite short') means 'simply, merely that and nothing else'. The first record of it in English dates back as far as 1747, but it is not really until the 20th century that it seems to have come into more than sporadic use. Its main role is to signify limitation or curtailment to the simplest possible form, with no unnecessary additions or flourishes (as in 'His full name is Fotherington-Smythe, but he likes to be known as Smythe *tout court*').

tout de suite

French *tout de suite* means 'at once, immediately' (its literal meaning, 'completely in sequence', is a mere memory, long defunct). It has had a curious double career in English. It was one of those French expressions that British soldiers brought back from the World War 1 trenches, in rather knocked-about condition. It was very common in the inter-war period, and for some time after World War 2, and when committed to print it took the form *toot sweet*, an attempt to render the rather mangled English pronunciation of the French original. There are sporadic records, however, from the late 19th century onwards, of its being borrowed in its original French form, *tout de suite*. Amongst the liberties taken with it by English is the jocular *the tooter the sweeter* for 'the sooner the better'.

tout ensemble

French *le tout ensemble* has two basic applications: it signifies 'the whole lot, everything together' and also 'the general effect' (*tout* here is a noun, meaning 'everything', and *ensemble* is an adverb, denoting 'together'). English took it over in the early 18th century and has used it in both modes, although nowadays the latter is much the commoner – particularly as applied to the impression created by an artistic production, a set of garments worn together, etc. It is often used interchangeably with *ensemble*, even though in French the two *ensemble*s belong to different word-classes.

tovarich

Russian *továrishch* means 'comrade'. It became the common mode of address amongst Russians when the Communists came to power following the Revolution, and in this role it found its way into English texts as early as 1918. It has since then become a convenient shorthand for giving a flavour of authenticity to fictional conversations between Soviet apparatchiks. Its spelling, though, has presented considerable difficulty: amongst the attempts on record are *tovarish*, *tovaritch*, *tovarisch*, and *tovaristch*, as well as variants beginning with *tav-*.

trahison des clercs

La Trahison des Clercs ('Treason of the Intellectuals') is the title of a book by the French novelist and philosopher Julien Benda (1867–1956), published in 1927. In it, he demanded that his fellow intellectuals should be uncompromising in their devotion to the truth, and not sell out to the blandishments of politicians, personal feelings, etc. The expression *trahison des clercs* began to be used in English in the 1930s as shorthand for the betrayal by intellectuals of the truth which they supposedly hold in trust – for example, if an academic were to compromise his or her principles for the sake of a seat in government. English also employs the translated version *treason of the clerks*.

tranche de vie

French *tranche de vie* means literally 'slice of life', and its connotations are exactly those of its English equivalent: an episode or portion of people's real lives in all their aspects – from the mundane and earthy to the exciting and uplifting – especially as represented vividly but naturalistically in drama, literature, painting, etc. The term was coined towards the end of the 19th century to characterize French Naturalistic literature (as epitomized by the works of Zola). It soon appeared in English, but in the translated form *slice of life* (which remains the commoner version today). The original French did not begin to make its mark until between the two world wars.

trecento

The *trecento* is the fourteenth century, or 'thirteen hundreds', in Italian art and literature. In the visual arts it was a comparatively fallow period, between the 13th-century giants Giotto and Duccio and the flowering of the Renaissance. Leading figures include Bernardo Daddi, Taddeo Gaddi, Ambrogio and Pietro Lorenzetti and Giovanni Pisano. Amongst writers, however, it was a golden age, producing Boccaccio, Petrarch, and the greatest figure in Italian literature, Dante, whose *Divine Comedy* was produced between 1300 and 1321.

tricoteuse

French *tricoteuse* means literally 'woman who knits' (it is a derivative of the verb *tricoter* 'knit', a word of unknown origin). But its specific application that brought it into English in the early 19th century is to the women who used to sit attentively at guillotinings during the French Revolution, and at the trials which provided their victims, knitting with relish as they followed every detail of the proceedings. It is from time to time used metaphorically of women who take a chillingly matter-of-fact delight in observing the downfall of others. It is also used in the antiques trade to denote a type of small sewing-table.

troika

Russian *troika* is a derivative of *troye* 'three', which is related to English *three*. English originally took it over, in the 1840s, as the name for a distinctively Russian type of small carriage that is pulled by a team of three horses abreast. It is also used for the team of horses itself. Then in the mid-20th century it began a new career as a term for any group of three, and in particular for a ruling body or administrative committee of three people with shared and equal powers – roughly equivalent to a *triumvirate*.

trompe l'oeil

French *trompe l'oeil* means literally 'deceives the eye' (French *tromper* 'deceive' is related to English *trumpery*). It is used for a technique of representation in art, and particularly in interior decoration, which attempts to make the viewer believe that a painted or modelled object is in fact the real thing. For example, a wall might be painted with shelves and books so realistic that one could be tempted to go up to it and try to take down a volume. Many of the surviving houses at Pompeii contain fine examples of *trompe l'oeil* work, with false archways giving on to distant but illusory vistas. It was also a characteristic feature of the Italian baroque. The first record of the term *trompe l'oeil* in English dates back to 1889.

tsunami

Any huge wave that causes inundation and destruction in coastal areas is likely to be called a *tidal wave* by the layman, but this causes great distress to oceanographers and allied experts. Such waves have more than one cause, and the terminology is distinct.

One precipitated by storm conditions and fierce onshore winds is properly called a *storm surge*, while one that results from the shock waves of an underwater earthquake or volcanic eruption is termed a *tsunami*. This word was acquired by English at the end of the 19th century from Japanese (Japan being an area much affected by such phenomena). It is a compound formed from *tsu* 'port, harbour' and *nami* 'waves'.

tu quoque

Latin is useful when it comes to wrapping up the frank or slightly scurrilous in a veil of apparent respectability, and *tu quoque* is a case in point. It means simply 'you too', and it is used to denote the sort of argument that descends to the level of saying simply that: 'you too!' – a retort accusing an accuser of having the same fault as his accused. A well-established example is 'Physician heal thyself', and the same sentiment is encapsulated in proverbs such as 'People who live in glass houses shouldn't throw stones'. The use of the term *tu quoque* in English goes back to the early 17th century.

U

übermensch, plural übermenschen

The concept of the *übermensch* was created by the German philosopher Friedrich Nietzsche (1844–1900). In various of his writings, and notably in *Thus Spake Zarathustra* (1883–92), he put forward the notion of the exceptional man, who by force of will had overcome the limitations of being merely human, and risen above the common herd to an exalted level of creativity and power. He called such people *übermenschen*, literally 'over-people' (he did not coin the term – it had been used earlier by Goethe, and it harks back to classical Greek *hyperanthropos*). The concept was much distorted by Nazi intellectuals, who took it as the model for their Aryan superman. It was essentially George Bernard Shaw who was responsible for introducing the term into English, both in its original form and translated into *superman* (although the earliest known printed reference to *übermensch* in English is actually in a 1902 edition of *Pall Mall*). It was his play *Man and Superman* (1903) which brought a version of the *übermensch* before British audiences.

ubi sunt

Latin *ubi sunt?* means 'where are they?' They are the opening words of many medieval songs and other works regretting the transience of human life, the loss of youth and friends now dead, and looking back with wistful nostalgia on past happiness (the first line in many cases runs *ubi sunt qui ante nos fuerunt?* 'where are they who lived before us?'). They have come to be used to denote this genre of medieval literature (which is vernacular as well as Latin: the Old English poems *The Wanderer* and *The Seafarer*, for instance, contain *ubi sunt?* motifs).

ultra vires

Something that is *ultra vires* is literally 'beyond strength, beyond powers' (*vires* is the accusative plural form of Latin *vis* 'strength, force, power'). The term is used in English, and has been since the 18th century, to denote any action which it is beyond the legal powers of a particular body to take (as in 'In granting the application before all objections had been heard the committee acted *ultra vires*'). It can be construed in English with *of* ('It was *ultra vires* of the committee to take this action')or even used quasi-prepositionally ('It was *ultra vires* the committee to do this').

ur-

The German prefix *ur-* combines the notions of 'originality, firstness' and 'primitiveness, existence from long ago in the mists of the past' (it is descended from Old High German *ir-* or *ur-*, which was a perfective prefix denoting 'thoroughly'). It began to infiltrate English in the second half of the 19th century, but it first made serious headway at the end of the century with the introduction of the German linguistic term *ursprache*. Literally 'original language, proto-language', this denotes a language from which others are descended, particularly one of an ancient pre-literate culture which has to be reconstructed from the evidence of its descendants. In the mid-20th century, textual critics introduced the term *urtext* 'original text', referring to the first version of a later much-altered text. These and other more minor introductions have led to the use of *ur-* in combination with native English words: in 1966, for instance, *Punch* referred to Leonardo da Vinci's design for an 'ur-tank'.

urbi et orbi

Papal pronouncements and blessings are said to be made *urbi et orbi* 'to the city and the world' ('the city' here refers to Rome). The import of this is that the Pope's message is for everyone. The Latin phrase was introduced into English in the mid-19th century, and is occasionally used figuratively to denote that an announcement is for general consumption.

V

vade mecum

Latin *vade mecum* means literally 'go with me'. *Vade* is the imperative form of *vadere* 'go', source of English *evade, invade*, etc and distantly related to *wade*, and the preposition *cum* 'with' was commonly tacked on to the end of pronouns it qualified. The term has two uses in English, both of which date back at least to the early 17th century. First, as the name for, and often the title of, a useful reference book, particularly one which can be carried around – the implication being that you have it with you at all times, to consult at need. The first known use of it is for the anonymous *Vade Mecum: A Manuall of Essayes Morrall, Theologicall* (1629), and in the 18th and 19th centuries there was a proliferation of books called 'the gardener's vade mecum', 'the housewife's vade mecum', etc; but now it has a decidedly archaic ring. The other meaning of *vade mecum* is 'something useful which one always carries around with one' – although this too is now rarely encountered.

va-et-vient

French *va-et-vient* is a noun formed from the third person present singular of *aller* 'go' and *venir* 'come'. It corresponds roughly in meaning and application to English *coming and going, toing and froing*. It can denote literal physical movement backwards and forwards or to and fro, but English, which took it over in the early 20th century, has used it more in the metaphorical sense of 'bustle, commotion', and also for 'interchange' or 'exchange'.

vagina dentata

The uncomfortable image of the *vagina dentata* encapsulates a range of dark subconscious human fears, mainly but not exclusively male. Literally in Latin 'vagina with teeth', the term was originally used by anthropologists for representations of such a phenomenon produced in primitive cultures, but it soon came to be used by psychologists too. Amongst the mental states it symbolizes are fear of castration, fear of sexual intercourse, fear of returning to the womb, and fear of rebirth. Use of the term in English dates from the beginning of the 20th century.

valet-de-chambre

A *valet-de-chambre* (literally in French 'chamber-valet') is a gentleman's personal gentleman, a male servant who looks after his male employer's clothes, serves his meals, and attends Jeeves-like to his other personal needs. The term was introduced to English from French as long ago as the mid-17th century, and it became so thoroughly naturalized that in the 18th and 19th centuries it was colloquially abbreviated to *valet-de-sham* and even *valley-de-sham*. It is now little used, however, although its shortened form *valet* (which actually dates back to the 16th century in English) is still alive and kicking.

vanitas vanitatum

'*Vanitas vanitatum*', begins the second verse of chapter one of Ecclesiastes, 'vanity of vanities, all is vanity'. This stern reminder of the futility of human ambition found a place in English as long ago as the 16th century. Latin *vanitas* (a derivative of *vanus* 'vain', and source of English *vanity*) is also used in English as an art-history term to denote a type of 17th-century Dutch still-life painting containing some object that functions as a reminder of mortality (eg a skull). Frans Hals was among the many artists who worked in the genre.

varia lectio, plural variae lectiones

Varia lectio is a term used in textual criticism to denote an alternative version of a text – a different spelling, for instance, or a different choice of words – that exists in another manuscript or printed edition. From the 17th to the 19th century it was common to anglicize the Latinism to *various reading*, which is what it literally means, but nowadays it is conventional to use the original form.

ventre à terre

French *ventre à terre* means literally 'belly to the ground'. In the 18th and 19th centuries, pictures of horses galloping flat out tended to portray them with their front legs flung out in front and their rear legs trailing behind, so that their underside was vividly shown as being parallel to and close to the ground. So it was that the expression *ventre à terre* came to be used to denote a horse (and occasionally other quadrupeds) moving along at top speed. English took it over in the mid-19th century. An over-literal interpretation of the idiom has led latterly to its occasional use for 'lying on one's stomach'.

verbatim

The classical Latin adverbial suffix *-im* (as in *sensim*, *pedetemptim*, *paulatim*, all meaning 'gradually') was the ancestor of a medieval Latin suffix, *-atim*, which likewise conveyed the notion of 'item by item'. From this was created the adverb *verbatim*, based on Latin *verbum* 'word', which means 'word for word', and is used to refer to the making of an exact copy of a piece of text, or to the precisely literal translation of a piece of text. It was adopted into English as long ago as the 15th century. Other similar *-atim* adverbs used in English include *gradatim* 'gradually' (which goes back to classical Latin), *literatim* 'letter for letter', and *seriatim* 'one after another'.

verboten

It seems that the introduction of *verboten* (past participle of German *verbieten* 'forbid') into English owes not a little to a perception of Germany as a highly regimented society, in which people generally do as they are told, and in which what they are told is often 'It is forbidden to do this'. Certainly in English the term connotes not just 'forbidden', but 'strenuously forbidden, on pain of unspecified retribution'. It probably became familiar to English-speakers via public notices (eg *Rauchen verboten* 'No smoking') – as is suggested by the first known example of it in an English text: 'Meads towards Haslingfield and Coton where *das Betreten*'s not *verboten*' (Rupert Brooke, *Old Vicarage, Grantchester*, 1912). *Betreten verboten* means 'No entry'.

verb sap

Latin *Verbum sapienti sat est* 'A word to the wise is sufficient' appears to be a sort of portmanteau aphorism, concocted from *Dictum sapienti sat est* 'What has been said is enough for anyone with any sense' (which comes from *Persa* by the Roman dramatist Plautus) and *Verbum sat est* 'One word is enough' (also from Plautus). Its nearest English equivalent is perhaps 'Need I say more?', accompanied by a knowing wink. It has been adopted and adapted into English in various curtailed forms since the 17th century, including *verbum sap*, *verbum sat*, *verbum sapienti* and *sat verbum*, but today *verb sap* is probably its commonest version.

verkrampte

The Afrikaans adjective *verkrampte* means literally 'cramped, restricted'. It is used by extension of someone who has very narrow, reactionary views, particularly on the question of apartheid and white supremacy. It started to appear in British English (both as an adjective and as a noun, meaning '*verkrampte* person') in the mid-1960s, as apartheid came increasingly to the fore as a political issue in the world at large. It was accompanied by its Afrikaans opposite, *verligte*, literally 'enlightened', which denotes broadmindedness.

vers de société

Vers de société is light, often witty and mildly satirical verse dealing with events in or topics appropriate to high society. A somewhat elitist genre, one of its leading exponents was the Englishman Frederick Locker-Lampson (1821–95). In the preface to his *Lyra Elegantiarum* (1867) he defined *vers de société* as verse in which 'sentiment never surges into passion, and where humour never overflows into boisterous merriment'. The French term means literally 'verse of society'; its use in English dates from the end of the 18th century.

vers libre

French *vers libre* means 'free verse'. The term was originally applied to the experiments of certain late 19th-century French and Belgian Symbolist poets (including Laforgue and Maeterlinck) in writing verse unbound by the traditional rules of metre, rhyme, etc. Their work had considerable influence on early 20th-century modernists writing poetry in English, notably Eliot and Pound (although Eliot once wrote that 'no *vers* is *libre* for the man who wants to do a good job'). English began to use the term *vers libre* at the beginning of the 20th century (and later followed it with the derivative *vers-librist* or *vers-libreist*), but the loan-translation *free verse*, dating from around the same time, is now commoner.

via media

Latin *via media* means 'middle road, middle way', and hence figuratively a 'compromise between two extremes'. Its use in English apprently dates from 1834, when John Henry Newman gave the title *Via Media* to number 38 of his *Tracts for the Times*. In it he praised the Church of England for taking the *via media* between Roman Catholicism and Protestantism of the Calvinist sort. *Via media* has continued since then to imply approval of compromise rather than its condemnation. The title of Harold Macmillan's *The Middle Way* (1938), subtitled *A study of the problem of economic and social progress in a free and democratic society*, was no doubt inspired by Newman's.

victor ludorum

Latin *victor ludorum* means literally 'winner of the games' (*ludus* 'game' is related to English *allude*, *elude*, *ludicrous*, etc). English adopted it probably in the late 19th century, using it for the overall winner of a sporting competition consisting of several individual events. It is a phenomenon particularly of school and college sports days: the athlete who gets the highest number of points from competing in the various different disciplines is the *victor ludorum*. It now has a rather dated air, redolent of vanished public-school glories, but it ekes out an existence in certain fixed contexts (eg it is used in the names of certain horse-races, notably the Victor Ludorum Hurdle for four-year-olds, run over two miles at Haydock).

videlicet

Videlicet is best known in English texts in its abbreviated form, *viz*. This is generally pronounced /viz/, but in fact the final letter originally had no connection with the letter *z*: it evolved from the abbreviation used for -*et* in medieval Latin manuscripts. It is a compound Latin word, formed from *vide*, a derivative of *videre* 'see', and *licet* 'it is permitted', the third-person present singular of *licere* 'be permitted' (source of English *leisure* and *licence*); and so it literally means 'it is permitted to see'. This evolved to 'it is easy to see, plainly', and hence to 'namely', which is where its modern use, introducing an explanatory example, list of items, etc, comes from. Its use in English dates back to the 15th century, and numerous abbreviated forms have been employed, including *vid*, *videl*, *vidz*, *vidzt* and *viz*, but it is only the last that has survived.

vi et armis

Latin *vi et armis* means literally 'by force and arms'. It was formerly used in English law as a term denoting a type of trespass that involves injury to someone's person or property. It has also had some currency as a more general term implying forceful compulsion.

vigneron

French *vigneron* denotes a 'wine-grower', someone who cultivates grapes and makes wine from them. It is a derivative of *vigne* 'vine'. English borrowed it as long ago as the 15th century, but it seems never to have become completely naturalized. It is still usually pronounced with an attempt at a French accent, and it tends to be used with reference to French wine-growers rather than as a general term.

vin du pays

French *vin du pays* means 'wine of the country'. It denotes a locally produced (and generally locally consumed) wine with no pretensions to international stardom. It has been used in English since at least the early 19th century. It should not be confused with *vin de pays*, which was introduced in 1968 as the official designation of the third level of quality of French wines, below *appellation contrôlée* and *vin délimité de qualité supérieure*. It appears on labels accompanied by the name of a particular region or *département* (eg *Vin de Pays d'Oc, Vin de Pays des Pyrénées-Orientales*). The category was brought into being to encourage higher-quality wine-making in the wine-lake areas of the south, and by the 1990s many *vins de pays* were achieving excellent standards.

vingt-et-un

French *vingt-et-un* means 'twenty-one', and English took it over in the 18th century as the name of a card game, the aim of which is to assemble a hand totalling as near as possible to 21 (court cards count 10). *Vingt-un* was an early alternative, but it had virtually died out by the 20th century. Around the turn of the 20th century it seems to have gone through the linguistic mangle of British army slang and come out as *pontoon* (influenced, of course, by the other sort of *pontoon*, the floating bridge much used by the army). *Pontoon* is now the general British term for the game, but in American English and in casino usage

317

vingt-et-un survives (and has been joined by the alternative name *blackjack*).

violin d'Ingres

The French painter Ingres (1780–1867) is said – probably apocryphally – to have been prouder of his limited skill as a player of the violin, which was his hobby, than of his painting. When he had visitors he supposedly subjected them to impromptu violin recitals when they wanted to be shown his pictures. So it was that French began to use the expression *violin d'Ingres* 'Ingres's violin' for any pastime pursued in addition to or in preference to one's main work. It began to creep into English in the 1960s: for example, Edward Hyams in his *New Statesmanship* (1963) described golf as President Eisenhower's *violin d'Ingres*.

virgo intacta, plural virgines intactae

Latin *virgo intacta* means literally 'untouched virgin' (*tacta* is the feminine form of the past participle of *tangere* 'touch', source of English *tact* and *tangent*). It is used in English as a legal term denoting a woman who is physiologically a virgin, with an unruptured hymen (the first record of its use in an English text dates from 1726). The commonest context for its use historically has been that of a woman whose marriageability is in question or who is seeking an annulment on the grounds of non-consummation. By extension, *intacta* is occasionally used on its own in English to denote 'unsullied'.

vis-à-vis

French *vis-à-vis* originally meant literally 'face to face'. Old French *vis* signified 'face' (it came from Latin *visus* 'sight, appearance', later 'face', which is related to English *vision*), but it has now died out, leaving its derivative *visage* as the word for 'face'. Before it died out, however, it found a place in the compound *vis-à-vis*, in which it has since become fossilized. This has a range of literal meanings, based on the notion of being 'face to face', including 'person opposite one, facing one', 'dancing partner', 'face-to-face meeting', and 'light carriage for two people sitting opposite each other', which were quite common in English in the 18th and 19th centuries; but they have now largely died out, leaving us only with the metaphorical 'in relation to'.

vivandière

Amongst the camp-followers or support services of armies in former times were women known as *vivandières*. Their function was to supply extra food and (alcoholic) drink to the soldiers over and above their standard rations. The French word comes ultimately from Latin *vivenda* 'things to be lived on, provisions', a derivative of *vivere* 'live' and source also of English *viands*. It was used in English in the 1800s with reference mainly to Continental armies of that and previous centuries.

viva voce

It was in medieval Latin that the phrase *viva voce* was coined. It means literally 'with the living voice': *viva* is the feminine ablative singular of *vivus* 'alive' and *voce* the ablative singular of *vox* 'voice'. It has been used in English since at least the 16th century to denote generally 'in speech, orally' (as opposed either to writing or to silent reading), but its most familiar role is as applied specifically to an oral examination, particularly one at a university which is additional to a written examination and which is often held to come to a decision about candidates who are on the borderline between passing and failing or between two classes of degree. In this sense it is most commonly encountered in the abbreviated form *viva*, as is the verb into which it has been converted (meaning 'examine orally'). It is notable for its retention of the ancestral English diphthongal pronunciation of the Latin long ī (to rhyme with *fiver*) which in so many other loanwords is being replaced by an /iː/ sound (as in *curriculum vitae*, *primum mobile*).

vive la différence

French *vive la différence!* 'long live the difference!' is an exclamation of approval of the differences between the sexes, usually uttered by men with the implication that life would be much duller for them if there were no women. It is not recorded in print in English before the 1960s, but is probably rather earlier than that.

vogue la galère

French *vogue la galère!*, literally 'let the galley be rowed!', is used figuratively to mean 'let's give it a go!, let's chance it!' It is first recorded in the works of François Rabelais (c.1494–1553), and there is evidence that it was familiar to some English-speakers by the early 16th century, but it did not begin to become assimilated into English until the 18th century.

völkerwanderung

The German historical term *völkerwanderung* is a direct translation of Latin *migratio gentium*, and means literally 'wandering of the peoples'. It denotes a mass migration of a people from one (part of a) continent to another, and is used especially to refer to the movement of various Germanic and Slavic peoples (such as the Goths and the Franks) into southern and western Europe from the 2nd to the 11th centuries AD. It began to be used in English in the early 20th century (although it was preceded in the 19th century by the now defunct *volkswanderung*).

volte-face

The word *volte-face* has a complicated history. English acquired it from French in the early 19th century (Sir Walter Scott is the first writer on record as using it in an English text, in his *Legend of Montrose* 1819). French in turn got it from Italian *voltafaccia*, which means literally 'turn-face', and is compounded from *voltare* 'turn' (a relative of English *vault* and *volume*) and *faccia* 'face'. It originally denoted literally a physical turning round, but that sense has never made much headway in English, and it is as a term for a 'sudden reversal of attitude', a 'U-turn', that it survives today.

vorlage

Vorlage is a skiing term. It refers to a position adopted by the skier in which he or she leans forward from the ankles, forming an acute angle in relation to the skis but keeping the heels in contact with them. It is used especially in ski-jumping. English acquired the word in the 1930s from German, where it means literally 'forward position'. The plural *vorlages* is used for 'skiing trousers'.

vox populi

The *vox populi* is in Latin the 'voice of the people'. It has been used in English since at least the mid-16th century for 'what the man in the street is saying or thinking'. However, it was not until the early 1960s that it, or rather its colloquial abbreviation *vox pop*, achieved a higher profile as a term for public opinion as gathered by radio or television reporters going out into the highways and byways with a microphone and asking people at random for their views on a pressing topic of the day. The Latin maxim *Vox populi, vox Dei* 'The voice of the people is the voice of God' (that is, the will of the mass of the people must prevail) may be attributable to the English scholar Alcuin (735–804), who used it in a letter to Charlemagne (although he used it in a way that suggests it was already a familiar expression – and he refuted it).

Other terms containing Latin *vox* that have been adopted by English include *vox angelica* 'angelic voice' and *vox humana* 'human voice', both denoting types of organ stop with voicelike qualities, and *vox nihili* 'voice of nothing', a philosophical term signifying a concept which, the closer you analyse it, the vaguer and woollier it becomes.

W

wanderjahr, plural wanderjahre

In former times, a *wanderjahr* was a year in which a newly qualified apprentice travelled around in order to polish his skills and gain more experience before settling down and starting a business of his own. The German term, literally 'wander-year', began to appear in English in the late 19th century, sometimes in its original form, sometimes translated as *wander-year*. The latter has died out, and the former survives mainly in metaphorical contexts.

wanderlust

The term *wanderlust* denotes an irresistible impulse to travel. English borrowed it from German at the beginning of the 20th century, and, thanks to the complete orthographical overlap with English *wander* and *lust*, has entirely anglicized its pronunciation (even though semantically English *lust*, with its specifically sexual connotations, is now far removed from the more general German *lust* 'pleasure, desire'). A further sign of its naturalization is the formation of the derivatives *wanderluster* and *wanderlusting*: '*Wanderlust* ... is used much more frequently in the United States along with its derivatives, *wanderluster* (Eng. *rambler*), *wanderlusting* and *wanderlust-club*' (H. L. Mencken, *The American Language*, 1936).

wandervogel, plural wandervögel

The original *wandervögel* were members of a youth organization founded in Germany towards the end of the 19th century by Hermann Hoffmann which was devoted to various rural pursuits, particularly hiking, in a conscious reaction against the stultifying life of the city. Their name means literally 'wander-bird', that is, 'bird of passage'. It first appeared in English in the 1920s, and still occasionally crops up (as in 'the interwar Germany of this book, a country of idyllically-envisaged landscapes peopled with shining-eyed *Wandervogel* [sic] and decayed nobility', *The Observer*, 6 January 1991), sometimes used more broadly for any rambler or hiker.

wehrmacht

Wehrmacht is the name under which the German armed forces went between 1921 and 1945. It is particularly associated with the armies of the Third Reich between 1935 and the end of World War 2. It means in German literally 'defence-force' (*wehr* is related to English *beware* and *wary*), and it is first recorded in English in 1935.

weltanschauung, plural weltanschauungen

German *weltanschauung* means literally 'world-perception'. It is a compound noun formed from *welt* 'world' and *anschauung* 'perception', itself a derivative of the verb *anschauen* 'look at'. English adopted it in the mid-19th century (the philosopher William James is the first English writer on record as using it), and employs it (along with the translated version *world-view*, which appeared around the same time) to denote a particular person's or group's conception of the nature of the world and of life in general – in broad terms, a 'philosophy of life' or 'outlook on life': ' "How serious was the threat of Communist subversion in Hollywood?" Note how abjectly the question panders to the *Weltanschauung* of the interviewee' (*The Observer*, 9 December 1990). A parallel German term occasionally used in its stead in English is *weltansicht* 'world-view'.

weltschmerz

Weltschmerz is a feeling of ineffable sadness and depression brought about by contemplation of the state of the world and its evils. The term connotes in particular a sort of fashionable apathetic pessimism. It originated in German (*welt* means 'world', and *schmerz* 'pain' is related to English *smart*), and English took it over in the late 19th century.

wunderkind, plural wunderkinder

A *wunderkind* is essentially a 'child prodigy'. English borrowed the term from German (where it means literally 'wonder-child') at the end of the 19th century, and has used it particularly with retrospective reference to great composers (such as Mozart and Chopin) and performers who showed precocious musical gifts as children. The 1930s saw the emergence of an extended sense, often faintly derogatory: 'dynamic young person who achieves early (but perhaps specious or short-lived) success'.

Z

zaftig

German *saftig* means literally 'juicy', but when Yiddish took it over as *zaftig*, it put it to a far more colourful use. As a glowing endorsement of plumpness in women, it transferred the adjective metaphorically to 'buxom, curvaceous, sexily plump'. Before World War 2 it had made its way into American slang (occasionally also in the form *zoftig*), and it remains vigorously alive there (in 1981, for instance, *Gossip* referred to Dolly Parton as 'zaftig'), but it shows no real signs of crossing the Atlantic.

zaibatsu

Japanese *zaibatsu* means literally 'wealthy clique'. It originated as a borrowing of the Chinese compound *ts'ai fa*, which is made up of *ts'ai* 'wealth' and *fa* 'powerful person or family'. To begin with it denoted any of a number of organizations, typically based on a single family, whose influence and control spread out like a spider's web over a number of commercial companies, but latterly it has been applied more generally to any business cartel or conglomerate. It is first recorded in English in 1937.

zaiteku

The term *zaiteku* denotes large-scale speculation on the financial markets by a Japanese commercial company. The term originated in Japanese (*zai* is Japanese for 'wealth'), and came into English in the mid-1980s. It often appears in the partially anglicized form *zaitech*.

zeitgeist

It was the poet and critic Matthew Arnold (1822–88), a fervent critic of British provincialism and advocate of Europeanism, who introduced the German word *zeitgeist* into English (the first record of it is in a letter written by him in 1848). In German it means literally 'time-spirit' (German *geist* is related to English *ghost*), which in English terms is 'spirit of the times' – that is, the characteristic outlook of a particular historical period, the intellectual, artistic and political concerns of its people.

zollverien

German *zollverein* means literally 'tax-union' (*zoll* 'tax' is related
to English *toll*). Specifically, it is the name of an association of
German states formed in 1834 under the aegis (and, largely,
under the thumb) of Prussia to co-ordinate tariffs levied on
imports and set up a free-trade area amongst themselves. By
1867 all German states except Bremen and Hamburg had
joined. It was the forerunner of German political unification in
1871. The word *zollverein* came into English in the 1840s, and
for a while in the latter part of the 19th century it was broadened
to apply to any free-trade area (the term *zollvereinist* was coined
to refer to someone who supported the notion of the British
Empire as a free-trade area).

DISTRIBUTORS
for the Wordsworth Reference Series

**AUSTRALIA, BRUNEI,
MALAYSIA & SINGAPORE**

Reed Editions
22 Salmon Street
Port Melbourne
Vic 3207
Australia
Tel: (03) 646 6716
Fax: (03) 646 6925

**GERMANY, AUSTRIA
& SWITZERLAND**

Swan Buch-Marketing GmbH
Goldscheuerstraße 16
D-7640 Kehl am Rhein
Germany

GREAT BRITAIN & IRELAND

Wordsworth Editions Ltd
Cumberland House
Crib Street
Ware
Hertfordshire SG12 9ET

INDIA

Om Book Service
1690 First Floor
Nai Sarak, Delhi - 110006
Tel: 3279823/3265303
Fax: 3278091

ITALY

Magis Books
Piazza della Vittoria 1/C
42100 Reggio Emilia
Tel: 0522-452303
Fax: 0522-452845

NEW ZEALAND

Whitcoulls Limited
Private Bag 92098, Auckland

SOUTHERN AFRICA

Struik Book Distributors (Pty) Ltd
Graph Avenue
Montague Gardens
7441
P O Box 193
Maitland
7405
South Africa
Tel: (021) 551-5900
Fax: (021) 551-1124

USA, CANADA & MEXICO

Universal Sales & Marketing
230 Fifth Avenue
Suite 1212
New York, NY 10001 USA
Tel: 212-481-3500
Fax: 212-481-3534